Paul Kegan

The Australian Wanderers

Paul Kegan

The Australian Wanderers

ISBN/EAN: 9783744662871

Printed in Europe, USA, Canada, Australia, Japan

Cover: Foto ©Andreas Hilbeck / pixelio.de

More available books at **www.hansebooks.com**

THE

AUSTRALIAN WANDERERS

OR THE

Adventures of Captain Spencer,

HIS HORSE AND DOG.

BY MRS. R. LEE,

AUTHOR OF "AFRICAN CRUSOES," "ANECDOTES OF BIRDS,"
"ANECDOTES OF ANIMALS," &c.

WITH ILLUSTRATIONS.

BOSTON:
LEE AND SHEPARD, PUBLISHERS.
NEW YORK:
LEE, SHEPARD & DILLINGHAM, 49 GREENE STREET.
1873.

PREFACE.

The favourable reception given to the "African Crusoes" has prompted an Australian wanderer to recite his adventures; and as the natural productions of the newer world are even more extraordinary than those longer discovered, it is the object of the present work rather to dwell upon them, than on the fast increasing riches of the settlements.

The author is desirous to express her gratitude for the assistance which she has received from private sources, and from the admirable travels which have been written on the same subject.

CONTENTS.

CHAPTER I.

                                                                PAGE

Captain Spencer recommended to leave India on account of his health—Hires a Malay Schooner—Embarks with his horse and dog—Cruises on the outskirts of the Indian Archipelago—Converts a Triton Shell into a tea-kettle, and a Clamp shell into a cup—A bird caught, which Captain Spencer names Charlie, and teaches to speak—Meets with the inhabitants of the Indian seas—The Organ-fish—The Cuttle-fish—The Diodon—Sea snakes—Captain Spencer, not gaining strength, determines to go to Australia—Touches at Timor to take in supplies—Description of Coëpang—Excursion ashore—A hunt—Timoree traffic—Departure from Timor... 13

CHAPTER II.

Arrival on the northern coast of Australia—Various sea animals—Albatross—Tropic and Frigate birds—Touch at an island, see natives—Go back to the continent—Enter a river—Catch a crocodile—The country on fire—See a Dugong—Return from the river—The Malays catch Trepang—Captain Spencer goes ashore—Finds a curious lizard—All go to an island to cure Trepang—See natives—Examine their rafts—Oysters found—Playfulness of a Whale at sea—Flies—Natives bring a young man for them to set his arm—Captain Spencer performs the operation—Description of natives—Charlie and Tiger (the horse) frighten them—Natives dance—The schooner goes to another island—Captain Spencer finds an Eagle's nest, and various birds—Goes ashore—Eagle shot—Captain Spencer stays all night—Violent hurricane and storm—Schooner lost—Malays crushed by falling of cliff—Captain Spencer enters a cave with Charlie, Tiger, and the dog Gipsy.................. 33

CHAPTER III.

Captain Spencer determines to start for Swan River—Secures objects from the wreck—Running fish—Attack from natives—Starts for Swan River—A log of wood converted into a shovel—A Hawk's-bill Turtle—Natives touch the baggage—Frightened away—Natives on shore taste pickled Oysters—Put on Captain Spencer's trousers—Insects—Birds—Impression of a cloven foot with a spur—Flight of Parrakeets—Scrub—Captain Spencer makes a grass hat—Albatross—Haze and mirage—Berries—Snakes—Porpoises—Sea-shells—Meteor—Gannets 67

CHAPTER IV.

Captain Spencer ascends a ravine—Flying Foxes—Green Ants—Hawks, Pelicans, Parrakeets, and Cranes—Mullet—Porpoises—Pandanus—Nutmegs—Pigeons, &c.—Mosquitoes—Sand-flies—Hears natives—Dangerous attack—Captain Spencer kills a man—He is wounded by a spear—Beautiful plain and lake—Water-lilies, &c.—Residence on the top of a hillock—Native graves—Sees Kangaroos—Tiger loses a shoe—Oats—Kangaroos—Skin prepared—Mocassins made—Frilled Lizard—Gipsy nearly killed by a Python—Kites and other birds—Cranes—Bitterns—Owls, &c.—Sow-thistle—Falcon—Shrike—Cuckoo—Captain Spencer rides to native huts—Spear-heads—Circles of stones—Bower-birds—Gourd—Cray-fish—Captain Spencer rides over the hills—Caves like temples—Paintings—Vampire Bats—Carved head—Kangaroo—Gouty tree—Vitex—Crabs—Reed—Beetles—Fire flies—Storm—Provisions collected for journey—The grass hat—A fresh start................. 93

CONTENTS.

CHAPTER V.

PAGE

Snake—Huts—Bark bedsteads—Ovens—Basalt—Luxuriant grass—Gorge—Another gouty-stemmed tree—Captain Spencer desires to go to the interior—Scrub—Fishes—Gum-trees—Large fish—Birds—Flying Opossums—Insects—Fusanus—Casuarina—Dragon-fly—Sun to the north—Tiger's hoofs worn—Tiger's socks—Mesembryanthemum—Jerboas—Bustard—Native grave—Melaleuca—Lark—Natives and dogs—Dogs rush on Gipsy—Captain Spencer saves the dog—Natives equipped for war—Captain Spencer separated from his arms—Dances to conciliate natives—Reaches his fire-arms—Frightens the natives—Tiger comes up, and they are still more frightened—Natives run off—Tombs—Opossums—Magnetic hills—River—Black Swans—Zamia—Captain Spencer poisoned by nuts—Conduct of his companions—Recovers—Yams—Moths—Peppermint—Grass-trees—Natives and dogs come upon Captain Spencer when cleaning arms—He frightens them away—Uninhabited villages—Yam-grounds—Howls of dogs—Splendid Pelargonium—Tiger attacked by a venomous Snake—In saving the horse Captain Spencer is bitten—Almost dies—Recovers—Natives blow at him—Hen-Turkey—Native hut for watching prey—Birds—Directs his way south—Water scarce—Tiger drinks all from one can—Proteæ.................................... 131

CHAPTER VI.

Bed of a river—Native women—Captain Spencer finds water by digging—Diamond birds—Charlie frightens birds away—Captain Spencer takes yams from women—Gives a horse-shoe in exchange—Conduct of the natives with the horse-shoe—Kangaroo—Howling of native dogs—Captain Spencer eats a dog—Holes of dirty water—Gipsy falls into one of them—Comes out covered with mud—Birds driven away by Charlie—Snake under saddle—A cry of distress—Finds the native whose arm had been broken and lamed by a thorn in the foot

—Captain Spencer saves him—Kinchela, name of native—
Speaks Malay—Tells his history—Conversation between the
Englishman and Australian—Captain Spencer goes to a well—
Kinchela cooks—Discourse about Boyl-yas—Kinchela afraid
of Tiger—Opinion of Captain Spencer among natives—Kinchela
ignorant of way to Perth—Promises to take Captain Spencer
to white men—Asks so earnestly to go with him that no refusal
can be given—Grubs in Grass-tree—Frogs—Charlie interferes
with Kinchela's lesson in English—Scarcity of clothes 164

CHAPTER VII.

Kinchela still afraid of Tiger—Zamia trees—Kinchela's first
lesson in honesty—Bed of a small lake—Improved cuisine—
Australians cannot boil—Fire-stick—Wild fowl—Birds—Kangaroo caught in Kinchela's fashion—Kinchela greedy—Reflec-
tions of Captain Spencer—Gums—Manna—Floss silk—Bee.—
Kinchela's memory of words—Cold rain—Kinchela catches
Opossums— Kinchela makes a cloak—Burnt grass—Catch
animals by burning scrub—Kinchela mends spear—Kinchela
talks of bad black men—Magellanic clouds—Higher hills—
Wallabies—Talperos—Emu—Emu oil—Cross the mountains—
Flies—Iguana—Kinchela's fear of a telescope—Beautiful sce-
nery—Flowers—Lake—Ipomea—Everlastings—Nest of Leipoa
—Banksias — Finches — Stork — Dragon-fly — Beetle—Fly—
Grubs—Captain Spencer carries Gipsy everywhere on his
knapsack—Native dogs—Wombat—Snake—Kingia — Grevil-
lia—Inga—Eugenia, &c.—Birds and insects—Buteo—Birds—
Scenery—Pieces of crystal and agate—Flowers—Mackintosh
given to Kinchela—Fungus—Natives frightened away by gun
—Python—Arrive at the ocean........................... 189

CHAPTER VIII.

Captain Spencer makes a signal to a vessel—Boat comes
ashore—Captain of the vessel comes in a boat—Offers assist-

ance—Captain Spencer and his companions go on board the French whaling ship, the Marie—Life on board the Marie—Native feast off a stranded whale—Natives pay a visit to the Marie—Kinchela Spoiled—Charlie learns French—Captain Spencer leaves the Marie—Scrub—Tiger very happy—Cranberry—Kangaroo—Kinchela has a fit of gluttony—Cliffs—Return to the sea-shore—Fishes—Musical Teredo—Salsolæ—Eryngium—Fruit—Plants, &c.—Reptiles—Birds—Crabs—Kinchela ill-humoured.. 228

CHAPTER IX.

Spinifex—Bark of Gum-tree—Excrescence on tree—Well—Rhagodia—Water scarce—Water from Gum-trees—Hot wind—Dew—Salt lake—Salsola—Mirage—Gum-tree roots—Emigrating birds—Cold wind and frost—Hakea—Curious stones—Absence of animal and vegetable life—Sand, quartz, iron—Scorching sun—No water, no food—Distress of Captain Spencer—Dog and horse suffer much—Tiger appears to die—Sorrow of Captain Spencer—Kinchela lies down to die—Captain Spencer gives himself up for lost, and becomes insensible—A shower in the night somewhat revives him—A Pigeon shows the way to some water—Captain Spencer rouses himself and reaches the place, drinks, and takes some to his companions—All go to the well—Kinchela and Gipsy eat Kangaroo skin and fall asleep—While sitting with his face between his hands Captain Spencer's hat is taken off—Sees Tiger with it in his mouth—Joy—Rest three days—Mountains—Country improves—Copious rain—Old Man.. 257

CHAPTER X.

Plenty of food—Yellow bean—Rough ground—Emus—Fishing—Natives—Painted man—Birds—Man and his wife—Captain Spencer rescues nets from flames—Rivers—Kinchela recognises the country—Finds a dead Kangaroo—Kinchela not allowed to take it—Building rat—Cold—Encampment of natives

—Kinchela's friends—Captain Spencer well received by them for his sake—Captain Spencer consents to stay the winter with them—The natives build him a house—Supply him with provisions—Two men, Warrup and Ugat, superior to the rest—Opinion of Tiger—Description of natives—A new tribe arrives—Their reception—Captain Spencer taken for the ghost of a relation—Corobbery—Dance of hill tribe—Warrup and Ugat talk of native customs to their guest—New sorts of food—Native manufactures.. 285

CHAPTER XI.

River overflows—Different modes of fishing—Cooking—Frogs—Cray-fish—Tortoises—Birds—Wind—Hatchet missing, and restored—Description of sorcerers—Sorcerers come to cure a boy—Restrictions concerning food—Native laws and customs—Women—Quarrel and combat—Boomerang—Large Kangaroo hunt—Tribe goes away and steals a young woman—Preparations for war—War-song—Departure in pursuit of the enemy—Captain Spencer follows—Encounter of the tribes—Captain Spencer fires, frightens, and pursues the guilty tribe—The young woman found bleeding to death—Taken home to be eaten—Captain Spencer goes away............................ 314

CHAPTER XII.

Return to the river—Beautiful scrub—Bauhinia—Marjoram—Ornithorynchus—Natives become more frequent—Watching necessary—Another native funeral—Beautiful country—Casuarinæ—Chirping bird—Sorrel—Wood-ducks—Spiny Ant-eater—Women carrying dead bodies—Old woman—Flowers—Herd of wild horses—Blue mountains—Overlander—Cattle cross the river—Meeting of Captain Spencer and Mr. St. John—Captain Spencer entertains the Overlander—Conversation between the two gentlemen—Astonishment at Charlie—Miners of Adelaide—Murray river—Arrive at the river Darling—Character of natives—Mr. St. John gives introductions to Captain Spencer—The friends part with regret................................ 346

CHAPTER XIII.

Captain Spencer romantic—Birds—Native—Captain Spencer catches him, and relieves his hunger—Fairy-like plains—Bull comes down the hills, and gentlemen on horseback after him—Insects, and their webs and nests—Harry Blunt attacks Captain Spencer—Harry caught and overcome; his companions stunned—Captain Spencer kind to the bush-ranger—Captain Spencer goes on—Forest flower—Wooden pear—Lemons—Flying foxes—Native cherry—Beautiful plants—Green frogs—Lizards—Out-stations—Shepherds—Laughing Jackass—Robin—Knife-grinder—Fish and its nest—Storm—Sorcerers make storms—Pine forest—Plants—Metamorphosis of beetle—Head keeper's station—Captain Spencer hospitably received—Tall black man's history—Harry Blunt's visits—Head keeper and wife very kind and hospitable—Untidy and deserted stations—Deserted townships—Ascend mountains—Meet drays—Ants—Come to the river—Arrival at Mr. Onslow's farms................. 374

CHAPTER XIV.

Description of Mr. Onslow's farm—Cordial reception of Captain Spencer—Clothes supplied—Conversations about Aborigines—Mr. Onslow wishes for Kinchela to enter his service—Kinchela refuses—Dingoes, sheep, cattle—Mrs. Onslow's garden—Hunt stray cattle—Wayside inn—Captain Spencer's courage and nerve—Tiger's good behaviour—Letter from stockkeeper Richardson, describing an interview with Harry Blunt—Endeavours to persuade Captain Spencer to settle in Australia—Conversation with Mr. Onslow—Description of woods—Mare kills a foal—English plants spring up in the neighbourhood of cattle—Tarantula—Native cat—Adventure of the pumpkins—Parting—Mr. Onslow goes to Sydney with Captain Spencer—Kinchela rides with them—Mrs. Onslow's courage when attacked by natives—Arrival at Sydney—Charlie—Attempt of Gipsy, Tiger, and Charlie to accompany their master—Harry Blunt taken—Captain Spencer obtains a mitigation of his sentence—Harry afterwards becomes a faithful servant to Mr. Onslow—Captain Spencer sends presents to all his friends—Arrival of all the travellers in Bombay—Letter from Mr. George Onslow about the Gold mines............................ 421

AUSTRALIAN WANDERERS.

CHAPTER I.

Captain Spencer recommended to leave India on account of his health—Hires a Malay schooner—Embarks with his horse and dog—Cruises on the outskirts of the Indian Archipelago—Converts a Triton shell into a tea-kettle, and a Clamp shell into a cup—A bird caught, which Captain Spencer names Charlie, and teaches to speak—Meets with the inhabitants of the Indian seas—The Organ-fish—The Cuttle-fish—The Diodon—Sea snakes—Captain Spencer not gaining strength, determines to go to Australia—Touches at Timor to take in supplies—Description of Coëpang—Excursion ashore—A hunt—Timoree traffic—Departure from Timor.

"Really, Spencer, your constitution, after the late campaign, requires some change, and you must for a time leave India. Why linger, when you know that there is a necessity for going?"

Such were the observations of Dr. Dynes to Captain Spencer of the —th regiment of Bombay Native Infantry, who pettishly replied, that "he would not go to Europe."

"It is not necessary that you should," said the doctor; "you can get as far as the Cape."

"I hate the Cape," growled out the patient.

"Well, go where you will," continued the good-natured adviser, smiling; "both mind and body need renovation, and I shall send you the proper certificate as my last prescription." So saying, he left the room, and Captain Spencer remained for some time in deep thought.

At last, turning himself impatiently on his couch, he muttered, "If it must be done, the sooner I set about it the better." The energy of the young man, of which he had a large share, being now awakened, his countenance brightened, his movements became more elastic. As he arose and walked up and down his room, his pace gradually quickened; and when his servant presented him with an envelope containing the aforesaid document, he said to him, "Yacoub, would you like to have a long holiday?"

"Yes, if Sahib please," replied the man, grinning.

"Very well; vanish!"

At these words the servant disappeared, wondering what was meant by the holiday; while his master, having slipped on his uniform, repaired to his commanding officer. After remaining with him for some little time, he proceeded to the port, stepped into a small boat, and was seen wending his way among the Malay craft then at anchor in the bay. He went on board several vessels which were waiting for freight or hire, and returned to his quarters before the heat of the day commenced.

Fatigued with his exertions, he threw himself on a sofa, but his mind was at first evidently too full of the future to sleep. One hand hung listlessly down by his side, and it was soon saluted by a cold nose, and the gentle touch of a tongue. "Ah, Gipsy, why do you disturb your master?" was the answer to this caress. "What will you do without me, my poor dog?"

At these words a small black and tan terrier leaped upon him, and nestling her head under his jacket, composed herself to sleep. After a pause, her master, patting her head, seemed to have come to a fresh resolution; for he said, "Gip, you shall go with me; we have never been separated since you were born two years ago. You shall go with your master, and help to take care of him; and what is more, Tiger shall go too. He is as playful as a kitten; he can sleep on deck—he can step in and out of a boat like a waterman—he can swim like a fish—and, still better, he has not forgotten how to fight with his forefeet. We'll all go together." Having thus settled matters to his satisfaction, Captain Spencer hugged Gipsy close up to him, turned round upon his side, and fell fast asleep.

The arrangements for the voyage were not long making. Leave of absence was granted for a year, certain; and if not returned at that time, it was to be extended to the soldier for at least another year. A pretty little schooner, with rakish masts and a comfortable cabin below, was engaged. She was manned by five Malays, who were well and favourably known in the port; she was provided with a small boat, and a kind of stall was knocked up on the deck for Tiger; but this accommodating steed, a half-bred Arab, grey in colour, and having a long white mane and tail, could, in case of bad weather, come down the cabin stairs and remain with his master. One of the Malays undertook to curry and attend to him, and an ample store of food was provided for his sustenance. Captain Spencer discharged some of his servants, gave others the long holiday of which he had spoken to Yacoub, with an allowance of wages through his agent; and taking leave of his friends in Bombay, started for a cruise on the western side of the Indian Archipelago. He did not like to go much between the islands, for fear of piracy; but he kept within their reach, that he might occasionally renew his stock of eatables. The idle and the dissipated wondered at him; his acquaintances said he was an odd fellow; and his friends, knowing how much " good stuff" there was in him, thought him right to please himself. Tea, sugar, hams, flour, biscuit, rice, and water, were placed in the small hold, with various other comforts; and poultry was lodged on the deck. The traveller furnished himself with books, drawing and writing materials, took a quantity of fishing-tackle, extra horse-shoes, various tools, a double-barrelled gun, a brace of double-barrelled pistols, a short sword, and a plentiful supply of ammunition. He also had a good chart, and a small but powerful pocket-telescope. A close friendship existed between Tiger and Gipsy; and as all the life of the latter had been spent with her master and the horse, she was perfectly happy when with them, wherever it might be; and as to Tiger, he emulated Gipsy in docility and attachment.

The little party proceeded smoothly; the health of the four-footed animals was preserved by now and then landing on one of the islands, and taking a run and a gallop; and for a time the invalid was pleased with the dreamy sort of life which such a scheme afforded. One great source of interest lay in watching the inhabitants of those seas, which are so varied, so beautiful, and at times so grotesque. A morning's amusement consisted of converting one of those enormous shells called Tritons* into a tea-kettle. Not that Captain Spencer was without this necessary utensil, but the singularity of the thing, as described to him, had struck his fancy; so, when one of the crew brought him the shell complete, with its lid, or operculum, he determined to exercise his skill upon it. Laying it upon the table in his cabin,

* Triton variegatus.

he with a gimlet bored a hole opposite to the part on which it rested steadily, and inserted a thick iron wire into it; with a pair of pincers he twisted this at the lower end, so as to prevent it from slipping through the hole; and at the top he bent it into a handle, round which he put some plaited hairs out of Tiger's tail. Into the operculum he inserted a smaller and shorter wire secured in the like manner, and the long canal of the shell served for a spout. In the evening, after being put on the hot ashes of the caboose fire, water was brought to him in it, boiling with great bubbles, as French people call it when fit for making tea, and he was perfectly satisfied with his own workmanship. He afterwards completed his tea-service by making use of the Clamp shell* as a cup, which on one of his excursions ashore he found attached to a rock by its thick tough bysus. He chopped this away with his hatchet, and then removed the velvet-looking animal within, covered with its beautiful spots, and lying in a heap in one part of the shell. He had chosen one of the least, for some of them weighed six hundred pounds; still his equipage was heavy, it must be owned; but it had the advantage of not being liable to break.

One of Captain Spencer's daily occupations was to teach a bird to speak, which one of his men had caught in the interior of an island. At first

* Tridacne gigas.

he thought it was was Linnæus called the *Gracula religiosa*, which now bears the name of Eulabes; but its beak differed, and he concluded, from its entire resemblance in other respects, that it must be only a different species; its talking powers, however, were even more remarkable. The Malay told him he had been attracted by its perfect imitation of himself and his companion, as they spoke, and he had easily captured it, owing to an injury it had received in one of its wings. In a short time the bird called Gipsy and Tiger, and talked most impertinently to its master, as Ned Spencer.

The invalid might have recruited his strength with bird's-nest soup, formed of a marine plant which his men called Agal-agal, and which, when made into nests, hung to the sides of shallow caves, like watch-pockets; but he did not relish its insipid taste. The Malays, however, procured a great number of these, with the intention of selling them on their return; and they frequently asked their master's permission to stay in some spots, where they dived for pearls. They brought him several specimens of their treasures, some of which were of a pale straw-colour, and others, taken from the shell called the Pinna, were quite black. Occasionally, as he stepped over a rough beach, during his excursions, he was amused with the Carrier Trochus, as it jumped over the obstacles in its way, gathering fresh fragments of shells and sand as it went along, lifting its superfluous burden by the action of its body, and trailing its operculum behind. The tentacula were generally stretched out, the creature bent down its thick pink proboscis, its large black eyes seemed to watch sharply for its food, and its carrier labours seemed almost ludicrous, from the idea they conveyed to the observer of being unnecessary.

Multitudes of fishes played about the rocks, particularly the *Scorpenæ*, which attracted notice by the extraordinary development of the spines about their head, also of their fins, and by their brilliant colours. There was a great variety of beautiful, branching Corallines, and sea-weeds of strange forms and splendid hues, showing a rich world of interest beneath the waters. In the Mangrove swamps they found the Close-eyed Gudgeon,* which, when it landed on firm ground, jumped about like a frog, slid along on its belly, or climbed the roots of the trees. They took some of the Fighting-fishes on board, and there kept them in water, to watch the fury with which they quarrelled, changed colour, and darted at each other, if they came in too close contact.

One night, as Captain Spencer lay asleep, he was awoke by a strange, singing and monotonous noise; and Gipsy at once started upon her feet,

* Periophthalmus.

and throwing up her head, uttered a howl which completely roused the whole crew, who rushed on deck together with their master, while the two who had remained up to watch and steer spoke and looked mysteriously. All was again silent, and then the same noise returned, accompanied by a booming sound, as if from under the vessel. They were not near land, the schooner having stood out to sea in apprehension of an approaching storm, so that the disturbance could not proceed from any terrestrial animal; and then it occurred to the Englishman that it was the sound made by the Drum or Organ-fish,* of which he had read; and when he again heard it, swelling and dying away as it were under his feet, he was satisfied with this explanation of the mystery. Not so his men, although two of them had heard it before; they shook their heads, and looked uneasily at each other, smiling incredulously as they lowered the nets by their master's order, and seeming to have expected their total want of success in making a capture. Night after night did Captain Spencer anxiously watch by moonlight, both for the sight and sound of these musical fishes, but in vain as far as they were concerned; he, however, saw some Cuttle-fishes, whose size quite verified all he had heard of them, for they could easily have taken a grasp of twelve feet with their long arms.

* Pogonias.

They were, however, too active to be caught, but stared with their cat-like eyes, and frequently and suddenly cast forth a thin, inky liquid from their necks, altogether being very hideous and grotesque.

The nets were torn by a curious Diodon, or Globe-fish, with golden eyes and black pupils, which swelled out its body, stuck out its spines, and bit and spat at those who took it into their hands. One morning a small, spotted shark snatched away a sheep-skin which was hanging at the bows; and snakes of varied form and size swam from island to island. Some of them were beautifully marked with bands, and were the size of a man's leg, lying lazily on the surface of the water, or forming graceful curves. One was caught by a Malay, which had enormous fangs; he formed a noose of a long piece of grass, which had been brought on board with Tiger's food, dexterously passed it over the head of the animal, drew it tight, lifted the snake out of the water, and only loosened it when the spine had been divided with a knife.

Amid so many interesting and beautiful objects, life was varied by occasional intercourse with the inhabitants of the gem-like spots of earth which studded the Eastern Ocean, who brought fowls, fruits, and vegetables alongside for sale. Occasionally Captain Spencer thought he saw some suspicious-looking craft, wearing a piratical appearance; but his men were faithful, and their Malay birth was a sort of security. Health and strength, however, did not return as quickly as he had anticipated; the heat was often intense, owing to the lingering remains of the rainy season, and he fancied that the frequent presence of mangrove-lined shores was unwholesome. Tiger began to droop, although every precaution had been taken to keep his shed cool, such as to cover its roof with boughs of trees or grass, and frequently to sprinkle these with water. Then his master determined to go still farther south; and he asked his chief navigator if he were acquainted with the Australian shores. The man replied in the affirmative, and said that he had frequently been on the northern coast, and bartered with the natives, who were very savage, treacherous, and difficult to deal with. Captain Spencer told him he did not wish to visit them, or any settlement, unless it were Sydney, where he could, if necessary, procure money; but merely to pass backwards and forwards along the north and north-western coasts, going ashore, as he had already done, when he felt inclined, and returning to the schooner when fatigued. The man answered, that it was very possible to accomplish this, but as it was sometimes difficult to land, and water and supplies very seldom to be procured there, they had better first proceed to some place where they could lay in a large stock. He recommended the island of Timor; and as Captain Spencer consented, they steered for this place, still keeping on the outskirts of the Archipelago, and so avoiding the larger islands of Java and Sumatra, which he had at first determined to visit, but the climate of which he now thought would be too relaxing.

After some days, constant sailing, high, sharp, and jagged pinnacles appeared in the distance; for these the master steered, and at night anchored opposite the town of Coëpang, in whose bay lay some of the southern whalers, to take in a supply of excellent water, which is conveyed from further inland to the beach by means of a pipe. When the bright morning sun lighted up the fleecy clouds which hung about the summits of the mountains, it disclosed rich woods and plantations at their feet. Little boats guided by Malays soon came round the schooner, and great surprise was evinced at seeing an English officer. They all asked him to land in their boats, but he preferred going in that of the schooner; and for the sake of assuming a more favourable appearance, he laid aside his jacket, and putting on an undress uniform coat, he and Gipsy went ashore for the purpose of visiting the Dutch Resident. They walked through several narrow streets, chiefly composed of bamboo houses, in which they met many passing to and fro, belonging to different nations, and frequently bearing with them fruit, poultry, eggs, &c., for sale. The Timoree men were but sparingly clothed; the women, however, wore long loose gowns: the former were easily distinguished by their athletic forms and crisp hair. Numerous shops lined the streets, which seemed principally to belong to plump, laughing, good-tempered Chinese, who, as they sat at their door eating their breakfast of rice with chop-sticks, asked the stranger to share their meal. Civilly declining their hospitality, and untempted by their merchandise, Captain Spencer pursued his way, and descended into a valley ornamented with beautiful trees, the most conspicuous of which were cocoa-nuts, placed beside the broad, floating leaves of the bananas.

Several good stone houses stood in the valley, and seeing a soldier leaning against the entrance of one of them, Captain Spencer supposed it to be that of the Resident. He spoke Dutch fluently, and his inquiry of the sentinel confirming his supposition, he asked to be shown into the presence of the great man. He was in truth a great man, for he was tall and fat, besides which he talked very loud and fast. His good nature, however, equalled his size, and he offered the stranger every convenience in his power to afford, and a day's sport into the bargain. Captain Spencer said his health would not allow him to undergo much fatigue, but if his Excellency would allow him, he would come early the next morning with his horse and gun, and ride over some of the neighbourhood of the town. The Resident said all should be ready for him, and extended his politeness so far, as to ask his visitor to inspect the fort at the present opportunity. The offer was accepted, and a servant was sent with him, not only there, but to attend and help him in transacting his affairs in the town.

This fort stood on a madrepore rock, commanded the port and the straggling town, and was washed on one side by a running stream. The view from it was very beautiful; the lofty mountains, their deep gorges filled with the luxuriant verdure of the tropics, and the lesser heights covered with vegetation, sloping off into plantations, altogether formed a sight not easily forgotten. Numerous paddy-fields, however, told the secret of those intermittent fevers, from which the Resident said the town of Coëpang greatly suffered.

Captain Spencer's guide took him to a place where he could change his rupees into the copper currency used in traffic; and carrying the load for him, then led him to the warehouses where he could best procure the provisions of which he stood in need. After superintending their conveyance to his boat, he followed the man to a Malay school, where clever, intelligent children were singing old hymns, from music noted in ancient characters, taught to them by the Dutch clergyman, who had converted many to Christianity. After this the Englishman rewarded the servant for his attendance, and returned to his floating habitation.

The next morning came Tiger's turn for an excursion; and his appearance was so superior to that of the native ponies of Timor, that he excited much admiration as he passed to the house of the Resident, who laid aside his pipe, offered refreshment, and entered into conversation with his guest. Speaking of the island, he said it was subject to earthquakes, one of which had a few years before destroyed the town; that water might be had in the northern part, but it was there tainted by a tree which grew close to it, but of what sort he could not tell; that the mountains were rich in various metals, but the custom of the mountaineers of sacrificing a life for every bottlefull of gold-dust which was collected, precluded all profit from that production; and that sixty Dutch soldiers had been sent to get some, but they had all been murdered. He spoke of the customs of the natives, and described the people as very superstitious; said that they always killed a number of pigs and ponies over the graves of their relations, in order to propitiate the evil spirit; that all those fine, wild-looking men his visitor had seen in the streets, were slaves to the Rajahs of the island, and implicitly obedient to their commands; that one or the Rajahs was at that time in the town, who was styled the Emperor; and in conclusion, his Excellency added, "By the by, although this fellow is polite and well-mannered, he is a great rascal, and makes nothing of cutting his wives to pieces if they give him cause for offence."

It was time for the traveller to start for his ride, and the Resident desired him to be taken across a well-watered and fertile country, among trees thickly inhabited by monkeys, into a valley, round which some lofty mountains rose in majestic grandeur. Some enormous trees bordered it, and a village was scattered among them. Here a subordinate authority, having been prepared by the Resident, met Captain Spencer, and regaled him with cocoa-nuts, bananas, mangoes, and honey, in a large, rambling house built near a beautiful stream, for the occasional recreation of the Resident. This repast was, literally speaking, a *hors d'œuvre;* for a meal, provided by the Resident, was served immediately in rather a novel order. Tea, coffee, and fruit came first; and an hour after a train of servants entered with fowls and rice, cooked into a number of different dishes.

In the evening Captain Spencer walked out with the Commandant, and shot some pigeons—a task of no small difficulty, unerring as his aim was, for they generally perched on the uppermost boughs of the loftiest trees. He found he was expected to stay all night; and dispatching a message to his schooner to account for his absence, he prepared for rest. The lights were merely some threads of cotton drawn through wax, and his bed consisted of a few mats; he was therefore very glad that he had brought a mackintosh cloak across his saddle; and after seeing Tiger well fed, and housed in a substantial shed, he rolled himself up in the said mackintosh, and passed, what appeared to him a cold night, in tolerable comfort, Gipsy bearing her share in imparting warmth.

Early in the morning, when the mists had cleared off the mountains in floating wreaths and flocky masses, the Commandant summoned Captain Spencer to resume his sport, and a large party of Malay servants and village-people added to their number. Each of the former was armed with an old Tower musket, which was loaded with common powder and stone slugs, the necessary quantity for each charge being put into a piece of bamboo. Besides the musket, all carried a large knife stuck into their belt. The combination of Malays and Timorees was picturesque; the latter, with their aquiline noses, having much the advantage in personal beauty. They proceeded to a plain, where, attracted by a large plant with a very handsome leaf, Captain Spencer was about to gather a branch of it. Before he could reach it, however, the

Commandant eagerly, and even roughly struck his hand down. He turned round with an astonished look, when his host bowed, apologised for his seeming rudeness, and informed him that that was "the Devil's leaf," and if he had touched it, it would have caused great soreness, pain, and terrible irritation for many months, if it had not killed him; especially as his hand had not been protected by a glove. Captain Spencer thanked the Commandant for his kind interference, and on looking more closely at the plant, he saw it was a kind of gigantic nettle.

The party was now stationed, each at some yards distance from the other, the deer were driven towards them, and several were brought down by the rude weapons, the stone slugs making enormous holes. The animals were skinned, and presented to the stranger, who restored the shot to the owners, and distributed some coin among the whole assemblage. To the Commandant he presented some of his better powder and shot, which were received with gratitude. On returning to his boat, which, by the messenger of the preceding evening, he had ordered round to meet him, he saw the curious mode of tillage practised by the Timorees. A piece of ground was enclosed and well watered, after which some bullocks were driven furiously across it, backwards and forwards in all directions; and this was all the preparation which the ground received before the sowing of the grain. Taking his game with him, in order to share it with his crew, Captain Spencer joined his schooner; and the next morning, when he started to pay a visit of thanks and farewell to the Resident, his chief man requested permission to go to a distant part of the island, in order to trade a little with the natives, he having brought with him a small stock of merchandise, in case of having an opportunity for traffic. Captain Spencer desired him to wait till he returned, and then they would all go together; for this would give him an opportunity of seeing more of the Timoree people, for whom he felt considerable interest. He finished his visit by presenting an English penknife to the Resident, who was delighted with the gift; and the schooner, passing by dark, limestone cliffs, with coral imbedded in them, anchored off the mouth of a small river, taking its rise in those noble heights, which give such beauty to the island.

Parcels of the Indian and European goods with which he meant to trade were made up by the master, consisting of silk handkerchiefs, coarse cutlery, gunpowder (which the natives of these places are very anxious to obtain), leathern straps, &c.; and after laying them down upon the shore, he returned to the schooner. The natives then came and examined them, after which they placed by the side of each packet the quantity of wax, honey, fruit, and cotton cloth of their own manufacture, which they meant to give, and retreated. The master, in his turn, went to their deposits, and not thinking the amount sufficient, left them all in the same state. The natives came a second time, and added some nutmegs and feathers, and returned to their hiding-place. With these the Malay trader was satisfied; he took them away, left his own goods in exchange, and finally embarked. This singular traffic being concluded, there was nothing more to detain them, and the schooner sailed for Australia; Captain Spencer not being sorry to leave a place, which, however beautiful, was decidedly unhealthy: a proof of this was given by one of his men being attacked with a slight fit of cholera, which disabled him for many hours.

Several weeks of Captain Spencer's furlough having now elapsed, without any great improvement in his health, he hailed the superior coolness of the breeze, as they left the island, with pleasure, and, full of hope and cheerfulness, welcomed the first glimpses of the Australian continent, with the full persuasion that he was now within reach of recovery.

CHAPTER II.

Arrival on the northern coast of Australia—Various sea animals—Albatross—Tropic and Frigate birds—Touch at an island, see natives—Go back to the continent—Enter a river—Catch a crocodile—The country on fire—See a Dugong—Return from the river—The Malays catch Trepang—Captain Spencer goes ashore—Finds a curious lizard—Go to an island to cure Trepang—See natives—Examine their rafts—Oysters found—Playfulness of a whale at sea—Flies—Natives bring a young man for them to set his arm—Captain Spencer performs the operation—Description of natives—Charlie and Tiger (the horse) frighten them—Natives dance—The schooner goes to another island—Captain Spencer finds an eagle's nest, and various birds—Goes ashore—Eagle shot—Captain Spencer stays all night—Violent hurricane and storm—Schooner lost—Malays crushed by falling of cliff—Captain Spencer enters a cave with Charlie, Tiger, and the dog Gipsy.

ARRIVED on the northern coast of Australia, Captain Spencer occasionally entered some of the numerous inlets with which it is indented, and at others crossed them, as the humour of the moment dictated, passing one or two which looked like the mouth of promising rivers; but he did not attempt to ascertain their course, "For," said he to himself, "I have no intention of making discoveries, and no desire to come in contact with the very barbarous people of these places. The rivers may flow as they will for me, and I am now getting so strong that I shall not have occasion to stay long on these shores, which hitherto have not appeared to be very tempting. Those slimy mangroves seem to abound on the shallow coasts here, as elsewhere, carrying their unhealthy atmosphere with them, and harbouring those vile mosquitoes, which are enough to frighten any one away; even at sea they reach me, and I must get further into the ocean."

During an extension of sea-room, fresh denizens of the salt water were met with, among which was a shrimp-like animal, probably a Pencus, which had a beautiful purple shield on its head, and a Hyalea, the purple grape colour of which cast a phosphorescent light around it. The Velella floated on an oval, but flat, cartilaginous membrane, on the under side of which was a mouth, surrounded by tentacula; on the upper side it had a crest which caught every little eddy of wind, and was whirled round by it without the power of resistance, so swimming along whether it pleased or not, according to the caprices of the breeze.

There was, however, nothing prettier than the Sea-snail,* with its beautiful violet colour, and frothy bubbles issuing from its mouth; the shell sometimes covered with tiny Barnacles, the animals of which had become violet in hue, while their coverings remained white. Then there was a Glaucus, looking like a deep-blue feather with a

* Ianthina.

white streak, shrinking from every object with which it came in contact, and punishing every animal that disturbed it by emitting a most disagreeable odour.

Captain Spencer had fitted a canvass bag on to an iron ring at the end of a long pole, in the manner of an insect net, by which he was enabled to catch many of these strange creatures. Having been once severely stung by an Acalepha, two feet long, the tail of which had a fin like that of an eel, he was careful not to touch any of them with his hands. The canvass bag had been thickly greased outside, therefore for a time held water, and so he was enabled to watch them while swimming. One very extraordinary creature* was so nearly transparent, that he took it out in order to observe it more minutely; and when he put it on to the head of a cask, it stood upright, and then crawled away like a beetle.

One evening, a large white Albatross† flew over the schooner, and remained for some time in sight. It seemed to float in the air rather than fly, and its grave, solemn motion, recalled Coleridge's wonderful poem of the Ancient Mariner so forcibly, that Captain Spencer would not have shot it on any account. As a contrast to this mysterious-looking creature, which seemed as if it never could be in a hurry, were both the Tropic‡ and Frigate

---

* Phyllosoma.   † Diomeda exulans.   ‡ Phaeton.

birds;* the former, with their extensive wings and *long* narrow feathers in the tail, appearing as if they never ceased their rapid flight; and the latter, with their wings stretching out twelve feet, swallowing all the flying fishes they could catch, most unceremoniously knocking over the Boobies,† which had already caught them, and making them relinquish their dinners. He was fortunate enough to bring one of these down while so engaged, and, on examination, found an inflated bag under its throat, to increase its internal volume of air, and the opening to which was placed in the middle of the shoulder-blade. Thus he ascertained the secret of its lengthened and powerful flight.

More Water-snakes too were seen; and one which was caught in his bag had flattened fangs, without a cutting edge.‡ To another he gave the name of the Sea-serpent,§ from its size, it being even larger than the Indian snake before taken. It was as big as a man's thigh, and was several feet long; a third kind had lids to its nostrils, and smooth and polished scales. There was no end of Star-fishes, with hard, round tubercles all over them; and a Gull, very much like that of the northern Skua, frequently made circles round the schooner.

Several coral reefs and small islands lay more or

---

* Tachypetes.   † Pelecanus sula.
‡ Hydrus australiensis.   § Hypotrophis.

less in the vicinity of the shore; and being curious to examine them, Captain Spencer ordered the steersman to approach them. When near, they saw some of the natives, women as well as men, swimming away from one of them, their progress apparently quickened by the sight of the schooner. In vain did the Malays hail them; one alone, or two together, held a large log with one hand, while with the other they impelled themselves forward, being almost upright in the water. Making for the largest island, some bold coral rocks at first forbade the landing of the Indian party, and they steered round it to find a more accessible spot. They at length cast anchor in a shelving bay, and Captain Spencer went ashore with three of the Malays to search for water. The beach was thickly strewn with the shells of enormous Whelks, for which probably the natives had been seeking; and getting a bag from the vessel, the Malays filled it with enough for more than one meal; and while they explored further, the two left on board caught what they called some Rock-cod, but which was not in the least like Cod, and these fishes had very large mouths, and were frequently five feet long.

No water was found, and the schooner proceeded still nearer to the continent. From the sudden bending of the coast to the south, they thought they must have been near some sharp promon-

4

tory; and shaping their course along shore, they passed some rocks looking like bastions, and found themselves in a considerable gulf, at the mouth of which they encountered a large, grey shark, with a short nose and white belly. As they advanced, they perceived that a river of some size fell into this gulf; and thinking it would be a capital watering place, Captain Spencer determined to go up it as long as there was depth enough for the schooner, and brave the mosquitoes. The mangroves disappeared after a little distance, the banks became low and muddy, Pelicans and Curlews frequented them, and occasionally they were covered with small, matted-looking bushes. Detached masses of rocky sandstone hills rose abruptly from the level plain, and in the far distance, long lines of dark-looking forest were perceived. Here and there a palm,* dwarfish to Indian eyes, raised its head of fan-like fronds, and tropical monsters of animal life accompanied tropical vegetation. Three or four enormous Crocodiles were passed, and a fifth being announced as very near the schooner, Captain Spencer fired at its head, and the ball lodged in it with such effect, that it turned upon its back, and floated with its feet uppermost. Captain Spencer ordered his men to get out the boat, put a rope round its legs, and tow it ashore; at first they hesitated, for they knew it was only

* Livistona.

stunned; so he stept into the boat with them himself fastened the line to one of the legs, and proceeded with it to the bank. Before it reached land, however, it gave signs of being still alive, and struggled; but they pulled vigorously, and jumping ashore, they dragged it with all their might, Captain Spencer at the head. Their task, however, suddenly became too easy, and turning round to look at their prey, they found that it had drawn its foot out of the noose, and was walking after the hindmost man with murderous intent, and its mouth open. All at once it closed this huge aperture with a snap like the shutting of a gate, and the man whom it seemed to have in its eye, fell, contracted himself almost into a ball, and rolled away. Captain Spencer then fired again, but he was obliged to give the reptile six balls in its head, before it was dead; it measured fifteen feet in length; the breadth of the head was two feet, and that of the shoulders more than five feet. The Malays skinned it with great pleasure; then cutting off the best parts of its flesh while their master amused himself by shooting some Ibises, they returned to the schooner; and the steaks which they produced at Captain Spencer's supper-table were like excellent veal.

Evening surprised the party in the river, and not thinking it wise to explore by night, orders were given to anchor in the middle of the stream.

The heat had been very great as they receded from the sea; and in the night was almost intolerable. The moon shone so brightly that Captain Spencer had read by her light till he was tired; the heat, however, would not allow him to sleep, and he fancied some storm must be approaching; he threw on his cloak and went on deck. Then he perceived that the whole country on one side of the river was on fire, and that if the wind had been in a contrary direction, they must have been enveloped in smoke. Whence this could arise he was unable to imagine; but as there had been no lightning to set the dry grass on fire—and in fact it was too near the winter for vegetation to have become dry enough to be so burnt—he concluded that natives were not far off, and consequently ordered his men to get out of the river as fast as they could. They had scarcely turned the head of the little vessel in a contrary direction when they heard a great splashing in the water; and looking over the side, Captain Spencer instantly recognised an animal swiftly passing them to be a Dugong;* probably making its way further down the river from the same cause as themselves; its tusks, just peeping from its moustached lips, were visible, but there was no time for closer inspection.

On passing round the western entrance of the gulf the next morning, the sea looked as if it were

* Halicore australis.

covered with reddish saw-dust. Guessing what it might be, Captain Spencer took some up in his bag, and pouring the water into his Tridacne cup, found that his surmise was correct. It proved to be an accumulation of tiny animals, which soon died, and sank to the bottom, and as they decomposed, stained the water of a bright crimson colour.

Not having procured any water in the river, they continued to steer close to the shore in the hope of finding some place where they could replenish their stock. It was characterised by sharp capes, shoals, and occasionally overhanging cliffs of red sandstone, which sometimes rose two hundred and ten feet from the sea, now and then opening and forming a gulley. At the entrance of one of these, some red objects were lying not far from the edge of the water, and by the help of his telescope, Captain Spencer perceived that they were pieces of broken pottery. When he told the men what they were, they said that their countrymen must have visited that place in search of Trepang. On inquiring what Trepang was, they replied that it was an animal which lived in the sea; they did not think it was a fish, but it was very good to eat; that it frequented this and many other seas, and they hoped he would give them leave to stop and catch some for themselves. Captain Spencer consented, and creeping still nearer to the shore, they at first only saw some Medusæ, but afterwards dragged up an animal, which he immediately recognised as the Sea-slug,* which the Chinese and inhabitants of the Indian Archipelago are so fond of eating. He told the men to fish for it; and after inspecting the gulley, and finding it accessible to Tiger, he started with him and Gipsy for a short excursion. He found a low and arid country behind the high cliffs, with patches of tall, reedy grass, off which, however, Tiger, who was by no means dainty, contrived to moisten his mouth. Several lizards were crawling about, and among them was one of very formidable appearance, and of whose presence he was made aware by Gipsy. She growled, gave a short bark, plunged at something, and then retreated, shaking her head as if scratched or wounded; she, however, made a stand at her enemy, and coming up to her assistance, her master found her engaged with a reptile about a foot and a half long, covered all over with rows of sharp, horny spines, and of a yellow colour spotted with brown over the tail, making a most fearful opponent.† As it was not required for eating, he called the dog off, and after a short gallop returned to his men, who had collected a considerable quantity of Trepangs. Just before descending he had passed a large mound of shells, and knocking a

* Holothuria.   † Moloch horridus.

hole in it, he peeped in to see what was inside; it was, however, empty, but the Malays told him it was most likely a native grave.

The Trepang was generally from six to eight inches long, of a tough, leathery texture, not at all tempting to Europeans, and with numerous tentacula round its mouth. It was necessary that it should be cured for keeping, and the Malays asked to go to a neighbouring island which looked convenient for the purpose; Captain Spencer complied with their request, and when their capture was embarked, they steered for this island. On nearing its shore, they saw several of the natives depart from the other side, men, women, and children, seated on small rafts, one of which being empty, floated towards them. They secured it for inspection, and found that it was made of slender poles, fastened together very ingeniously by wooden pegs, and broader at one end so as to resemble a fan. After it had been examined, Captain Spencer desired it to be launched and pushed off, that it might be taken ashore by the tide; on it he put a handkerchief, some biscuit, and a knife. He desired his men to shout with all their might to the supposed owners; but they refused to answer, and watching with his telescope, he saw the raft arrive, and a man take the presents from it, which underwent the scrutiny of the others also; two tasted the biscuit, but immediately spat it out again, and they left that and the other things on the shore and ascended the cliffs.

All hands quitted the schooner, which anchored in twelve fathoms water close to the beach. A fire was made, and preparations were commenced; the cooking utensils were brought ashore, the Mollusks were split open on one side, put into boilers, and placed on the ashes, which were constantly fed with bushes, where they were to boil for eight hours. That night, and perhaps more, must be passed on the spot, and Captain Spencer determining to remain quietly where he was, let Tiger roam at large, and amuse himself on the island. Some of the spare poles were placed close to a hollow in the rock close by; and these and some bushes were converted into an excellent shelter. The men said they should have to press the Trepang with heavy stones, and stretch it open the next morning with pieces of stick, and then dry it in the sun, after which it was to be smoked over the fire, and that the length of time this would occupy must depend on the effect of the sun; but at all events they should be glad of a longer time than the usual period of rest. It was a good opportunity to give Charlie a little liberty, for so the bird was named, and try how far he would avail himself of it; for now his wing was perfectly well, he might at any time make his escape. When put down upon the ground, he seemed somewhat at a loss to understand his position, and at first had some difficulty in stretching his wings; by degrees, however, he rose higher and higher, and then flew rapidly backwards and forwards; at last he took the direction of the mainland, and seemed to bid adieu to his former companions, screaming and calling out, "I'm coming, I'm coming!"—"You are going, I think," said his master, as he watched him to the opposite shore, and in spite of the reasonableness of the proceeding on the part of the bird, somewhat disappointed, for Charlie was a great favourite and source of amusement, and Captain Spencer thought he was gone forever.

On walking under the rocks the Englishman found some delicious Oysters attached to them, and he called one of the men to collect a number. Having some vinegar on board, he amused himself by pickling a stock of them for future purposes. While standing by the fire with the Malays, he asked them what they meant to do with their Trepang. They replied, that they should sell it to the Chinese, and as this was the black, or best sort, called batoo, they should get forty dollars for every hundred and twenty-five pounds; but that the grey was not worth more than half that money. They added, they should like to catch some sharks, for they could cut off their fins and cure and sell them to the same people at the same rate of profit. Sponges and Madrepores with various shells, lay scattered upon the shore of this interesting island, which was evidently a frequent resort of the natives, for they found various traces of them, some of which were roots which they were apparently going to cook; also a spear, the shaft of which was made of mangrove wood, and was seven feet eight inches long. The lance, or head, was a sharp splinter of quartz, fastened on with a strong gum and plaited grass; altogether, in a skilful hand, making a fearful weapon. Shoals of Mullet played round the island, and many were caught, cured with the Trepang, and packed in barrels for future use; and a bush smelling like Rosemary awakened all the home feelings of the Englishman, going as far back as when his nurse used to wet his hair with rosemary tea, to make it thick.

Provisions were fast disappearing, and a return to Timor was contemplated; but Captain Spencer was beginning to feel interested in the scenes which opened around him, and he determined, by going ashore more frequently with his gun, to delay the return as much as possible. He knew he could procure any number of Rails,* for he had seen them in hundreds when last ashore; and who could tell what other good things might be procured? besides which, who could return from Australia without having seen a Kangaroo? The faithful Charlie came back in the evening after he

* Rallus littoralis.

had been let loose, and at sunset his deep voice was heard saying, "I'm coming, I'm coming, Ned Spencer!" so it was settled that he should in future have more liberty, for he had perched himself on his master's shoulder as a place of refuge, and consequently was likely to return to him on other occasions.

A distant but violent storm, accompanied by torrents of rain, had cooled the air; the Trepang, Mullet and Oysters, were safely stowed away in their proper places; the schooner returned to the main coast, and Captain Spencer, finding his way ashore, was not disappointed of the Rails which he had promised himself; besides these he procured a few species with shorter and more feeble wings,* and he loaded Tiger with a full meal for days, not only for himself, but all his crew. The grass was of a better sort, and the Malays laid in a stock of it for Tiger; so that all seemed to prosper. In some places he met with sand dunes, where vegetation was stunted, and the only thing which grew freely there was a pale, pink Convolvulus, whose trailing stem was an inch thick and thirty yards long. At the bottom of the cliffs was an abundance of Oysters and Neritæ; and a curious Sea-urchin, with hair-like spines, afforded his men a feast; but the fishes were not tempting, being chiefly of the Silurus, or Cat kind, which, on being

* Eulabeornis castaneoventris.

taken out of the water, made a singular noise, and showed a broad back of silvery green and a white belly. Several small hillocks at a distance, and smoke not very far off, made him fancy that he saw the dwellings of natives, but on looking through his telescope, he ascertained that the former were gigantic ant's nests.

One evening, while sitting on deck, resting himself after a hard day's sport, he was startled by what he supposed to be the report of a gun at sea, but one of the Malays told him it was only a Whale at play; and, if he would look with his glass in the direction whence the sound proceeded, he would see that it was so. Following the man's advice, and very much amused at the idea of a playful Whale, he beheld several fin-backed Whales lashing the sea in sport, suddenly leaping out of it, and falling again with a noise resembling cannon. Ashore, life seemed to become more beautiful and abundant: the Palms told that they were still between the tropics, the Cycas also presented itself, but as yet its fruit was not ripe enough to be useful; the Grevillea Cancerina, with its curved red blossoms, like crab's claws, was of great beauty; and flowers from bulbous roots were springing from the earth in totally new shapes and forms. To his game he added various Pigeons, one of which had dark-blue plumage and a white head, and afforded a delicious repast.* For the first time he now saw a Butterfly,† which had a large yellow spot on the upper edge of the upper wings. White Cockatoos came in flights over his head, and he brought several down with his gun, so that the stock of provisions was increased beyond the apprehension of not lasting; for it seemed as if he had only to go ashore to procure plenty. He had, however, more abundance than he liked of hornets, small scorpions, snakes, centipedes, &c.; and flies, the greatest of Australian torments, of which he had hitherto had but a gentle warning, assailed him in full force; these are the sand-flies, so minute that they are not seen, but which lodge on the eyelids, enter the nostrils, mouth, and ears, and cause almost unbearable irritation: his poor horse and dog snorted and sneezed, rubbed their heads in the grass, and jumped about as if they were mad. At last, tired out with these tiny pests, he took his way back to the schooner. Certainly, thought he, the country has become more interesting; still it is nothing to eyes accustomed to India; and if I could but shoot a Kangaroo, I would go back directly. As he walked along pondering on the past, his companions followed; Tiger well contented to stop for half a minute at a time to nibble on the way, and Gip, who always assumed her master's tone of mind, was

* The Wonga Wonga.   † Papilio Sthenelous.

perhaps also pondering on the past, for she walked steadily by his side, only pricking up her ears now and then as a frog jumped out before her nose, and occasionally looking up at Charlie as he swooped down and said, "Gip," to show he was close by.

On descending the cliff, Gipsy had preceded her master a little, and all at once she paused, put her head first on one side, then on the other, and jumping up, commenced a most outrageous barking. A sharp turn disclosed the cause, for there Captain Spencer saw two of his men amicably seated on the shore among a party of natives. The latter were, although somewhat lanky, very fine, athletic-looking men, with all the characteristics of their race; but nevertheless there was a manly bearing about them which prepossessed the Englishman in their favour. The head and nose were large, and some had the latter pierced for the insertion of a piece of wood or bone; the brow was very prominent, the eyes sparkling and deeply set; the lips full, the mouth very wide, the hair crisp, and frequently tied behind in a sort of club; the shoulders broad, the muscles of the arms well developed, the hands and feet small and well shaped, but the hips also small, and the lower limbs spare and slight. Their complexions were brown, approaching to black, the upper parts of their bodies were tattooed, and the scars projected at least half an inch from their bodies, which made a very ugly appearance; they had no clothes whatever; the older men had had one of their front teeth knocked out, and several of them were painted with black and white earth.

On the ground, in the midst of the group, lay a young man, whose left arm was very much swollen, and a third Malay was fomenting it with rum and water; they could speak a very few English words, and were without weapons. When they heard Gipsy bark, they started to their feet, saying, "Ho! ho!" and then, on perceiving Captain Spencer, saluted him by bowing almost to the ground, exclaiming rapidly and shrilly, "White fellow! very good." When Charlie, however, mocking even their tones, cried "Ho! ho! I'm coming. Come back again, Ned Spencer," they seemed perfectly stupefied with alarm. They stood as if awed; and when Tiger suddenly appeared from behind the rock, their fears came to a climax, and all fled except the disabled man, who was left upon the ground. Charlie, however, went on board the schooner; one of the Malays took Gip and Tiger, and Captain Spencer proceeded to the relief of the young sufferer. His men said, they thought they could understand that a fall had brought him to this condition, and the swollen arm was broken. After bathing it for about half-an-hour longer, the swelling had much decreased, and then Captain Spencer found that the upper arm was fractured, and that the poor creature had also received several severe bruises. He tried to entice the other natives to come back to him, and as they gradually recovered their alarm, they appeared from behind the rocks, but did not at first approach; he made signs to them that he would return, and then went to the schooner, where he tore up some linen into bandages, and taking his medicine-chest with him, hastened back to the shore. Seeing one of the men with a piece of bark in his hand, he asked for it; it was readily given, and he proceeded to set the limb, not without trepidation, it is true; but he had more than once assisted the regimental surgeon in such operations, and he tried to do all he had seen done on such occasions. After putting the arm into its proper position, he bandaged it with a double-headed roller; by the aid of a strong knife he cut the bark into strips in imitation of splints, and tied these pieces on with some string which he had in his pocket: taking off his silk cravat he converted it into a sling and lodged the arm in it; but how he was to tell the natives it must be kept there for a month, he could not imagine. He administered some medicine, rubbed the patient all over with a lotion, and made up some powders which were to be taken every night. He closed his eyes and laid his head down to imitate going to sleep, in the hope of conveying an idea of the time of swallowing them; and endeavoured to make the longer interval comprehended by the help of the Malays. The young man fixed his large eyes upon him with an expression of gratitude, and his friends carried him away; but before they mounted the cliffs they took their spears from the rock in which they had hidden them, and besides this description of weapon, each held a short stick, which the Malays told their master they used in throwing their spears.

Very little water at a time had been procured at this place, which little had descended to the sea through a fissure in the rock. Captain Spencer therefore ordered his men to steer to the south-west, it being his intention, after he had procured a proper quantity, to return along the northern shores, on his way to Timor. As the schooner receded, the natives, who had been watching it from the top of the cliffs, danced about with very extraordinary gestures, which, the Malays said, showed their friendly intentions, and bawled out—"Very good, very good!" till their visitors could no longer hear them; upon which Charlie made a little excursion in the air, echoing, "Very good, very good!" till Captain Spencer shouted with laughter, in which the bird joined with all his power. On the whole, these men were favourable specimens of the aborigines of Australia; but the remarkable carriage of their head puzzled Captain Spencer; and on mentioning it to his chief Malay, the man told him they were obliged to keep their eyes nearly shut to exclude the sand-flies, and therefore threw back their heads when they required to look at anything. Frequently a degree of suppuration was caused by these tiny creatures during the night, which it was necessary to wash off the next morning, before the eyes could be opened.

The schooner again anchored close to an island, about a mile from the continent, which had attracted Captain Spencer from its promising appearance for procuring water. It was formed of two ranges of cliffs, with a valley between; and as they were to stay there two or three days, the search for water was postponed till the next morning. The night was tranquil, and the day dawned with a splendour which gave every token of fine weather. Two of the Malays went ashore before sunrise to reconnoitre, and met with traces of natives, for whom they sought in all directions. They had, however, suddenly decamped at the approach of the schooner; but the marks of their footsteps showed the way to a pool of water, and the men returned for implements with which they might enlarge it, and after breakfast they began their work. Captain Spencer proceeded to examine the island, first shooting some of the quails, which abounded there, and sending them back to the vessel. After going through the valley, in which he saw a very large and vigorous umbelliferous plant, and which made an impression on him by being almost the only one of the family which he met with in his Australian travels,* he and Gip scrambled on to the top of one of the cliffs to look around him. There he found an enormous nest built upon the ground, and rising two feet from it; the branches of trees and collections of fragments in it would have filled a small cart. There were no eggs, but masses of seals' hair, and that of terrestrial animals, and small bones of quadrupeds and birds. He stood looking at it, and then exclaimed, "It *was* an eagle,† then, which I saw yesterday soaring over my head, and this its eyrie. I must try and shoot it, for I should like to take its measurement." From this point Captain Spencer, through his telescope, saw a fresh and tempting tract of land on the opposite shore, and descended to get ready and pay it a visit, in doing which he disturbed whole flocks of sooty terns,‡ noddies, oyster-catchers, and sand-pipers, which took fright at him. The heights seemed to have been seldom visited, and he had excited an immense commotion among the winged tribes, whose different characters he could not detect in their hasty flight.

* Azorella.
† Haliaëtus leucogaster (Kaup.); Ichthyaëtus (Gould).
‡ Onychoprion fuliginosus Anous (Gould).

Ordering the boat to be made ready, Captain Spencer breakfasted, and then prepared for a long and last excursion to the mainland while in this latitude. The men were to make sundry repairs in the rigging, and clean his cabin thoroughly during his absence, and were also to catch, salt, and smoke birds and fishes for the ensuing voyage. He took with him a large quantity of ammunition, with which Tiger was chiefly loaded, and he hoped not only to kill the eagle, but a kangaroo, the object of his present ambition. On leaving India he had, for the sake of convenience, caused holsters to be fixed to his saddle, and into these he now thrust his pistols and many spare charges. He filled a bag with biscuit and dried provisions, and in another put some of the roasted quails which had been shot and cooked before breakfast; he slung a couple of tin cans full of water by a leathern strap across the saddle; and as he surveyed his preparations, said to himself, "All these things I mean to fill with game when I return." He took his gun in his hand; a short sword, an axe, and a large knife were stuck into a belt round his waist; and he filled his pockets with odd things, such as pincers, and several boxes of copper caps. On the beach he found Charlie much too busy picking up insects to accompany him, and who, when he saw his master going away, looked up at him, saying,

"Good-bye, Ned Spencer; make haste back to Charlie—ha, ha, ha!"

The shore was rocky, and the surf beat high upon the fragments of rock lying at the foot of the bluff which the traveller now approached, and of whose lofty proportions he could only form a just idea as he approached close to it. It was a bold headland, at least five hundred feet high, consisting of the usual red sandstone, interspersed with granular quartz. Before he dismissed the boat, he sought for a track by which he might ascend the cliff; and after some difficulty found a part that was accessible to such good climbers as the trio now together; then telling his men that he would fire a gun from the top when he wished to go again on board, and not to be uneasy if he did not return at night, he and his companions scrambled to the summit, and the boat and her crew returned to the schooner.

On arriving at the top, the air was so fresh and balmy, so laden with sweet odours from an extensively wooded district not far off; the grass was so green, the country was so chequered with rich yellow patches, which were evidently the flowery districts of abundant vegetation, that even flies, which here, as elsewhere, abounded, were disregarded, and the telescope was lifted to the eye to ascertain if natives were near. None were discovered. Gipsy jumped and barked with delight, and Tiger danced, and curvetted, and kicked, and seemed quite inclined to run off altogether, very much to the discomposure of his master's property on his back. It was the month of October, the end of winter in those latitudes; the grass was still young and tender, the flowers were just beginning to come into blossom, and insects, birds, and all living things seemed to rejoice in the glories of creation. A large eagle was performing circles in the air, probably the inhabitant of the eyrie on the island, and it caused the first disturbance in this scene of beauty; for it evidently had an intention of pouncing on poor Gipsy, who was quite unconscious of her danger till the eagle suddenly dropped upon her, when she uttered a scream of terror. At that instant, however, the unfailing aim of her watchful master took effect; and the monstrous bird rolled upon the ground. It was not quite dead when Captain Spencer went up to it; but a blow from the back of his hatchet put an end to his struggles, and he longed to skin it, or at least to preserve its beautiful brown and banded feathers. He could only draw a few from its graduated tail, stick them on one side of his foraging-cap, and leave the body where it was, in the hope of securing it on his return.

Several beautiful Kingfishes* flew past the sportsman while busy with the eagle, as if they

* Alcyone pulchra (Gould).

had been relieved from the fear of an enemy, and took their way to the shore; they were of a new species to him, and were of a brilliant blue, orange, and red-wine colour, forming a contrast to a sober-looking Crow,* which now came forth to pick up his food from the ground; in fact, the death of the eagle seemed to form a jubilee among the birds, so many now issued from their hiding-places, and appeared so joyous that the sportsman could not find it in his heart to disturb their happiness.

Day was beginning to close, when exercise and fresh air made the Englishman hungry; he took the load from Tiger as well as his saddle and bridle, and suffered him to graze at pleasure. There were no trees near enough to afford shelter; and accustomed to bivouac in all sorts of localities, he and Gip seated themselves on the grass where they were, and ate their meal, drawn from the stock brought from the schooner; cold quail and biscuit being most acceptable. By this time the sun and heat of the horse's body had warmed the water in the cans; so the traveller rose and followed Tiger, whom he saw drinking at some distance from a stream which flowed through the grass, and fell into the sea on the opposite side of the bluff to that where they had landed. The cans were refilled there, and he again sat down to rest. A range of curiously-shaped, flat-topped hills closed

* Corvus coronoïdes.

the horizon to the east; and a belt of dense and dull-looking forest formed the southern boundary of the landscape, where the ground seemed to sink. Not a trace of human life was to be seen, and, alas, many miles had been walked that day, and no kangaroos had been perceived. Captain Spencer swept the horizon with his glass to fix on the direction towards which he should bend his steps with the morning's dawn, for he almost made a vow he would not return without one of these animals. Gipsy, however, had been much more fortunate, for she had again been roaming, and disappeared among some thorny bushes, whence, in a few minutes, she brought a small animal of the marsupial kind, and laid it at her master's feet. It was a Kangaroo-rat,* which she had nipped in the back of the neck, and as it was better than no kangaroo at all, he determined to take it to the schooner.

It was now necessary to look for some spot in which the party might pass the night comfortably; and then, for the first time, the traveller became conscious that an alteration in the weather had been gradually taking place; the breeze had dropped, and thick masses of clouds were gathering all round. He felt that a storm was approaching, and he sought for some shelter; he saw at a distance what he took for a native hut, but the

* Hypsiprymnus or Macropus minor.

telescope only showed an ant-hill, which he knew to be likely to crumble and overwhelm him on such an occasion; he sought for bushes under which he might creep, but those around him were too low to do him any good; he then proceeded to a rising ground, from the top of which he looked around him. A still more heavy mass of the thick, black clouds had gathered in the north-west, which foreboded a fearful tempest, not far off in point of time and distance. It was getting dark more rapidly than usual, from the loaded state of the sky, and there was no time to mount Tiger and seek better protection; so he returned to the bottom of the hill, placed himself on the lee side, and prepared for the night with his saddle for his pillow: he carefully secured his fire-arms and powder from the chance of getting wet, and Gip curled herself round upon his knees; Tiger trotted up to him, laying back his ears, as the first drops of rain fell, and cast himself down by his master's side, who rolled himself and his dog in his cloak, spread his ample mackintosh over them all, to its utmost extent, and prepared to endure patiently that which was unavoidable, saying to himself, it was "the fault of those rascally kangaroos that he was thus exposed."

Often as Captain Spencer had spent the night in the open field, he had seldom, if ever, encountered such an one as this proved to be, in so defenceless a state; and his great fear was, that from the violence of the hurricane all their coverings would be stripped from them; fortunately, however, they remained firm, thanks to the shelter of the hill; but the lashing of the waves upon the cliffs, the furious lightning which ploughed along the ground, the roaring of the mighty thunder, the sheet of rain, were nothing to the all-absorbing rush of the wind. Two or three times a dull, crashing, but awful sound was heard during a slight lull in the storm, and the ground shook under the little party, disturbing Tiger, who lifted up his head, and making Gipsy tremble. "Down, good beasts," said their master; "you at least are safe, but where are my poor men, and my schooner, and Charlie?—he can fly to land, but I tremble for the good Malays."

After hours of unabated fury, at length the storm passed over; and, wearied with anxiety and watching, Captain Spencer slept till the bright sunbeams darted upon him. Rousing himself, and immediately recollecting all the past events, he hastily swallowed a few mouthfuls of food to give him strength, placed all his effects on Tiger's back, and departed for the shore. It took him some little time to reach the edge of the bluff; the mists which rose in consequence of the preceding rain had disappeared, and nothing obstructed his view: the whole place was clear, and the schooner was not in sight. "She stood out to sea," thought he, "and she was a strong little craft. She may yet be safe." He fired his gun, and anxiously awaited an answer: not a sound was heard, except the dashing of the waves, swelled by the previous disturbance. He stayed some time, anxiously looking to sea-ward, both with and without his glass; and then, full of melancholy forebodings, he slowly bent his steps backwards and forwards by the edge of the bluff, stopping at every few paces to look for the approach of the vessel, and firing again and again. Tiger and Gipsy strayed, and each found food; but their master was too full of anxious forebodings to think of eating; at length he determined to go quite round the headland; but ere he reached it, daylight was gone, and that memorable 6th of October never was erased from his memory. With Gip in his arms, and Tiger for his pillow, there, on the open ground, listening to every sound, and fancying, each time he dozed, that he heard the cries of his men, lay the soldier, who started up at daybreak, determined to search the shore itself.

The suspense was ended; for that morning's light showed him the sea covered with the fragments of his schooner: he raised his glass with a shudder, and felt thankful that he could not discover a human form among them. Following the direction taken by the floating wreck, he reached the extreme end of the bluff, and at some little distance saw a well-worn track, doubtless made by natives, which led to a much easier descent to the shore, and he determined to follow it; he thought that his men had escaped by the boat, or had remained on the island, or were perhaps even now waiting for him at the foot of the cliff. As he advanced he perceived that enormous masses had been detached from the top of the headland, and cautiously peeping over at the first point where he could with safety plant his foot on the edge, the whole dreadful truth was revealed. The crew *had* tried to escape in the boat, and had been about to shelter themselves on the farther side, where the fragments (the crash of which Captain Spencer had heard the first night) had fallen upon them to their utter destruction. It was with difficulty that the stout-hearted soldier prevented himself from falling over the brink of the cliff in his agony and horror; but he reeled back a few paces, and then nerving himself, he went hastily down the side, followed by Gipsy and Tiger, who both seemed to know that something was the matter. They passed a comfortable-looking cave, and the little stream from above dripped in tiny cascades from rock to rock; but Captain Spencer could not then take much note of such things; he set his foot on the flat beach, turned round a sharp angle of rock, and beheld two of his men, one of whom was the master, lifeless on the sand, and evidently killed by the fallen rocks, for their bodies were dreadfully mangled; another was nearly buried under a huge mass, and the other two had disappeared altogether. Pieces of the boat were strewn about, and combined with those of the schooner in telling the tale of desolation.

Tiger had started at the first glimpse of the master's body, and would not advance a step further; Gip ran round and round the three bodies, licking their faces and hands, and whining and moaning her lamentations for her good friends. Her master stood with his eyes fixed upon them, deploring the sudden fate of his good and faithful servants, and thinking what he could do for the burial of the bodies. He tried to scoop a hole in the sand by means of the broken spars, and succeeded with two of them; but he was unable to move the third from under the superincumbent mass; he therefore heaped as much soil upon him as would cover him; and although they were not fellow Christians, they were fellow men, and he obeyed the impulse of his heart, by repeating as much of the burial-service of his Church as he could recollect over them, and praying most heartily to his and their God. This exercise opened the heart which had become rigid from grief and horror, and he concluded his orisons by fervently expressing his gratitude for his own preservation. Leaving the spot with a more tranquilized spirit, he retired to the cave which he had seen on his way down to the shore, to ponder upon his present situation, and to form plans for the future. Tiger, who had made an ample meal in the morning, entered the cave with him, and threw himself down near the entrance; and Gip and her master, after convincing themselves there were no inhabitants already in it, took possession of the interior.

CHAPTER III.

Captain Spencer determines to start for Swan River—Secures objects from the wreck—Running fishes—Attack from natives—Start for Swan River—A log of wood converted into a shovel—A hawk's-bill Turtle—Natives touch the baggage—Frightened away—Natives on shore taste pickled oysters—Put on Captain Spencer's trowsers—Insects—Birds—Impression of a cloven foot with a spur—Flight of Parrakeets—Scrub—Captain Spencer makes a grass hat—Albatross—Haze and mirage—Berries—Snakes—Porpoises—Sea-shells—Meteor—Gannets.

For a time Captain Spencer sat with his head buried in his hands, and could scarcely realise his own position, so filled was he with grief and horror at the loss of his five men, drowned as it were for his sake. His horse and dog seemed now to be of double value; and as he sat with one arm round Gipsy's neck, it occurred to him that Charlie had not made his appearance. "My poor Charlie too!" he said; the word Charlie was repeated, and he started; but as all was again silent, he thought the sound must have proceeded from an echo in the cavern. "All dead!" he exclaimed, as his head again dropped. "All dead! all dead! Charlie's coming, Ned Spencer!" exclaimed the bird, and thus signified his escape. He hopped up to his master, who hugged and caressed him, poor, wet, sandy, and miserable-looking creature as he was, as if another dear object had been preserved. The bird had probably been frightened by the hurricane to take refuge in the cave, or had crept out from under the masses of fallen rock; at all events, he was overjoyed at finding his master and his companions. Gip, who had hitherto been rather jealous of him, actually licked him; and Tiger raised his head and fixed his large eyes upon him in a most amicable manner.

This circumstance roused the energy of Captain Spencer, and the necessity for immediate exertion presented itself. The desolate nature of the country on which he was thus cast, the dangerous reputation of its inhabitants, and many other evils stood before him with almost appaling force; yet the more he thought, the more did his natural courage and piety revive. "Shall I," said he, "who have faced death hand to hand with the enemies of my country; who have fought my way through ranks of foes, and held England's possessions against a besieging army, fear a handful of rude savages? Nevertheless," added he, "they are perhaps more formidable because they are treacherous, and defy the laws of honourable warfare." Throwing himself on his knees, he again thanked God for his own preservation, and prayed fervently for aid and support.

Strengthened and refreshed by prayer, the wanderer began to consider what was best to be done. Three ways seemed to present themselves, one of which was to remain near the coast on the chance of seeing a vessel; but when he recollected that all the time he had already been there he had not beheld a sail of any kind, this was rejected. The second suggestion was to return along the northern coast, and so reach Port Essington; but he fancied he was nearer to Perth on the Swan River, and if he had to travel, it might as well be in a totally new country; and he accordingly decided on proceeding close to the western shore, in the hope of perhaps seeing a vessel which was going to that port, or at all events reaching that settlement in some way or other. His chart, his sextant, were gone, he had nothing but his compass to guide him; but he deemed it an easy matter to steer in a south-west direction, which must lead him more or less near to the last mentioned colony. His pocket-book, containing letters of credit, was sewn inside his waistcoat; and the latter being cashed there, would enable him to take passage for India.

Captain Spencer's resolution being formed, he glanced at two of his companions as promising to be most serviceable in helping him through his undertaking, and he knew that his unfailing prowess as a shot would procure him food; but he resolved to remain where he was for a few days, to see if any useful articles would come ashore from the wreck, especially gunpowder and shot. It seemed to have been like foresight that he should have provided himself with so much ammunition, and made so little use of it, and he thought if the chest did not come up he had still enough. His chief difficulties would be want of water and clothing; "but," said he in a more cheerful tone, "you, my poor beasts, obey every sound of my voice, and, please God, we shall get through our troubles; so let us try to sleep." Thus speaking, he stretched himself on the ground, and the four were soon at rest; Charlie having perched himself close by on a ledge of sandstone.

Early in the morning, Captain Spencer took Tiger to the top of the cliff to get his food, and then descended to the beach, where he picked up some pieces of plank and brush-wood, which had been driven ashore, and setting fire to them with a little gunpowder, he contrived to make a hot meal for himself and Gip of some quails which he had shot above, though he felt quite sorry to pluck off the pretty fawn, or reddish, coloured feathers from their breasts; he stewed them in one of his tin cans, and ate them heartily, in spite of the failure of sauce and seasoning. On going to the sea-shore a multitude of objects met his view which would be very useful, and among others, two very large pieces of tarpauling. The ammunition-chest, to his great joy, was sticking fast in the sand; and having the key in his pocket, he opened it, and found the powder but little damaged; he spread this out on the tarpauling to dry, and was so intently occupied, that he scarcely observed the progress of the sun, till its descent warned him it was time to collect all his treasures, and take them to the cave. Among the latter was a barrel of flour, which he also emptied and dried; he then made some cakes of it, and baked them on hot ashes, as an addition to his evening meal. Tiger had several times peeped over the cliff as if to see whether he were wanted, and at sunset trotted down the path to settle for the evening. Charlie had both fed and amused himself upon the beach, but not approaching too near the water, of which he seemed to have an instinctive horror, thereby proving that he had been drenched during the storm. "You must be turned into a pack-horse, Tiger," said his master; "so come and be loaded for your new office." The docile creature stood unmoved as his master put the things upon his back, and walked steadily with his burden to the cave, where, after being unloaded, he laid himself down. Captain Spencer hearing Gip express herself in impatient tones, went to see what was the matter with her, and found her pulling with all her might at the sleeve of his thick over-coat which had hung up in the cabin, but which was now half-buried in sand. "Good dog," said he, patting her head, and the efforts of both freed the garment. Then putting it under one of the cascades to wash out the sand and salt water, it was the next day dried in the sun.

The night was warm and tranquil; and the next morning, on returning to the beach, Captain Spencer saw a number of fish, which appeared to be running about upon their elbows, to the great astonishment of Gipsy; and he could not help smiling at the dog's look and the ludicrous action of the fish, with their three free spines on their head, one of which had a tuft at the top, their gills like a hole, and their lower fins looking like great splay feet.* They were about nine inches long, and ran at each other with their mouths open; but the moment Captain Spencer came up to them, they all at once disappeared in the slimy matter which had collected round the mangroves growing on one side of the inlet. Their pectoral fins were supported by a sort of arm or stem, and on this part they walked, the fins themselves looking like hands. On trying to catch one, Captain Spencer saw it swell itself out till it looked like a ball on four feet, of a yellowish brown with black stripes. Gipsy seemed to think that she was also come to the beach to look for what might be found, and ran about with her nose close to the sand; at last she **stopped** and began scratching with all her **might,**

* Chironectes.

and her master, attracted by this, came to her assistance. To his great delight he found it was the trunk which contained his clothes, and which he emptied; but as he carried them to the cave, and saw the pile of articles which he had selected, he was sure he could not secure them all, and he was losing time, and uselessly consuming provisions to linger where he was; he therefore discontinued his search, and remained at the cave to arrange his property. He had secured some needles and balls of coarse thread, and cutting one of the sheets of tarpauling into pieces of sundry dimensions, he manufactured bags for holding gunpowder, flour and other eatables, cases for his fire-arms, and a knapsack for himself to carry. He kept the other piece of tarpauling entire, as a waterproof covering for all the rest, and for Tiger in bad weather, to which he fastened strings made of untwisted ropes, thrown ashore, so that it might be tied underneath the horse. From his own clothes he made what he thought a judicious selection of shoes, and woollen articles of dress, linen, and plenty of handkerchiefs and light things, which he thought might conciliate the natives. He hoped that the tin cans would convey a stock of water from place to place, and he hailed with considerable joy two hams, which he now cooked, and which had been but little injured by immersion in salt water.

All these preparations for his arduous journey occupied Captain Spencer a longer time than he had at first calculated on, and five days had elapsed before he thought of starting; during which time his horse and bird fed as usual, and he caught a sort of Guard-fish; and, besides this, met with one with a long muzzle like a Chelmar, cockles, and small and well-flavoured oysters, which had attached themselves to the mangroves, and in which he often found pearls. These trees were not numerous at that spot, therefore the traveller was not injured by them, but became still more strengthened for the long route which he had to traverse, and which he contemplated with an indefinable sadness, in spite of his faith, and the excitement which new adventures bring to the young and courageous. Gip had, during the last three days, taken an independent walk on the top of the cliffs, and each time brought back a Kangaroo-rat; thus cheering her master by the promise of her future services, which would spare his ammunition, and not only make it last for procuring food, but give him the more for self-defence. Each day he became more expert in cooking, of which all soldiers who have seen service know something; and as to Charlie, he was more intelligent than ever, repeating every word his master spoke, and applying his phrases to all circumstances which were similar to those under which he had learnt them.

The night before he left his quiet retreat, Captain Spencer was awoke by a low growl from Gipsy, as she raised her head and pricked up her ears. "Be quiet, Gip," said her master; but although she did not move, the animal continued very uneasy, and now and then gave a stifled bark. At length Tiger was roused, and stood upright in the cave; and on seeing a sudden disturbance, Charlie exclaimed, "What's the matter?" Then Captain Spencer also rose, gun and pistol in hand, which he always kept loaded, and looked out. How many dark forms he saw before him, and on the beach, and ledges of the rock, he never knew, but the moonlight disclosed a formidable number who had spears in their hands. They advanced; and two, more daring than the rest, came close to the cave, each carrying a thick heavy club. "To him, Gip!" said Captain Spencer, and the dog immediately seized one of them by the leg; while Tiger, who seemed to understand what was going on, burst out on his hind legs, striking all within his reach with his fore-paws, knocking them over down the rocks. Those who were behind paused, and Captain Spencer, who only wished to alarm, called Gipsy off, and fired one of his pistol-barrels into the air; the ball whizzed over their heads, and they retreated; he cautiously looked after them, and saw them hastily making their way upon their rafts to the island, with their double-bladed paddles; and he concluded that they had discovered him from thence by the smoke of his fire. "This decides my departure," said he; "it is better to go before they have recovered from their fright, and start with to-morrow's dawn; but this night I and Gip will watch."

On the morrow Captain Spencer packed his things in as small a compass as he could, eating his breakfast during the operation; he carried them to the top of the cliff, and there loaded Tiger, who was an apt and obedient servant when his master wanted him; the whole of the load was secured by the tarpauling, and he was much amused at seeing Charlie seat himself on the top, saying, "Let us be off; all's right." No more was seen of the natives, even from the height, by means of the telescope. The travellers followed the outline of the coast, except where its deep and frequent indentations rendered it more expedient to go straight across the projection. Captain Spencer had lost all trace of the day of the week, and consequently could not distinguish the Sabbath; but as far as prayer and praise were concerned, each day was Sunday to him, and it seemed as if, in that wild country, and in his isolated position, he must unceasingly invoke the aid of his Heavenly Protector, and admire His wonderful works. To all who have read Scripture, it is in these scenes that the very words of Holy Writ rise unconsciously to the lips, as if they alone, in their grand simplicity, could express the feelings; and those who, in their intercourse with their fellow-men, would refrain from using them as being irreverent to do so, find themselves involuntarily speaking in the language of the Bible.

The steady pace at which Captain Spencer began his long march, as all experienced soldiers do, made Gipsy walk by his side the first day, and the novelty of carrying a burden curbed the dancing propensities of Tiger. As for Charlie, he kept up a dignified demeanour at first, as if he would not interfere with the grand conveyance which he had chosen for himself. "This steadiness is too good to last," thought Captain Spencer, as he took off the load, and prepared for rest, dinner, and siesta, during the heat of the day. On rising to resume his journey, he examined the country with his glass, saw the jagged coast on one side, and on the other, at a considerable distance, the land seemed to be more covered with large districts of flowering bushes, and here and there a patch of untidy-looking timber, while in the far-off horizon some hills seemed to rise, some with flat summits, which betokened their sandstone formation. Altogether, mind and eye ached with the immensity of space around him, some of which he had to traverse. it was monotonous, yet it was **grand**; but the apparent absence of animal life was oppressive, and he thought of the many leagues which he must journey before he could find a civilised companion. A few birds, eagles, and crows, and others which were strange to him, were high up in the air; but with these exceptions, he and his unreasoning companions, as they are called, seemed to be alone. He had read something about the country in which it had thus pleased God to place him, and knew that it was unlike any other in its features and productions; yet he hoped that the little knowledge which he possessed of natural history would be of some help in procuring sustenance, for he thought the great laws of creation must be the same everywhere. As he stood gazing around him, and absorbed in his reflections, a soft, velvet-like touch upon his cheek made him start, and turning round he saw Tiger, who went up to one of the cans as if to ask for water. "What, already is there a scarcity?" said his master; "if you have not found any, I must let you have some from my own stock; poor fellow! it is lucky that Arab horses do not require as much as others do; nevertheless, instead of going on now, I had better begin to look for some. Come along, Gip." "I'm coming," said Charlie, and flew before him. He directed his steps towards a clump of trees covered with pale yellow **and** feathery blossoms, perfuming the air with their delicious odour; they proved to be acacias, which, from growing near a small stream, had acquired greater size than the neighbouring bushes of the same sort. These bushes were also beginning to flower, and Captain Spencer concluded they must form one of the scrubs described as so formidable both to man and beast; he stooped down to examine this scrub, and found that no description had done justice to its inaccessible nature; it was full of sharp, woody, and branching thorns, often eight inches long, frequently crossing each other, and he thought with dismay of the probable necessity of making his way through such obstacles. There was water, however, under the trees, and by raising the turf with his axe, and scooping the earth out with his hands, he made a hole big enough to enable him to fill his cans; and calling his companions to him, he resolved to remain there all night. Then Gipsy, with her usual sagacity, dashed into the scrub, and brought her accustomed tribute to the meal, producing two or three rats, which, as usual, were good to eat.

The following day Captain Spencer strolled towards the sea, in the hope of finding something with which he might be able to scoop out earth when he met with water underground, as the last had been. On looking over the cliff he discovered a log of wood which had been washed ashore.

"Why should I not shape that into something like a shovel?" thought he; "it might do for any soft sort of soil;" and he determined to secure it. Leaving Gip at the top, where he stood looking down, whining and wagging her tail, afraid to follow, and yet not liking to stay behind, he leaped from ledge to ledge of the rock like a birdcatcher, till he reached the bottom. The log was too heavy for him to carry, and while pondering on the possibility of conveying it up the cliff, a much more valuable prize saluted his eyes in the shape of a huge hawks-bill Turtle. To dash into the surf, push it ashore, and turn it on its back, was the work of two minutes; but then came the same difficulty as had puzzled him concerning the log. His only plan, he thought, would be to chop both to pieces on the shore; but during the time this would take, he dared not leave his packages above unguarded. In this dilemma he turned his head, and saw Gip at some distance, running down the cliff with ease. "A native path," thought he; "Tiger shall come down and drag them up." Gip jumped with delight on reaching her master, and her curiosity was excited by the turtle. Going up to examine it with her nose close to the creature, she received such a blow fom one of the fins, that she thought herself killed. On recovering her fright, however, she became very angry, and uttered a cry of such mingled fear and rage, that her master could not help laughing; he took her up in his arms and soothed her, but on inviting her to battle with the reptile, she hung her head and tail, and crept behind him, still showing her teeth.

Captain Spencer again mounted the cliff in order to fetch Tiger; and looking around with his glass, he was so convinced of the absence of other human beings, that he thought he might with safety leave his packages, with the exception of the cans, closely covered with the tarpauling, and pass the day and night on the shore. His first business was rudely to chop the log into the shape of a shovel, and with the chips he made a fire; he then chopped off the head of the turtle, and the fins, and these he put into one of the cans with some water; he divided the upper from the lower shell, and to his pleasure found the turtle full of eggs; he put the rest of the flesh into the can, and set it on to boil, while he strewed some of the hot wood-ashes on the ground, and roasted the eggs in the turtle's shell. Gip had her share of them; and the whole party went to rest. Rising again at break of day, Captain Spencer and the dog invigorated themselves with more eggs, and prepared for remounting the cliff. Charlie flew into the air, Gip preceded her master, and Tiger followed, the cans, the turtle, and rude shovel slung across his back by the pocket-handkerchiefs and cravat of Captain Spencer.

The moment the dog reached the summit she began to bark furiously; and convinced that there was something wrong, Captain Spencer cautiously raised his head a little above the cliff, and saw a body of natives, armed in the usual manner, examining the contents of the tarpauling. They had paused on hearing Gip bark, and one of them had raised his arm in order to spear the poor animal, when Captain Spencer sent a ball flying over his head, and the smoke of the powder went into the faces of all; then freeing Tiger from his burden, and springing on to his back, he leaped into the midst of them, the horse's mane and tail floating in the air, and he firing off a bullet from the second barrel of his weapon. "Boyl ya! Boyl ya!" screamed the natives, running away with the utmost rapidity, not daring even to look behind them; Gip went barking after them, and Charlie flew screaming out, "I'm coming, I'm coming! here's Charlie!" the one acting in the defence of her master, the other expressing his delight at a noise and bustle. In their hurry one of the men left his throwing-stick behind him; and Captain Spencer found it to be eight feet long, smaller at both ends, and at one of these a barb, looking as if made to fit the spear. By its side lay a strong cord, made of twisted woody fibres, both of which he left where they had been lying, after they had undergone his examination.

The route was complete, and calling Gip off from the pursuit, Captain Spencer, gave way to a violent fit of laughter, joined by Charlie; but it was a lesson to him never again to leave his things exposed; and as he watched the Australians with his glass, and saw them disappear down the cliff at a distance, most thankful was he that they had not surprised him when below.

Some days elapsed without any variety of incident, the wanderers making steady progress, and gaining much ground, when being again near the edge of the cliff, Captain Spencer heard some of the natives chattering below. Lying down flat, he peered over, and was highly amused by watching their proceedings. There was a numerous party, and among them some women; one with a grass mat tied at her back, from which peeped out the head of a child, and a large bag in her hand; another had a kangaroo-skin cloak over her shoulders, and a fire-stick, which was a hard, tough piece of wood, lighted at one end, but not blazing; a third was hugging neither more nor less than Captain Spencer's valuable Triton tea-kettle. On the ground lay a dog with a long, narrow head, like that of a lurcher, which seemed to be of Malay origin. The women stood quietly looking on, while most of the men were squatted round some object which was in the midst of them, and making an immense noise. Presently several put their hands to their mouths, and immediately after rose, spitting and stamping their feet, and the jar of pickled oysters came to view; they yelled, they tossed their arms up, and while the owner was thinking how he could recover his oysters, two of them took the jar, and threw it into the sea. Nor was this all: one of them rose from the ground, deliberately placed a pair of Captain Spencer's trousers on his head, which occupied the seat, while the legs floated over the shoulders. This was too much; rolling himself from the edge of the cliff, he gave way to a hearty fit of laughter, which being echoed by Charlie, caused a sudden sensation below, and he heard the people stealing away with voices hushed into a whisper. They were well-made, dressed their hair in various ways, some decorating it with feathers; most of them had a nose ornament; and their language sounded as if it were very melodious, and composed of words of many syllables. Among them were two who had a much lighter complexion than the others, probably owing to Malay blood, and they seemed to be the chiefs of the body.

Fearing a re-action, and perhaps a surprise, Captain Spencer pushed on as speedily as he could, not stopping to bivouac in the middle of the day. On the next he travelled more leisurely, and watched Charlie pursue a butterfly with a golden body, green and blue wings, and spots like black velvet,* which he vainly tried to save from destruction. Grasshoppers chirped so loudly at night that he could not sleep, and he took that opportunity of polishing and sharpening his shovel with his knife, thereby rendering it much lighter to carry. While so occupied he heard a bird with a full melodious whistle, slowly uttering five or six successive half tones; but he could not get near enough to have an idea of its plumage. Various Beetles had that day attracted him, one species of which was very round, of a yellow brown, and spotted. The flies† still continued to distress all except Charlie. Large Cranes had more than once appeared in the air, a flight of Pigeons‡ crossed over the scrub, and Quails with black spots on their breasts, and some curious Ducks§ had given him a large stock of good eatables, in the preparation of which he had now become very expert, as he split and roasted them on hot ashes: a greater abundance of animal life, especially of the winged kind, made him think that their scarcity hitherto might have been occasioned by being frightened away from the coast by the hurricane.

The impression of a large cloven hoof on the short turf had excited some sensation in Captain Spencer's mind, for he knew that no animals owning such an one as that were indigenous to Australia. Could he be near any cattle station? surely

* Prianiceps. † Paropsis.
‡ Geophaps plumifera. § Amas semipalmata.

there were none so far north as he was then; perhaps it might be a stray bull which had become wild, and had thus wandered. He settled that it was so in his own mind, but yet he dwelt on the circumstance, and he looked for it again and again. A piece of depressed ground, however, settled the question, for this had not dried since the rain had lodged in it, and retained the marks of the foot more correctly than the previous print; he now, therefore, ascertained, from the impression of a spur, that one of the buffaloes introduced in the northern part of the continent, of which the Malays had told him, had strayed to this point, and the hope of soon reaching a settlement was abandoned. That he was still within the tropics was evident from the existence of some Palm-trees; he diverged from his path to go to them, and finding a young one, he cut off the top, and boiled and ate it for his supper without fear of its indigestible qualities.

Tired of always seeing the same things, the traveller longed to go further inland, yet he dared not do so to any extent, from the fear of completely losing his way; he, however, came to an enormous, round projection of land, and determined to march straight across it. In doing this, however, he was annoyed by the scrub which presented itself; no longer Acacia, but Atriplex of the most matted and entangled kind. It was like navigating to follow any track in which the mass of vegetation was thinned; but now and then, in parts which had been burnt, and consequently cleared, a beautiful crimson Kennedia had started into being. Poor Tiger was much wearied by lifting his feet straight up to get them out at all, and then stamping them down to crush the stems, and obtain a free footing. Now and then a beautiful creeping plant would make its way from underneath, in the shape of a yellow papilionaceous flower, which Captain Spencer believed to be a Dolichos.

A cloud seemed to pass over the travelling party, when Charlie, who had been flying above, gravely took his seat on the top of Tiger's back, muttering to himself, "All's right! all's right!"—and looking up, his master beheld a vast flight of Grass Parrakeets taking a direct southerly course, and emigrating, probably in search of food; he fired among them, and brought down several; though it grieved him to destroy such pretty creatures. "The worst part of my present life,' said he, " is, that I am obliged to kill so many innocent beings; but I must eat." "Must eat," echoed Charlie; thereby confirming the necessity of the destruction.

At length water was scarce, and Captain Spencer was again obliged to seek some in the vicinity of a clump of green-looking trees. He pushed his way to them as well as he could through the scrub, and then made his first acquaintance with one of the distinguishing features of Australian vegetation, for they belonged to the great tribe of Myrtles and the genus *Eucalyptus,* of which there are so many species, gum-trees as the settlers call them, and to which other English names have been also given, according to their fancied resemblances in taste and smell, such as the Peppermint tree, the Mahogany, the Box, the Paper Bark, &c. Their appearance was peculiar, and the trees had a dull, untidy look, owing to the manner in which the leaves hung from the twisting of the leaf-stalk, which caused them to present their edges, instead of flat surfaces to the observer. The bark hung in picturesque festoons, and he recognised it as the same which he had applied to the fractured arm of the man on the coast. Under the trees was a pool of water, which had evidently been visited by natives, for the edges had been trodden down by many naked feet; but, tired of the scrub, he turned again towards the shore, Charlie going before him, and pursuing a curious Dragon-fly[*] with a bright brown and black body, and an appendage to its tail like two small leaves. Hawk-moths[†] were also flying about near the pool, for the sun was fast declining. The moment he was outside the scrub he threw himself on the ground to rest; and then observing that the grass was very long and silky, it struck

---

[*] Petalura.   [†] Deilephila.

him that he might contrive a covering for his head, which would be cooler and lighter than the hot cloth and leather of his cap; and he consequently selected some of the longest blades, and endeavoured to work according to measurement, somewhat on the model of his military head-cover, only he was decided on having a very broad brim all round. This occupation carried him far into the night, and intruded upon the next day; but he determined not to leave it till finished. Do what he would, however, the crown obstinately assumed a conical shape, and so added to his height, which was already six feet, and the brim would hang and flap about his face; the former he could not remedy, but he procured some long thorns from an Acacia tree, and weaving them into the brim, it stood out wide and stiff; moreover he, to his great satisfaction, contrived a button and loop, which fastened it up in front at pleasure; he put his eagle's feathers on one side, and flattered himself that he looked something like the picturesque models of banditti of which he had seen drawings; but the conceit was soon taken out of him, when Gipsy saw him put it on; for, fancying he was dressing himself up for fun, she ran round him, jumped and barked, and it was some time before she could be quite reconciled to this new head-dress. "Gipsy, you are no judge," said her master, as he put his cap into his knapsack; and at that moment

Charlie, whose chase had been very successful, flew to him, saying, "Ned Spencer! Ned Spencer! ha! ha! ha!"

Another Albatross was seen near the sea, and this time came near enough for the traveller to perceive that it had a rose-coloured beak, that its head and neck were of a deep brown, and that the dark back gradually softened into white underneath; the noise which it made was like that of an old goose. Gip evidently expected her master to shoot it; but he could not eat it, and collections of natural history would have been very cumbersome to carry, so the bird passed over in peace. On the same day a thick haze came over the sky, and so much mirage appeared, that he saw overhead the distant objects to which he was coming, and among others, at what distance he could not tell, a deep ravine too wide to cross, and which would therefore force him to go inland, and skirt its sides. At night a heavy dew fell, and but for his mackintosh, would have wetted him through; and when he had lain down, and covered himself, Tiger, and Gip, with the tarpauling, he was amused at seeing Charlie also creep under it, saying, "I'm coming, I'm coming!" All four formed a loving party, and he felt that he had the very best substitutes for human companions.

The next morning Captain Spencer visited the cliffs before he turned inland, for he had full faith in the mirage, though at what distance the ravine might be he could not tell. On going there he saw some small shrubs, among which were Acacias* of a new description, and a Pittosporum,† loaded with ripe, many-seeded berries, which Charlie ate, and therefore his master followed his example, having no fear of their being poisonous. Several snakes were near them, black and yellow, and black and green, which glided into holes in the ground, leaving the marks of their undulating course on the sandy ground of which the cliff was formed, and which he had often seen before without knowing what they were, thereby finding that they were numerous, and exciting his gratitude that neither he nor his followers had been bitten. A land-slip and depression tempted Captain Spencer to go down to the sea-shore, and there he saw whales at a distance, and porpoises swimming one after the other in such a manner that they resembled the drawings and prints which he had seen of the Sea-serpent, and he could scarcely persuade himself that they were really not that far-famed monster. Again did he catch a turtle, which Gip would not approach; and again did he bathe with two of his companions. There were plenty of different kinds of shells on this part of the coast, and among them he recognised Cypreæ, Coni, Volutes, and Patellæ, also some enormous Venus's

* A. ligulata. † P. oleifolium.

Ears,* one of which he formed into a drinking cup, and another into a strainer; from the former he twisted off the holes through which the inhabitant thrusts its tentacula, and filed the edge quite smooth. That same night a large meteor crossed the sky out at sea, leaving a long train of light behind it, and exploded into a shower of star-like sparks. Numerous Petrels of different species hovered about; and the next morning a large flight of Gannets, extending many yards in length and breadth, passed along at the rate of at least thirty miles the hour. They were evidently going to the south, and some thousands must have been there, for they were an hour and a half in their passage over the spot where Captain Spencer was. Charlie sat on the top of the cliff staring up at them, and muttering to himself, and when the last was gone, he burst into a loud "Ha! ha! ha!"

From this point the party proceeded along shore at the foot of the deep red cliffs, till the truth of the mirage was proved, and they reached the mouth of a wide inlet, through which a river was flowing to the ocean.

* Haliotes gigantea.

CHAPTER IV.

Captain Spencer ascends a ravine—Flying Foxes—Green Ants—Hawks, Pelicans, Parrakeets, and cranes—Mullet—Porpoises—Pandanus—Nutmegs—Pigeons, &c.—Mosquitoes—Sand-flies—Hears natives—Dangerous attack—Captain Spencer kills a man—He is wounded by a spear—Beautiful plain and lake—Water-lilies, &c.—Residence on the top of a hillock—Native graves—Sees Kangaroos—Tiger loses a shoe—Oats—Kangaroos—Skin prepared—Moccasins made—Frilled Lizzard—Gipsy nearly killed by a Python—Kites and other birds—Cranes—Bitterns—Owls, &c.—Sow-thistle—Falcon—Shrike—Cuckoo — Captain Spencer rides to native huts—Spear-heads—Circles of stones—Bower-bird—Gourd—Cray-fish—Captain Spencer rides over the hills—Caves like temples—Paintings—Vampire Bats—Carved head—Kangaroo — Gouty tree—Vitex—Crabs—Reed—Beetles — Fire-flies—Storm—Provisions collected for journey—The grass hat—A fresh start.

To ascend the inlet at which he had now arrived on one side, till he could cross the river flowing through it, and then return towards the coast on the other, seemed to Captain Spencer to be the only feasible plan which he could pursue; for although he, Gip, and Tiger could swim well, the current was immensely strong, and the bed of the river full of rocks, so that he would have found it difficult to resist being carried out to sea by the force of the water, and certainly the light Gipsy, and Tiger with his burden, could not get across.

The idea of being taken by this ravine into a new part of the country would have caused no regret, had he not reflected, that as yet he had made but little way in the many leagues of distance which he had to traverse ; but there was no help for it, and he consoled himself with the prospect of seeing the interior of a country which he knew to be beautiful, but which had not as yet presented many of its charms to his eyes. He retreated for the night to a distance from the mangroves, and only unpacking what was absolutely necessary to allay thirst and hunger, he wrapped himself in his cloak, and, sheltered by the cliffs, the whole party slept for a few hours.

The next morning, even before the sun had risen high enough to light up the western ocean, Captain Spencer was ready for starting. The sea was calm, but a heavy tide rolling in shore, gave it that ong, heavy swell, which conveys an idea that the whole of our planet must more or less partake of the vast movement. None but a very rugged path could be found between the banks of the river and the high cliffs which bordered them ; but Tiger picked his way through, Gip leaped from stone to stone, and for a time Charlie rode in his usual place on the top of the baggage, as if afraid to trust himself out of sight in a new scene. In their passage close to the mangroves, they disturbed numbers of those bats which are called flying Foxes,* and which his Malays had told him were good eating; but he had never tried them; and now, as they flew past and around him, their musky odour rendered him still more unwilling to convert them into food. With his Indian dislike to mangroves, he hastened on, and was well pleased, after walking for two hours, to find that they altogether disappeared, thereby leaving him a wider path, skirted on one side by the rushing, tumbling river, and on the other by a thick belt of trees of various kinds, which, in their abundance, frequently spread their branches across the way, to the discomfort both of master and horse; for when they knocked against them, a swarm of green ants, which built their nests among the leaves, dropped upon them and bit them severely. According to his usual custom, when anything annoyed Tiger, his master sought to relieve him from it; but there was no kind person to perform such an office for himself; and the painful attacks of these little creatures made him rejoice in the brim of his grass hat. The ears of Tiger, however, suffered so much, that he stamped and kicked; and Captain Spencer contrived, when he rested for the night, to make coverings for them out of one of his handkerchiefs, and hanging from each was a long shred of the same material, which he hoped would also keep off the flies.

* Pteropus edulis.

The height of the cliffs, and the dense vegetation rendered the air less fresh than above, but it was far from disagreeable; these heights were still composed of coarse ferruginous and siliceous sandstone; and from the foliage numbers of beautiful parrakeets rushed out, pursued by black-shouldered hawks; and from the former Captain Spencer did not hesitate to derive two or three meals. Now and then a row of pelicans, with their solemn looks, told him that fishes were to be had in the river; but these heavy birds slowly flew away at his approach, wheeling off in circles near the ground, and then soaring upwards. Large cranes* also came to feed by the water side, and with their accustomed fearlessness of man, would probably have suffered him to go by without being disturbed; but when Tiger appeared he was too much for their courage, and they flew away as if unwilling to go Plenty of mullet in the river explained the presence of these birds, as well as that of some wild ducks resembling teal; and he determined to follow their example of having fish for dinner. Unloading Tiger, he prepared a line and hook, which he took from one of his jacket pockets, and cutting a pole from one of the trees for a fishing-rod, he baited the hook with one of the unknown insects hovering over the water, and seating himself on a fragment of rock, he soon captured a plentiful sup-

* Ardea antigone (Native companion).

ply; and, as he drew them out, he observed that they were of a much paler red than when they inhabited the ocean. Experience had not taught them to avoid man, and they seized on his bait with avidity: but on hearing a great splashing at some distance, they darted away with the utmost rapidity. A shoal of porpoises had just arrived from sea, and rapidly advancing, overtook the hindmost; and then Captain Spencer knew it would be in vain for him to compete with his finny rivals; so while Tiger browsed on the herbage growing between the pieces of fallen stone, he made his fire, roasted his mullet, and he and Gipsy enjoyed an excellent repast.

The trees under the cliffs were of various kinds; but the Pandanus,* having the air of a palm-tree with simple fronds, and Nutmeg,† were the most abundant; the traveller tasted some of the fruit of the latter, and found it very insipid; but it was still very young, and in this sheltered ravine was probably never out of fruit and flower. The brightest and most exquisitely-coloured parrots and parrakeets, displaying all the most brilliant plumage which could be conceived, filled the air with their cries as they came to feed upon the nutmegs; and equally beautiful, though not so gay, were some white pigeons, which came for the same purpose. Of these Captain Spencer secured a pro-

* Pandanus pedunculatus.   † Myristica insipida.

vision for himself and Gipsy. Various climbing plants crept up the trees, and the bright orange fruits of the Pandanus, having attained something like maturity, afforded an agreeable refreshing pulp at the bottom of each scale, in the manner of the scales of an artichoke.

Small lateral creeks, or rather fissures, now and then broke the monotony of the vegetation, and at the end of the afternoon's march, the party reached a circular opening, down which a rivulet dropped in tiny cascades. The water of the river, though drinkable, was still a little brackish; but this was deliciously fresh, and here Captain Spencer determined to remain the whole night. Tiger was freed from his load, the fire was made and lighted, the fish were split, impaled, and placed over it. Gipsy lay down with her paws crossed to watch the operation, and Charlie, who was always near when in a new place, perched himself upon the rocks, hopping from one to another to catch his insect supper. The birds and fishes were cooked, and all four having feasted to their satisfaction, laid themselves down to rest in their accustomed fashion, as much covered as possible to avoid the mosquitoes; but the first heavy sleep of fatigue over, rest was gone, in consequence of their old enemies the sand-flies. Gip adopted her usual remedy, which was to creep under the coat which she herself had secured from the wreck, and on which her master generally slept, where she nestled with one paw over her nose. Poor Tiger, however, had no such remedy, and started and fidgeted, and at last stood up. Captain Spencer turned up the collar of his coat, and buried his face in it, but it was of no use; he also got up, and tied a handkerchief over Tiger's nose and mouth, and enveloping the whole of his own face in another, and tucking his hands under his sleeves, he seated himself with his back against the cliff, regretting the heights, where at least he had been free from mosquitoes, and wishing for some mosquito-gauze, through which he could have seen; for he well knew the continued torment to which he should be liable whenever he was near water. During his disturbed sleep he fancied he heard some footsteps, and Charlie muttered, Tiger pawed the ground, and Gip withdrew from her covering and barked; but no molestation followed. In the morning, however, to his great annoyance, Captain Spencer discovered that there was not only a well-trodden path from above to the spot where he had passed the night, but that there were marks of recent footsteps, which proved that none of them had been mistaken.

Hastily swallowing his breakfast, and throwing to Gipsy hers, while he saw that his fire-arms were in good order, and loading Tiger, Captain Spencer, fearing some hostile attack, departed early from his bivouac. As hours passed away, and fresh beauties presented themselves to his view, apprehensions of evil from the natives subsided, and laughing to see how Tiger snorted away the flies, and Gip rubbed her nose in the bushes, as they walked on with their eyes almost closed, according to the native fashion, he had some thoughts of resting, when Charlie, who had been occasionally flying ahead of them, quickly returning, exclaimed, "Ned Spencer! Ned Spencer!" and perched upon his master's shoulder. Advancing a few paces into a spot cleared of trees, and full of masses of fallen cliff, the soldier stood opposite to his enemies mounted on the top of the cliff, and awaiting his approach. They were headed by a man much taller than the rest, whose face was painted white, to show that he was in mourning; and he and the others had their spears fixed in their throwing sticks, and uttered the most savage yells. They pointed with firce gestures towards the sea, as if ordering the stranger to return. But the sight of Captain Spencer with Charlie on his shoulder for a moment astonished them; and the bark of defiance with which Gipsy greeted them, so different to the howl of their own dogs, which never bark, arrested them. Then, when Tiger appeared, they fell back, and evidently talked to each other concerning the whole party; and wishing to conciliate, Captain Spencer, unable to find anything white as a signal of peace, broke a bough from a tree, and, holding it up, advanced towards them. Many of them retreated still further; but the tall man loudly addressed them, with passionate gestures, on which they screamed, jumped, bit their beards and spat them out again, and at last the chief hurled his spear; Captain Spencer avoided it by stepping on one side, and thinking that he ought now to show his power, he fired one ball from his pistol over their heads. As it whistled through the air, they stared, and endeavoured to follow it with their eyes; but they stood their ground; and when again excited by their head man, a shower of spears was about to be hurled at the party, when the able marksman paralysed the aim of the principal person, by lodging a bullet in his arm. Again were the weapons lowered, and the Englishman tried to advance; but their leader, in a still greater fury, evidently ordered them to throw their spears. Springing behind a piece of rock, the traveller saved his life; but one of the spears carried away a part of his valuable grass hat, and another became transfixed in the load on Tiger's back, who raised his head and neighed loudly, while Gipsy continued to bark, and Charlie to scream overhead. Now, thought Captain Spencer, if ever a man were justified in taking away life in self-defence, I must destroy that fellow; and, crouching down, and resting his gun upon the rock, he fired at the tall enemy, and sent a bullet into his heart. The man instantly fell, and most of his companions crowded round him, while two or three again hurled their spears. The second barrel of the gun sent a third bullet into the leg of another man, and then all crowded in confusion round the body of their companion, and went away as quickly as possible in the greatest state of alarm and distress; at which time Captain Spencer again heard the syllables, "boyl-ya" muttered in an under tone.

The first impulse of the traveller was to utter his short and fervent thanks to the gracious Preserver of his life, and then to leave the spot as quickly as possible. On turning round to summon Tiger, he beheld the poor beast on the ground, and in the greatest alarm he ran to his assistance. Anxiety gave way to joy, when he found that this faithful friend was unhurt, having been brought down by one of the last spears, which destroyed the equilibrium of the baggage. After reloading his gun and pistol, he repacked the baggage, and Tiger was as ready to start as he was. Gipsy had been behind the rock with her master, and so escaped unhurt; and Charlie issued from a hole, saying, "All's right! I'm coming!"

Anxious to avoid further surprise, Captain Spencer endeavoured to find a way of getting up the cliffs; but this being impossible, he pushed forward at a brisk pace, and went on without stopping till nightfall, by which time he had gained a considerable distance. He chose a convenient spot, where there was grass for Tiger, and he and Gip ate cold bird and flour-cake, as he would not light a fire for fear of discovering his whereabouts to the natives. Then he discovered that he was stiff and uncomfortable from a slight wound in the neck, made by the spear which carried away part of his hat. Another spear had made a deep indentation on the surface of his powder-flask, and "this hair-breadth 'scape" seemed to promise him that he should be allowed to reach home, regiment, and friends, in safety. He kept the spears which had pierced his hat and upset Tiger's load, thinking they might be useful in killing quadrupeds, and so save his ammunition. One of them had a head of stone, deeply notched like a series of fish hooks; and had it entered his flesh, could not have been extracted without either cutting or tearing him terribly; the other was headed by a sharp piece of wood, harder than the shaft of the spear. He bathed his wound well with cold water, put a soft handkerchief over it, and thus alleviated the pain in some degree. When he settled for the night, and had time to think, he felt greatly distressed at having been obliged to kill the native; and, restless and feverish, it preyed upon him, although it had been necessary for his own preservation. Tiger and Gipsy were foot-sore from their forced march, and he suffered them to sleep in quiet, while he watched over their safety. He did not know if Charlie were apt to talk at night, or whether the disturbance of the day had made a deep impression upon him; but more than once, during those long hours, he frequently moved his head from under his wing, held it first on one side and then on the other, and after saying, "Such a row! all's right!" went to sleep again. When the morning began to break, Captain Spencer, rousing Gipsy, ordered her to watch, and, quite exhausted, he threw himself on the ground, and slept soundly.

Refreshed by three hours of good rest, Captain Spencer and Gipsy breakfasted upon the scraps of their now scanty stock, and all proceeded at a steady and uninterrupted pace for several hours; at that time the cliffs began rapidly to decline in height, and the river, though still broad, became more tranquil in its course. Anxious to get out of reach of the mosquitoes as soon as it was practicable for Tiger, Captain Spencer clambered with him and Gip to the top of the cliffs; and on arriving there stood for some minutes in silent admiration of the beautiful scene displayed to his observation. A large plain lay below and before him, in which the river, whose course he had been following, spread into a wide basin or lake, covered with white and blue water-lilies, and here and there a head of the pink Nelumbium in the midst of them; its banks were adorned with reeds and flowering plants; the long grass of the plain was five feet high, and very silky; and small hillocks and beautiful shrubs, some of which were in flower, and clumps of trees, were spread over the surface. A ridge of sand-hills, with whimsically-shaped heads, looking as if they had been put on by the hand of some mighty man in sport, skirted the eastern part of the plain, and their sloping sides, covered with verdure, almost reached the lake, making this park-like country, hitherto untrodden by the foot of the white man, seem to be a pleasure-ground; a dense forest to the south closed the horizon in that quarter.

On descending into the plain, Tiger could not resist nibbling the delicious bearded grass, and her master could not help laughing at Gipsy, who jumped, and played, and tumbled among the long blades, and yet never got out of them, till, knowing how tired the poor little animal was, he placed her on the top of his knapsack, while he sought for the best spot in which to find a resting-place. He made his way toward the hills, in order to get above the region of water and mosquitoes; and where, on something like an eminence, he could see around him, and detect the approach of enemies. No traces of natives having been recently there could be found; and he concluded those with whom he had had his late encounter had not taken that direction.

On the way to the hill a place had been cleared amongst the grass, and a mound of earth was seen, ornamented with small sticks, some painted with red horizontal marks, and others, which had been scraped, had the shavings twisted round them. At a short distance from this were two heaps of stones; and taking a large one from the top of the lowest, and peeping in, Captain Spencer discovered a skeleton; he covered the hole again, and concluded that all three mounds were graves, and looking round him, thought he saw some of the inhabitants of the neighbourhood, in the long grass, at a great distance. Notwithstanding his late encounter, he always hoped to be friends with these people, and knew if he could overcome the first hostile feeling, he should probably succeed, for all savages act from impulse, and this once gone by, they will, generally speaking, listen to amicable overtures. Whether men or any other animals, however, the dark moving objects which he saw suddenly disappeared.

Captain Spencer had chosen the highest hillock he could find, and thought it would be a commanding position from which he could watch the approach of an enemy. It was easy of ascent, and on reaching the top he first surveyed the country around with his glass, and, to his great delight, those which he thought were men again leaped up, and proved to be kangaroos. Here, then, all his preconceived notions of Australia were to be realized; and forgetting dangers, savages, mosquitoes, and all disagreeables, he said to his weary companions, as they toiled up the hill, "Cheer up, boys!" "Cheer up, boys!" was echoed by a voice over his head; Charlie caught the lively tone, and again and again bade them all be cheerful. For a moment, however, Captain Spencer's pleasure was clouded by seeing Tiger walk as if he were lame, and apprehensively he examined his feet. Fortunately, however, it was nothing more than the loss of one of his shoes; so when the horse arrived at the top of the hill, he took off the rest, and tied them carefully together, thinking he would present them to some native, who would be glad of the novelty, and Tiger must in future go bare-footed.

On the top of the hill an irregular surface presented itself, and in one of the depressions he saw a hole; fearing that it might harbour some beast or reptile, Captain Spencer thrust a spear into it, and found that it was a cave of small extent, and would form a safe hiding-place for all his baggage when he wished to quit it, and might be easily made to conceal it by covering the mouth with grass or bushes. The area of the whole summit was quite sufficient for his purposes of rest and cooking. The most urgent necessity now, however, was to allay hunger, and Tiger being unloaded, began to satisfy his appetite on the long grass, while his master examined the state of his larder. "These bones must do for us to-night, Gip," said he, "for I am too tired to get anything else, and to-morrow we will be afoot early and shoot a kangaroo. We shall have a glorious stock of provisions before we go further south;" then beating the grass all round to dislodge any unwelcome companion, he frightened away some beautiful lizards, and frogs of brilliant colours, and in a short time the whole party was asleep, with a feeling of security which made their slumbers more refreshing.

Early the next morning, by means of the shovel, the hiding-place was completed, and Tiger having descended the hills, and Charlie started on his foraging excursion, Captain Spencer and Gipsy took their way in search of kangaroos. The attention of the former was, however, immediately arrested by a tract covered with a yellowish grass, and on approaching it, he found that this was a sort of oat,* and not only would it afford the most invigorating food for Tiger, but yield meal and cakes to his master. Although he had not had any breakfast, Captain Spencer turned his "sword into a reaping-hook," cut some down, and calling

* Panicum.

Tiger, placed it on his back and bore it to the hill, where he spread it to dry upon his large piece of tarpauling. Gip took to her usual hunting, and had already caught and devoured her former food, the kangaroo rats; and munching some of the oats as he went along, the traveller again started in quest of his long-wished for spoil, this time guiding Tiger to the spot where he might feast.

Turning to a small tree which grew like a young elm, but which had a dark-green, pointed leaf, he cut it down for fire-wood. The timber was very hard, and dark inside, with a white rim outside it an inch in thickness; and leaving it to take up at his leisure, he pursued his way to the kangaroos, from which he had been twice diverted; Charlie flying up to him occasionally, and talking like a child from happiness.

Tall, dark figures, some of which were at least nine feet high, raised their heads from out of the grass, and the wary sportsman stopped; then making a circuit, and keeping his dog close to him, he made good his way to some trees, near which the kangaroos were feeding. Again did the kangaroos prick up their ears, and again did their enemy pause; but as they seemed inclined to make off, he fired at the nearest, and it lay dead upon the plain. The report of the gun made the whole herd decamp at their utmost speed, and Gip started after them, not in the least daunted by their, to her, unusual appearance, or their novel, leaping gait; she sprang after them like a mad thing, and fastening upon the ear of the smallest and hindermost, she there hung. The poor bewildered beast made for a tree, and placing its back against the trunk, kicked with his hind legs. Had not Gipsy attacked it on one side, she would probably have been torn to pieces by the strong nails of the kangaroo; but she kept fast hold till her master came up to her, and with his knife killed the animal, as if he had been a deer-slayer. He was puzzled what to do with this abundance of game; but calling Tiger to him with all the force of his lungs, the good steed heard, and galloped to him at full speed; then laying one portion of the spoil on his back, Captain Spencer walked by his side to the hill, and repeated his journey for the second kangaroo. Charlie, however, who had heard his summons to Tiger, had also come to him, and placing himself on the top of the last kangaroo, screamed out, "Ha! ha! ha! all's right!"

The whole of the rest of the day was spent in skinning the kangaroos, and cooking their flesh, that it might keep the longer, for which Captain Spencer's only resource lay in the tin cans, into which he put large pieces of his game, and boiled it. The kangaroos belonged to the species which has a nail, and a tuft of hair at the end of the tail.*

* Macropus unguifer.

"And now," said he to himself, "when I have killed an Emu, I shall be happy to quit Australia the next morning." "The next morning," echoed Charlie, "ha! ha!"

For some time had the traveller seen with dismay that his shoes were wearing out; and now that he found the kangaroo leather to be thick and pliant, it occurred to him that if he could but prepare it, he might make some moccasins and stockings, and shoes would thus be supplied. There is no telling how much may be done when the invention is sharpened by necessity; so he dug a hole near the lake, into which the water soon rose, and throwing some pieces of bark, procured from the neighbouring trees, into it, he steeped the skin with them, to imbibe the tannin which they yielded, and let them remain there for some days; then taking them out, he stretched them on the ground, fastening them down with pegs, and he scraped and beat them till they became perfectly soft and even. By these means, which he adopted as long as he stayed by the lake, he acquired a valuable stock of leather, which was of more use in many ways than he at first anticipated.

There was no end to the treasures which the plain and its neighbourhood afforded, and Captain Spencer determined to profit by them to the utmost: he made a flail with two pieces of stick, fastened to each other with a thong of leather, **and** threshed his oat-grass; he then procured two large stones from the range of hills, with which he ground the seeds into meal, Charlie helping himself very often during the process; and on this occasion, when he reached the hills, Gipsy gave a muffled bark, and jumping away from what she had seen, ran to her master, and asked him, as well as she could, also to behold the strange sight. It was another remarkable lizard,* of even more singular appearance than any he had yet met with; its colour was a yellowish brown, variegated with black; its small eyes were placed in a ridge on the upper part of the head; the eye-lids, and indeed the whole animal, were encased in scales of various sizes, which more or less projected, and a scalloped frill began at the back of the head, and extended along the sides of the neck, reaching as far as the chest; it stood upright when Gip approached, was supported by several cartilaginous spines, which proceeded from the tongue-bone, and the outside of it was clothed with scales. When Gipsy went away, this strange appendage was contracted into five plaits, and lay like a tippet upon the shoulders; the tail was twice as long as the body, and the claws of the feet were hooked. It did not avoid the approach of the strangers, as if it trusted in its frill as a sure defence; and for a long time did Captain Spencer examine this creature as nearly

* Chlamydosaurus Kingii.

as he could, and regret that his drawing materials had been lost in the schooner.

At length, shouldering the stones, Captain Spencer turned towards his temporary abode, and as he continued for a time to skirt the foot of the hills he heard an agonised shriek from Gipsy, who was behind him. Turning his head, he to his horror saw the faithful creature almost enveloped in the folds of a Python. Twice had the reptile twisted itself round the body of the poor dog, who was almost breathless from fear and pressure; but quick as thought her master dropped the stones which he was carrying, and being an accomplished killer of serpents in Indian fashion, he knew what to do in Australia, and struck the Python on the tail with his axe, so as instantaneously to render it powerless. It was then easy to release Gipsy, and deprive the snake of its head as well as its tail; and taking the poor dog up in his arms, he felt her all over with the greatest anxiety, fearing that some of her bones might be broken; but his succour had been timely, and she was not seriously hurt. She, however, trembled excessively, and licked her master's hand incessantly. He left his pieces of stone for the time, and carried her to his abiding-place, rubbing her as he went along; he there laid her down on his coat, and he did not leave her till she was fast asleep. It was many days, however, before she recovered the squeeze and the alarm, and often awoke in a fright, looked up in her master's face, and repeated her caresses. It was still longer before she would hunt again; and he left her constantly to keep guard over the baggage, at first taking care not to go out of hearing, in case she should announce the arrival of visitors, and be too frightened to defend herself.

Finding that he and Gipsy could not devour two kangaroos, while they were good, when he procured others, Captain Spencer cut the meat into strips, and dried it in the sun; a plan which answered perfectly, and by which means he had always materials in store for a capital stew. He also met with very small marsupial animals, resembling mice,* which afforded much sport to Gipsy when she was well enough to catch them, and which he split open, and dried with the kangaroos.

The number of birds which frequented the beautiful spot where Captain Spencer sojourned, would have kept his gun in constant requisition, had he not sought to spare his powder and shot as much as possible, even seeking for small stones to supply the place of bullets, so much did he fear to be without them in case of an attack from the natives, who, though unseen by him, he was sure were not very far off; for he frequently, when he looked towards the hills, saw thin columns of smoke ascending above them. With the Kites, and other

* Acrobata pygmæa.

birds of the kind, he often had a regular fight at meal-time; they tried to snatch the meat from his hands; and he now and then amused himself by throwing pieces of it into the air, and seeing them catch it as it fell. Then the noise and struggling between them was almost deafening; and on these occasions Charlie, who had been taught to abuse his brother birds, would creep into the hole in the hill, saying, "Great rogues! great rogues!" A few Crows would hover about, but they did not openly snatch their morsels; and slily coming round at the back, dragged them away, if they were for an instant laid down. Many flights of Cockatoos came into the plain to feed on the numerous and beautiful Orchidæ which grew there; and never did they pass overhead without exciting Gipsy's anger. They seemed to be her particular aversion, for which Captain Spencer could not account, till he recollected that, not long before they left Bombay, she had had an encounter with a tame one belonging to a lady friend, in which combat Gip was by no means victorious.

Several species of Crane frequented the shores of the lake, in which were numerous fishes. One had white plumage; but the most common was a very large species, which, when he was close, walked familiarly up to the stranger, and even suffered his caresses, but which instantly took flight whenever Tiger appeared, who, as soon as he descried his master in the plain, danced up to bid him welcome; it was of a pale gray, with a reddish tinge on the head.* The Snipes there were large; and it was most entertaining to see the Plovers use the spurs on their wings when they had a battle with the Crows and Kites. Waterhens and Divers frequented the lake; Musk Ducks with their strong odour, others like Sheldrakes,† Shovellers, and also common Teal. One sort he watched till it roosted in trees, swinging itself backwards and forwards, and whistling in a peculiar manner. He surprised a Bittern among the reeds, and then could not resist the impulse to shoot it for supper; some exquisite little grey birds, like Reed-warblers, always flew out of the rushes as he approached; and at night he distinguished the almost noiseless flight of the Goatsucker, with its soft plumage;‡ while a melancholy Owl§ worried him with its hootings.

The oatmeal cakes had been made over and over again, and no Scotchman could have had more pleasure in munching them than Captain Spencer and Gipsy enjoyed, while Tiger revelled in the grass, which waved like rye,‖ and for a time was always to be seen in its vicinity, when his master required him. For two days, however, he had

* Ardea rectirostris. † Tadorna Rajah.
‡ Podargus brachypterus. § Athene boobook.
‖ Panicum lævinode.

moved away to another place, and at night showed symptoms of having eaten a little too much. This excited his master's curiosity; and going to him on the third day, he found him devouring the common sow-thistle* with as much avidity as if he had been an European horse; when he called him, he only looked around and neighed, as much as to say, "I shan't come;" but instantly repenting, he trotted up to his master, and put his nose into his neck. "Your coat shines, old fellow," said the latter, "as it used to do in India, although I do not often curry you; but you grow enormously fat, and I must take a few rides upon your back to keep you a proper size, and fit to travel; so mind, to-morrow we will have a ramble to the other side of the hills, that I may see what lies beyond." That same evening, as Gip and her master were taking their meal, Charlie, who always hovered about near home at that time, and closed the day by having a long talk with Captain Spencer, gave a sort of scream over his head, and calling out his name, dropped on to his knees, and hid himself under his jacket. Gip, who was lying with a piece of kangaroo between her paws, started up; but her amazement was still greater when she looked down again, for her meat was gone. Charlie had been pursued by a powerful falcon, with a white head and neck, which, disappointed of its living prey,

* Sonchus.

had snatched the morsel from the dog. "Tolerably impudent, that," said Captain Spencer; "if I settled here, what a falconry I would have!" Charlie was too much frightened to learn his lesson, and his master spoke to him in vain; but he was surprised to hear himself imitated in another quarter; he paused to listen, and then he heard the calls of different birds, and now and then a shrill whistle; he himself whistled in various tones, which the bird repeated, even catching the tunes he uttered, and then giving a few of its own clear, ringing notes. It came again and again; and when he had recovered his agitation, this excited Charlie's jealousy. He exerted himself to the utmost to out-do his rival, and as soon as it began, he tried to drown its sounds by his own. He at last fled in a rage to the tree where it was, and frightened away a Shrike, as big as a Thrush, of a dull, brownish black, and a white bar across its wings. This was a daily amusement; the human whistler generally giving the signal when he commenced his supper, and each bird trying which could follow him best. The Shrike, however, never seemed to catch words very distinctly. Birds of splendid plumage were to be seen, which were wholly new to the traveller; and Pigeons of singular beauty abounded. One had bronzed wings, and another* resembled a quail in size and habits,

* Geophaps plumifera.

ran along the ground, had a long, pointed crest, and fed in families of eight or twelve. One of the Cuckoo tribe* looked something like a pheasant, but had two toes before and two behind, like a parrot; it climbed trees, and as it ran in the grass, made a noise like whir-r-r-r. Multitudes of Swallows, Finches, and other kinds hovered round the traveller's resting-place, to pick up the grass-seeds and scraps which had accidentally fallen: and seeing this, he scattered some on purpose, by which means he gathered round him all the feathered tribes of the neighbourhood; and sometimes, while they were scrambling for their morsels, Gipsy's aversions, some black, some white, with scarlet and sulphur crest, some rose-colour, and accompanied by Parrots and Parrakeets of rainbow hues, all dashing in among the lesser birds, would assert the right of the strongest, and bear away their prizes. On all these occasions Charlie was evidently very much annoyed, and hopped up to his master, repeating, "Great rogues! great scoundrels, Ned Spencer!"

In pursuance of his design, Tiger was one morning desired to stop and feed at home, and received an unusual portion of cleaning from his master; the saddle and bridle were put on, and when Captain Spencer mounted on his back, he capered and danced about half mad with delight, while Charlie

* Cuculus phasianus.

flew overhead laughing with all his might, till the Shrike began to imitate, and then he flew away, muttering about rogues and scoundrels. The first point to which Captain Spencer rode was that of some native huts which he had discovered with his telescope; they were built like bee-hives, and thatched with long grass; the entrance was small, and placed opposite to the wind which most frequently blew there; they were entirely deserted, and on dismounting to examine them, all that could be discovered inside were some fragments of agate for the making of spear-heads, with the stones used in chipping them into shape; one of them had been left half finished, and was of a pretty green colour. Outside the huts were several circles of large stones, paved at the bottom, and heaps of broken shells were scattered around, as if they had been crushed by the lesser stones lying about; rude troughs of bark, and places where grass-seeds had been evidently ground, some of the meal still adhering to them, were mixed with these circles, and broken shields, also of bark, were close by.

On riding away from the village, Tiger almost stepped upon what his master thought was a bird's nest; but it was the playground of the Bower-bird,* formed of twigs and grass, so as to make nearly an arch, and on the ground underneath and

* Chlamydera nuchalis.

about were pieces of broken shells, bright pebbles, which evidently came from the sea-shore, feathers, flowers, and fruit-stones. At the time he could not comprehend it; but he afterwards came upon another, and there saw speckled brown and white birds enticing each other to run backwards and forwards under the arch. On returning through the plain, he saw two trailing plants of the Gourd kind, one with red and white oblong fruit, and the other with fruit the size and shape of an orange, of a bright scarlet; he ventured to taste them, but they were much too bitter to swallow.

"I think, Gip," said Captain Spencer, when he reached home, "that you ought to try and run about now; I am sure you are quite well;" so taking her in his arms, he carried her to the banks of the lake, where he placed her on the ground. She had recovered from the pressure of the snake, but was a little stiff for want of exercise; however, she in a short time ran about gaily, though a little nervous, and started at the frogs which hopped before her; but all at once she gave a cry, and looked at her master, as she always did when she had made a discovery. On reaching the spot, he could not help laughing at the poor little animal, for one of a regiment of Cray-fish had nipped her nose, as she placed it within reach of its claw. This was an important addition to the already long list of eatables; and fetching a bag from the hil-

11

lock, he carried many of them home, plunging them into boiling water to kill them immediately for his supper. They accounted for the broken shells which he had seen at the huts, and which at the time he thought must have belonged to Crustaceæ. "I do not think I have sufficiently explored this lake," said he; "and after having been to the other side of the hills to-morrow, I will see more of it."

At first Gipsy started as usual with her master, but when she found where he was going, she hung her tail and head, and whined. "Go home, good dog!" said her master, pitying her natural apprehension; she did not wait to be twice told, and scampered back at full speed, not, however, without now and then stopping to give a wistful look at Captain Spencer. Tiger and he scrambled up the rude acclivities, and on reaching the top of the ridge, he found that it formed the boundary of the fertile country in which he had stationed himself. They overlooked an immense district of scrub and shrubby trees, intermingled with small patches of Eucalyptus, some of which rose to a lofty stature. As far off as he could distinguish anything, he saw a range of blue hills running N.N.E. and S.S.W., much more lofty than those on which he stood, and yet not very high, which sent off lateral branches, and gave indication of basaltic structure in places; the branches evidently consisted of horizontal strata of ancient sandstone, and he thought that behind them was that mysterious interior, which was by some supposed to contain a large inland sea, and by others to consist of a desert district of sand. Dark and gloomy ravines seemed to exist between the hills; and now and then a silver-like thread marked the course of a small river, in the vicinity of which rose the smoke of several fires.

Cautiously descending the further side of the hills which bordered the plains, Captain Spencer found that they were composed of nearly horizontal strata of different coloured sandstone; but rain and time had caused the soil to crumble in some places, leaving that which still stood in various forms, such as pillars, overthrown obelisks, gigantic, statue-like pieces; and one part looked so like a ruined temple, that he made his way towards it in spite of the wiry spinifex scrub which he had to encounter. A little imagination would have persuaded him that these fallen masses were the works of a race which had now disappeared; some of the pillars were encircled by an insignificant-looking, but sweet-smelling Jasmine, and on others were magnificent creepers. Still further on he found caverns, and dismounting, he was desirous of entering them in the hope of finding fossils. In this he was disappointed; but he there met with what astonished him much more—paintings of gigantic figures, which showed a greater degree of civilization among the natives than he thought they possessed. The roof of one of these caves was sloping, and on it was portrayed a huge, grim personage, in red and white colors on a black ground, having red rays all round the head, and a circle of yellow round each eye; other faces on the sides were merely surrounded with a rim of blue and red, and none of them had any mouths; on one was a necklace, and this seemed to be intended to represent a female.

Surprised and interested in his discovery, Captain Spencer visited these caves several times, and found others at a little distance, but which did not all contain paintings; in one of them was an enormous black hand, which produced a startling effect, from appearing to issue from a crevice in the wall; and in this cave he disturbed a number of vampire bats as he entered, which flew out with a screeching noise, and filled the air with a disagreeable odour, resembling mildew; they settled on a bamboo-looking tree close by, which they almost bent to the ground by the weight of their numbers. He then came to another cave, in which was a rude painting of a man carrying a kangaroo, and also a number of those animals with a spearhead flying among them. What the pigments were which had been used, Captain Spencer could not tell; but they were evidently mineral, and were not to be defaced either by rubbing or washing. Some little distance from the caves, a human head was carved on the surface of the rock, and not at all resembling an Australian in features. It was the best specimen of artistic skill which had yet appeared, was two feet long, and fourteen inches broad; the ear was in the right place, and it seemed to have been cut with a better instrument than the stone knives and hatchets which he had heard that the natives alone possessed. The edges were round, as if it had been done some time; and further on was a figure without a mouth, dressed in a red gown, which reached from the head to the feet.

Hours were passed in the examination of these extraordinary works of art, and then hunger pressed Captain Spencer to return; he and Tiger again clambered up the hills, and in so doing disturbed a species of kangaroo, which he had not found in the plain,* and which he shot and slung across the saddle before him. He passed many trailing plants, such as Convolvuli and Ipomeæ; and as he descended on the other side, he came upon a very extraordinary tree,† the stem of which, at the bottom, swelled into a protuberance like an old-fashioned decanter; and it had horizontal branches, with palmate leaves. He got off his horse to examine it; and cutting the trunk

* Petrogale brachyotis (Gould.) † Sterculia.

with his hatchet, he found that the wood was stringy, and contained an agreeable, mucilaginous pulp, some of which he carried home as a variety of food for supper. A beautiful trailing Vitex, with a white blossom, covered the rugged sandstone in many parts; and in the plain some bright blue flowers, very like those of the borage, attracted his attention; while a tree like a horse-chesnut carried his thoughts far away.

As soon as Captain Spencer left the hills, Gip, who was on the watch, ran to meet him, and Tiger's friendly salute was that of taking her up by the skin of her back, and giving her a good shaking, which proof of love seemed rather pleasing to her than otherwise. The kangaroo was placed in safety for the night, and prepared the next morning; after which Captain Spencer more minutely examined the lake and its productions, preferring the middle of the day on account of the mosquitoes, and taking his shovel in his hand. Here he found such treasures that he returned to the spot several times. Of animal productions he met with Unios, or fresh-water muscles, of which he took away a great bagful, also some of the numerous other Mollusca with which the shore abounded.* A whole army of Crabs was marching from one spot to another, each with the left claw much larger than that on the right side; water-beetles, and

---

* Planorbis, Ancyclus, Paludina, Cyclas.

small, merry Cicadæ abounded. The greatest of the treasures, however, was the fresh-water Turtle, which was excellent eating.

Of vegetable food, Captain Spencer secured some of the tubers of the Cooper's Reed,* and the Bulrush,† which he had heard of persons eating in England, and which, when well roasted, were so farinaceous that they formed an excellent substitute for flour. Nor did he neglect to secure some of the seeds of the Water-lilies, especially those of the Nelumbium, which his Indian experience told him, when roasted, were very like coffee. A plant very like the Papyrus was plentiful; but, as evening approached, he did not stop to gather it, the more especially as he was very wet from wading into the water in search of provisions. As he returned to his hillock heavily laden, he observed there was an unusual appearance of insects; when Tiger came home for the night, some green flies were annoying him very much; beetles with tiny plates, or lamellæ, on their antennæ, knocked against his face; and Charlie, as he returned, chased a large Sphynx moth. When the sun had quite sunk, one part of the plain was brightly illuminated, which told of the gambols of fire-flies, and which the traveller was accustomed to see in India, though probably not the same species. As he and Gip supped together, the howls of some

* Arundo phragmites. † Typha Chara.

animal saluted his ears, which made Gip prick up hers; and he imagined it to proceed from the native dogs. Charlie began to croak, and mutter to himself, as he always did when he was disturbed. These mysteries were explained by thick, heavy masses of clouds, which were gathering to sea-ward, and the traveller prepared all his coverings to escape a wetting. He defended himself and companions. with the tarpauling and skins; Charlie crept into the cave with the baggage; and glad was his master that he had repaired the tarpauling with the bags, and used the kangaroo leather in their stead. Before he lay down, however, fearing that the water would stand in the hollow where they were placed, he dug a sort of sluice, by which the rain, when it came, as it did with tropical fury, in torrents, ran off down the hill, and they remained perfectly dry.

Although not injured by the storm, it had broken into the general routine of everything around him; it had swelled the lake, and consequently there would be some unhealthy exhalations; and it was probably the last for a long time, when the dry season would come for months, and the traveller began to think that he ought not to linger in that plentiful spot as he did; and once convinced of the necessity of departure, he made preparations for it; resolving all the time, that if he were ever to settle in Australia, he would come there; for he thought the bed of the river might be improved so as to admit of navigation, and if not, that it at all times afforded a plentiful supply of water. The grass was of the most superior kind, and covered an immense tract; the climate was delightful; the abundance of Eucalypti and Acacias, at a little distance, would afford materials for building, thatching, tanning, &c.; and the stones on the hills would serve for many purposes. There had been no drawbacks that he had seen, except a few reptiles, which would soon desert the haunts of man, or be extirpated; and surely the natives might be conciliated. He wound up his eulogium by saying, "None but those who have lived in the countries where ferocious beasts abound, can appreciate the feelings of security which their certain absence affords. I shall take care to inform the good people of Perth what a treasure they possess within their reach, though at some little distance, I suspect."

That day Captain Spencer began to collect food for his march, and in the course of his researches he stumbled on some Cycas trees, growing in a sandy, rotten soil, and which were from ten to twenty feet high, full of half-ripe fruit. He cut down two, on which this fruit was the least advanced, and extracted the pith-like sago from the stems; then gathered some of the cones of the others, and when he took them to the hill, he cut them into slices, and dried them with the pith, so as to be put into bags. He had always remarked that there was a great scarcity of butterflies; but on this day he discovered some of the Meadow-brown, one with a broad yellow spot on the wings,* and those which live on the chalky soils of Great Britain; he also saw some of the Bower-birds on some high trees, as if seeking their fruit.

While his flour of various kinds was drying, and the kangaroo meat and fishes curing in the sun, Captain Spencer washed his clothes in the lake, soaking them in the water, stamping on them in the manner of the Indians, and occasionally beating them, for he thought the absence of soap could alone be made up by manual labour; which labour, however, wore out the materials much sooner than common washing or friction would have done; and he saw with dismay that his linen was likely to disappear. In his washing labours he disturbed several water insects, but they were unknown to him; and on his return by a different path, he was surprised at some plants which resembled Carrots; he was rather suspicious of any vegetable which bore such a leaf, but he pulled one up, and to his surprise found that its root perfectly carried out the resemblance, and after cooking it, he was convinced that it was wholesome food. He therefore procured a stock of them,

* Papilio Sthenelus.

chiefly to surprise Tiger with after a long march. Much of the meal of various kinds was made into cakes; a few cured Unios were added to the animal portion; and a new grass hat was not forgotten. It was not any improvement on the first, it must be owned; and the manufacturer was painfully convinced of his want of talent for that peculiar department. The arms and tools were well cleaned and put in order, and Tiger received two or three most careful dressings. The moment the baggage was put on his back, he altered his demeanour: he seemed to consider that he was then a horse of responsibility, and gave up dancing and jumping; while Gip also began her journey at a sober pace. The only one of the party whose spirits became raised on the occasion was Charlie, who delighted in movement and bustle of any kind; and when the party started, flew round and round, screaming, "Hurrah! I'm off! ha! ha! ha!"

CHAPTER V.

Snake—Huts—Bark bedsteads—Ovens—Basalt—Luxuriant grass—Gorge—Another gouty-stemmed tree—Captain Spencer desires to go to the interior—Scrub—Fishes—Gum-trees—Large fish—Birds—Flying Opossums—Insects—Fusanus—Casuarina—Dragon-fly—Sun to the north—Tiger's hoofs worn—Tiger's socks—Mesembryanthemum—Jerboas—Bustard—Native grave—Melaleuca—Lark—Natives and dogs—Dogs rush on Gipsy—Captain Spencer saves the dog—Natives equipped for war—Captain Spencer separated from his arms—Dances to conciliate natives—Reaches his fire-arms—Frightens the natives—Tiger comes up, and they are still more frightened—Natives run off—Tombs possums—Magnetic hills—River—Black Swans—Zamia—Captain Spencer poisoned by nuts—Conduct of his companions—Recovers — Yams — Moths —Peppermint—Grass-trees—Natives and dogs come upon Captain Spencer when cleaning arms—He frightens them away—Uninhabited villages—Yam-grounds—Howls of dogs—Splendid Pelargonium—Tiger attacked by a venomous Snake—In saving the horse Captain Spencer is bitten—Almost dies—Recovers—Natives blow at him—Hen-Turkey—Native hut for watching prey—Birds—Directs his way south—Water scarce—Tiger drinks all from one can—Proteæ.

From a former study of the maps of Australia, and a guess at the distance which he had come, Captain Spencer imagined that he had reached a bulging projection of land which lies on the western side of the continent; and deeming it superfluous to go round it, and so keep close to the coast, as he had at first intended, he determined to shape his course directly south, and to march across it.

Scrub began to take the place of grass; but **Tiger** managed to get through it, and from it rose a tall, strong gum-tree, whose stem took an oblique direction. Upon it was crawling a large Lizard,* measuring at least six feet in length, and making a disagreeable noise. When Gipsy saw it, she begged so earnestly to be taken up, that her master lifted her on to his knapsack; and glad was he, a few minutes after, that he had yielded to her entreaties; for a light-brown snake, with dark-stripes on its back, slipped through the grass where it had been coiled up; and as it hid itself in the scrub, he saw by its flattened head that it was venomous; ant-hills again occurred, and he perceived that these clever architects mix much clay with the sand of their dwellings, in order to cement it. He came upon paths worn by natives, and met with what he at first thought to be mere temporary screens, but which he afterwards found to be more permanent dwellings. They consisted of several boughs of trees stuck into the earth, and then tied together, on the top of a forked stick, so that they were entirely open in front. About them were sharp pieces of chipped basalt, and long narrow troughs of bark, which had all the appearance of bedsteads, placed round a spot where there had been a fire. The circles of stones were repeated, and in them were some remains of eggs, which had

* Iguana.

been roasted; and he at once guessed that they were ovens, from which the owners had probably made a hasty retreat. He dismounted, and going to the top of the hills, which he was still skirting, he saw a large body of people carrying on their usual occupations. They had, then, been close to him while living in the plain, and why he had been left unmolested, he could not imagine; for his preservation, however, he poured forth an especial prayer of thanksgiving, and entreated for a blessing upon his future journey.

The ground was for some time swampy; and as long as that and the sand-hills lasted, the annoyance of flies and mosquitoes continued. Basalt, however, began to show itself, and they decreased; the ground became harder, but of course the supply of water was less abundant, and a short, dry herbage took the place of the long, silky, and luxuriant grass in which Tiger had been lately revelling. Strange birds flew over their heads, for which Charlie always prepared by flying closer to the party. Valley succeeded to valley; these often with such steep and rugged banks, that Tiger's load had to be carried for him piecemeal, because of the slanting position he was obliged to assume; but he scorned to be led, and never missed his footing. He and Charlie provided for themselves; and as his master and Gip used their ample stock but sparingly, there was no occasion to renew it for many days.

In a deep, narrow gorge, more like a crevice than the bed of a river, a happy discovery of water was made, which in some measure tempered the oppressive atmosphere in that great crack of the earth. Growing in a nook of the rock, Captain Spencer saw another gouty-stemmed tree, the enlargement of which took place at a greater distance from the ground than in the first. He examined it, and could scarcely avoid pronouncing it to be a Capparis, very different to the previous gouty tree in all but its stem; its branches were loaded with hanging fruit about the size of a cocoa-nut, having a brown outer rind, and a shell beneath, which was easily broken. Within were several seeds, surrounded by a soft white pulp of very agreeable flavour; and he gathered some, which he added to Tiger's load. It was so like the other gouty or bottle tree in shape, that he could scarcely persuade himself that two of different genera, or even families, should so resemble each other in form; and he cut the stem, and from it he also extracted a pith, which came out in strings like macaroni, some of which accidentally fell into one of the cans of water, to which it imparted a slightly acid flavour, and transformed it into a very agreeable beverage. Tiger took such a fancy to it, that he pushed his nose into the can, like a spoiled horse as he was, and almost took it by main force. Some of this pith was also collected and put into the bags; but as the traveller went on, he pondered on the similarity and differences of the trees, and not arriving at any conclusion, he then thought that he must have been mistaken in both of these singular vegetables; but he afterwards found that there were two distinct kinds.

The plentiful supplies which Captain Spencer had hitherto met with admitted of no apprehensions for the future, and it flashed into his mind that it would be a noble undertaking to go directly across the continent from west to east; and the spirit of discovery became stronger in him every day; but fortunately for his own preservation, he recollected the fearful accounts which had been brought of the interior of that vast continent by those who had penetrated furthest; and common sense whispered in time, that it would be foolhardy to rush unadvisedly upon what threatened destruction. Yet, as he turned unwillingly from the idea, he involuntarily exclaimed, "Our wants are so few, we are so inured to climate and exposure, and my beasts are so well trained, that we should perhaps stand a better chance than those travellers whose numbers alone impede their progress, from the quantity of water and provision which they require."

The way for some time presented nothing that

was bad, the depressions in the ground amounting to furrows, which seemed as if they took the direction of the coast, and perhaps, in rainy seasons, conveyed the water of the interior to the ocean. This idea was confirmed by occasionally finding some pools of water in them, which had not yet been dried up by the sun; and they were so cool and shady, that they presented tempting resting-places. Captain Spencer, however, did not remain long in them, for fear of being surprised there by the natives, and also from some apprehension that they might engender fever. In one of them he found some long-necked Turtles, and caught some fishes of the Perch kind; nor were the opportunities of washing linen and bathing neglected.

On the plains above, eternal scrub beset the wayfarers, which assumed various shapes, all of which were different, and at times impossible to cross; often composed of different sorts of Acacia, the leaves totally unlike those which Captain Spencer had been in the habit of seeing; then of Atriplex, which well deserved its name of horrida, but the young shoots of which Tiger nibbled with much satisfaction. Again, there was the Callithrix, with its yellow flowers. "What European," said he, "could form an idea of these scrubs without seeing them? Even if I were to say that they were like exaggerated furze-bushes matted together in every direction, they could scarcely comprehend the impenetrability of Australian wastes." The old author's* term, "*quasi diabolus*," as applied to the prickly Spinifex, recurred to his memory; and while he smiled at it, he never forgot it when he travelled through or thought of a scrub. The only use which he could find for such bushes was to form hiding-places for the rats and mice which Gip dragged from under them, or to rid Tiger of the flies when he plunged his head in for that purpose.

It was in the water lying in the crevices that the objects of greatest interest existed; and in order to catch the Jew Fishes,† Captain Spencer fastened the hook and line on to one of his spears, and baited the former with pieces of tortoise; besides these were Perch, some small, and others of the Carp kind, yellow in colour, and having dark longitudinal lines. On one occasion he was surprised by a Saw-fish, which had probably come up the ravine in a high tide, and could not get back again; it was, however, in a very languishing condition. He found a large fish,‡ which had evidently entered the river for the purpose of spawning, and it proved an excellent addition to the larder for himself and Gip who now ate fish like a Newfoundland dog. The gum-trees were not very plentiful in these spots, but occasionally a tall, rugged stem so far above the lesser trees, and threw its long,

* Dampier. † Gristes. ‡ Sciæna.

sprawling arms about, which bore tufts of bright green, poplar-like leaves at the ends of them, and on which sat multitudes of tiny birds. The bark, like coarse white paper, hung in a profusion of shreds, strings, and festoons, from the trunk and larger branches. Thousands of Pigeons of various kinds—Parrots, with their short, low flight—Parrakeets like rainbows—Cockatoos of great beauty, and Hawks, would occasionally rest on the tops of the trees, as they passed on their journey, or fed on the fruit of a shrub with stiff leaves, covered with berries like red acorns, enclosing two bitter seeds. Owls made a sort of barking noise in the most retired parts; where also were Flying Opossums;[*] bird's nests, out of which he now and then took one or two eggs; a Craticus,[†] with a strong, straight bill, hooked at the end, and magnificent plumage, excited Charlie's ire by its imitations; but he rovelled in the abundance and variety of insects, the principal of which were two kinds of Danais; one having light green transparent spots on its dusky brown wings. He also feasted on a butterfly very like that of the Cabbage butterfly of England, and countless numbers of beautifully coloured flies, beetles, bees, and wasps. A species of Sphex, and a green Chrysis, seemed very much to affect a Tournefortia,[‡] with silvery white leaves. A Fusanus, with globular fruit, like a small apple or Sibe-

[*] Petaurus Sciardus.   [†] C. destructor.   [‡] T. argentes.

rian crab, but which had a large rough kernel, was most refreshing in the middle of one very hot day: he also observed a species of the Fig-tree* tribe, with several other plants which the traveller scarcely expected to find there; but when there was nothing remarkable in them of rarity or beauty, he passed them with a casual glance. Not so, however, a huge Eucalyptus, nearly covered with a rich drapery, formed by a luxuriant creeping-plant, which bore the appearance of a vine, from its hanging bunches of fruit, resembling black grapes both in taste and colour, and the seed within very like coffee.

A gradual change had been taking place in the vegetation of the country, the only persisting feature of which continued to be the several kinds of scrub; and Captain Spencer now came upon another of the wonders of the land; the Casuarina, with its articulated, leafless branches, looking like a gigantic horse's tail, over which one of the Honeysuckle kind† flung its trailing branches; he thought also that he perceived some plants of Indigo; and a prickly Solanum close by wounded his fingers, as he attempted to gather it for inspection. It was Charlie who generally called his attention to the insects as he pursued them; and one day he heard a great buzzing noise from a Dragon-fly,‡ which was trying to escape him; the

* Ficus. † Loranthus. ‡ Thopha saccata.

bird brought it to him at his desire, and he found it had a brown body, very clear wings, and a bag on each side of its head; he afterwards saw one of the same kind with white bags in the same place. There was a plentiful appearance of short-nosed Beetles, with little tubercles all over the wing-cases; and others, with long horns, and red patches of colour, formed by minute scales, became quite troublesome.

A narrow river, which had once flowed freely, was now dwindled to a thread, making the traveller apprehend a time of suffering and scarcity. As he sat down by it, he laid his compass on the ground; and although the sun had constantly been behind him as he walked, he started when he was so plainly convinced that it was to the north of him, and that he had passed the southern tropic; he knew it must be so, and could not help laughing at himself for thinking it strange to look for warmth and sunshine from that point of the compass. Having for a few hours since he left the river, traversed a sterile region, he perceived Tiger walking as if he were lame, and he stopped to examine his feet; the removal of a stone restored him to his usual gait, but his master was dismayed to find how much the constant marching had worn his hoofs, now they were no longer protected by shoes, and had often encountered rough ground; he determined to rest, therefore, for a short time, and try to cover them with the thickest of his kangaroo leather, and shoe him as he had shod himself. He accomplished this with some little difficulty; and when he put the coverings on to the beast, he slipped about as if he did it on purpose, and pawed the ground, and looked at his master as if to tell him how uncomfortable he was; nevertheless, a little perseverance reconciled him to them, and Captain Spencer was surprised to find how long they lasted. As Tiger was sliding about the first day, a pale, bluish-green looking patch of vegetation at some distance attracted his master's attention, and going up to it, he found it to be a Mesembryanthemum with pale pink flowers, many of which had fallen, and a five-sided, insipid, but juicy fruit had begun to show itself. In the same place was matter of rejoicing to both himself and Gipsy, for the latter caused some Jerboas to spring from the bushes; they leaped away rapidly, and Gipsy chased them till they suddenly disappeared into the ground, where they burrowed. Captain Spencer procured his shovel, and digging at the hole, he found that each habitation was composed of a common central shaft, from which several passages radiated to a distance.

Some of the Jerboas were secured, and when cooked were of good flavour. Far more acceptable, however, was a large Bustard, weighing at least twenty pounds, which he shot, and dragged to his resting-place, where he dried some of the flesh for future occasions. A native grave was near this spot; and as he had his measuring tape in his pocket, he ascertained that it was twenty-three feet long and fourteen broad; the ground was raised, and over it were laid some branches of a tree, which evidently belonged to the Myrtle family,* and which he concluded to be the Melaleuca, so abundant in some parts of the country. The next morning, as he was preparing breakfast, a bird rose from the top of a neighbouring bush, singing with a clear, melodious note, like that of a lark, and after soaring to a great height in the air for a little time, came down again with fluttering wings. Gipsy looked up in her master's face, as much as to say, "Won't you shoot it?" and he answered her by replying, "No, Gip, I cannot shoot a Lark, it puts me too much in mind of my own country." Gip was satisfied apparently that there was some good reason for denying her request, and started off to cater for herself as usual, soon returning with food to the bivouac. Tiger would eat any vegetable substance which was offered to him; but not so Gip; she spluttered and threw it about, and never having yet known want, she had not in this respect been obliged to disobey her natural taste.

Having made the usual provisions for starting,

* Melaleuca.

Captain Spencer pursued his way along a sandy, rugged soil, rising occasionally into ridges of no great elevation, but sufficiently so to obstruct the view. Thinking that the country at the back might be better than that in which he then was, he determined to cross these ridges; but just before he loaded Tiger, Gipsy barked, ran to and fro with great uneasiness, and the tramp of many feet was heard approaching; she gave tongue; head after head appeared, and a large body of men mounted on to the top of the bank, with evidently hostile intentions. They were accompanied by dogs, which snarled and appeared to be very savage; and two of them rushed down the ridge upon poor Gipsy. Her master, unmindful of his own safety, flew towards her, placed her in a cavity of the rugged bank, and in his excitement easily put a fragment before her, which he afterwards found it difficult to dislodge, from its weight, and which, though it did not quite conceal her, opposed an effectual barrier to the attacks of her enemies. By this time the spears had been placed in the throwing sticks, ready for hurling at him, and the people were yelling, and making all their accustomed frantic gestures of anger and defiance. They were probably on their way to meet their enemies, for they were equipped for war, and coming suddenly upon a white man, were enraged at his appearance; their shields were upon their arms, and they had clubs as well as spears; they were painted red and yellow; their Opossum cloaks were hanging at their backs; their thick hair was either fastened up behind, or encircled by a fillet, and many had it adorned with dogs' tails or emu's feathers. Not a friendly bough was near to show his own peaceable intentions, and for a moment the Englishman thought he was lost; for in running to save Gipsy, he had separated himself from his fire-arms, which he had laid upon the bank in order to load the horse. The alarm excited by the appearance of Tiger on former occasions darted into his recollection, and he looked round for him, but he had trotted off to take a last nibble of an inviting patch of grass before he started; and then it occurred to Captain Spencer, that on the northern coast the natives had danced to show their amicable feelings, and now he would dance to show his. He immediately began to caper with all his might, and it was many a long month, perhaps years, since he had jumped about as he did then; for it was no graceful sliding and bending, with the feet scarcely lifted from the ground; it was real, jolly dancing, and had the desired effect, for the natives paused. If he relaxed for an instant, however, they again raised their spears; but the day was won; he of course danced towards his fire-arms, and in one of his attitudes he took up his pistols, and fired one of the barrels over their heads. Before they recovered from their panic, he fired a second, and all decamped with the utmost speed. By this time Tiger came galloping up to him, and he ordered him to stand on the top of the bank in a most conspicuous situation, where he neighed loudly, and where his mane and tail spread out like a banner. The two dogs were still trying to get at Gipsy; but he knocked one on the head, and the other, after a severe blow, made its escape, running with a howl after its owners. After taking his favourite from her place of refuge, where she lay in an agony of apprehension, he peeped over the ridge, and saw the party hurrying off at an immense rate, in a direction quite contrary to that in which he wished to go; and then calling Tiger down, he examined the dead animal, and found it had a long sharp nose, and was more like the wolf, or the fox, than any of the European breeds. Charlie had flown after the natives, calling out, "Hurrah! hurrah! ha! ha! ha!" as if to give them their last fling; and then when Tiger was loaded, he perched himself on the top of the baggage, saying, "All's right, Ned Spencer!"

As he journeyed on, the traveller had leisure to think of his late adventure, and the ejaculations of gratitude for his escape which had immediately risen to his lips now assumed the form of deep thanksgiving to his Great Preserver; nor was this less fervent because no blood had stained his hand on this occasion. Then the ludicrous side of the picture came uppermost, and he could not help laughing at the ridiculous figure he must have made; such a contrast to the gay Edward Spencer, the hero of the Governor's and military balls in Bombay, dancing only when and with whom he chose, and now forced to dance to a set of savages to save his life. It was a good lesson, he thought, and he half-determined never again to give himself airs. Certainly he, for the remainder of his life, laughed whenever he thought of the capers of that morning.

Traces of the native Australians were now to be seen every where; such as tombs of stones, placed east and west, and made of pieces of rock, which had been only seen in distant places, and sea-shells; heaps of ashes where fires had been lighted, and trees which had either fallen from fire, or at least had been charred by the flames. The number of Gum-trees increased, and some of them were in blossom, each flower looking, at first, like a goblet, with a pyramidal cover, which was pushed off when the stamens burst into a starry circle; the leaves were dull, and the white trunks were decorated by hanging strips of bark, which assumed fantastic shapes. Up one ran an animal about the size of a cat; and as the tree leaned to the side, Gip pursued, but it was not quick enough, for the Opossum crept into a hole and disappeared. Some kangaroos were shot; and patches of grass were here and there found in the midst of a low scrub. Hills of sand, cemented by oxide of iron, with compact quartz and gypsum, occured more than once; and Captain Spencer began to suspect that the metal in these had attracted his compass, and that he had made too much easting; he did all in his power to counteract this by taking a south-west direction, for he exceedingly dreaded greater uncertainty of route, and missing Perth altogether. In spite of his faith and courage, when tired with a long day's journey, his heart would occasionally sink, as he passed day after day without any traces of civilised man; and thought that heat was increasing, with its attendant evil, drought. The quantity of water being already so greatly lessened in the river which he had lately passed, he became doubly anxious to reach the settlement to which he bent his steps. As if to ease his apprehensions, he after this came to what was evidently a permanent river, on the banks of which were large Casuarinæ, and on it some black Swans majestically sailing; he secured two of these for food; and after a rest of about four hours, he refilled his skins and cans, and marched on. Melaleucas were also growing by the side of this river, with their small, abundant blossoms; and some of the leaves having fallen into one of the cans, he fancied that they had imparted to the water a flavour like that of tea; and when he came to some more of them, he boiled them, in the hope of finding a substitute for this invigorating beverage; but he could not relish it, and did not try the experiment again. His path was made more uncertain by the scrub, through some parts of which he could not penetrate; and he had been constantly obliged to carry Gip, for she was so small that she crawled under the bushes, and could not get out again without the axe being used to chop a hole for her release.

Captain Spencer was surprised by what he thought the re-appearance of the Cycas, but going up to the tree which had attracted him, he found it to be of a different species, and concluded that it was a Zamia. He gathered some of the fruit, and finding it agreeable, he ate it, and proceeded on his journey; he had not, however, gone far, before he felt incapable of proceeding, from the most violent sickness, and without being able to choose a place where water and grass were to be found, he laid himself down in the clearest patch of scrub in the immediate vicinity. Finding himself get worse, he with the greatest difficulty took the baggage from Tiger's back, and then flung himself on the ground, arms, hat and all, with a can of water by his side, for his thirst was excessive; he did not doubt that he had been poisoned, and it seemed to him very uncertain whether he should survive the agony he was then enduring. Both Tiger and Gipsy seemed to know that there was something the matter with him, and would not leave his side. Charlie, when he saw that they all stopped, came bustling up, and stuck himself into a bush, saying, "Ned Spencer, what's the matter?" then he put his head on one side to listen for the usual answer, and finding no return to his chattering, he went through the whole of his vocabulary, over and over again, till the poor sufferer wished he had never taught him a sentence. There he lay for hours without being able to move hand or foot, not even to cover himself. But Gipsy nestled up, and tried to comfort him, and Tiger laid himself, when night came, as close as he could to him, while Charlie descended from his bush on to the horse's shoulder. At length the pain abated, and Captain Spencer thought, as he dozed, that he might never wake again; he slept the whole of that night, but was awake before his companions had opened their eyes. To his surprise and thankfulness he was well, though weak; but as his appetite was not yet returned, he determined not to eat more than was necessary that day. Rousing his companions, they fed, and by the time they had breakfasted he was able to lift the things on to Tiger's back, who neighed, and did not attempt to play, and so hinder the progress of loading.

Gipsy almost impeded him with sundry jumps, Charlie flew round him, perched upon his shoulder, and screamed "All's right!" and so they set off. They rested for some hours during the heat of the day, and in the evening reached a fine open plain, with here and there a clump of trees, where Captain Spencer encamped for the night, and ate with his usual appetite.

On crossing the plain Captain Spencer was surprised at finding the soil full of large holes, which made it very difficult for Tiger to keep his footing; he, however, trusted him to his own guidance, knowing that he was sagacious enough to pick his way properly, and he found that these holes arose from digging up a number of tubers resembling Yams.* A short, pointed stick, broken in two, showed the tool which had been employed in taking them up; but overjoyed at so wholesome a discovery, he used his shovel, and procured several in a very short time: he roasted some for supper, and having that morning shot some cockatoos, he made a thick soup with the two, and was perfectly renovated from his late illness. He remained the whole of that day, digging up as many as Tiger could carry, and converting some of them into meal, with which he filled his almost empty bags, and imitated his oatmeal cakes, which Gipsy condescended to partake of. As for Tiger, he enjoyed the mash which

* Dioscorea.

his master made for him as if it had been oat-gruel. It was a general feast; for Charlie had the previous evening devoured as many of the Sphinx and Ghost Moths as he could catch. The former had triangular marks on their wings, and measured three inches across. Some locusts, too, had made a loud, rattling, and most disagreeable noise, as they settled on one of the neighbouring clumps of Eucalyptus; they were large, had brown bodies, two inches long, rough legs, a square-shaped head, with red and yellow marks, half an inch broad, a long proboscis, which was not put out except when feeding; their wings were perfectly transparent, and they altogether were very handsome insects. Chancing to crush some of the leaves on which he saw them, Captain Spencer found that they had a flavour of peppermint;* the whole tree made a beautiful appearance; the bark was of varied tints, the leaves were unusually thick, were narrower, brighter, and greener than those of other gum-trees, and the fragrant blossoms looked like a mass of white fringed stars, which yielded a quantity of honey. On one tree he caught an Opossum, and saw several others on the neighbouring trunks.

More uneven ground was crossed, and at last the travellers found themselves in a swampy valley, in which Tiger greatly rejoiced, for he there

* Eucalyptus peperita.

met with the same long, silky grass which he had before eaten, and which he attacked the instant he was free from his load, first, however, taking a good roll in it. "Poor fellow!" said his master, "I have not been well enough to rub you down lately, but to-morrow you shall have a good scrubbing." Some kangaroos seemed to relish the same grass as that which delighted the horse; for they were numerous there, and were of a different species to those before seen. But that which now interested Captain Spencer, was the appearance of some curious tufted masses of long, narrow, sharp leaves, growing on the top of a round stem, of various heights, most of which fell back, and hung round the stem. This stem was rough from the scars of fallen leaves, and was frequently five feet high. From the middle rose a scape ten feet high, with a spike on the top, a foot long. "These must be Grass-trees," said Captain Spencer, "and are a good sign of my progress, for I must be getting to the south to meet with them.'

The dew was heavy but refreshing, and welcomed on account of its rarity, especially as the party was well protected by coverings; for with the instinct which all animals more or less possess when tame, Charlie now always crept under them with the others: and as it was a spot abounding with all sorts of necessaries for his wants, Captain Spencer decided on halting in it for a short time, to repair clothes, moccasins, tarpauling, and Tiger's socks. He examined his stock of ammunition, and, thanks to Gip, who caught so much for him, the Tortoises, Fishes, Unios, and vegetable food, it was still plentiful; but his gun and pistols wanted cleaning, and while intently at work at them, Gipsy rushed into his arms, followed by several native dogs, and their masters at a distance; he gave one of the first such a blow with the stock of his gun, that he thought he must have killed it, and hurled the second and third to a distance. The first, however, got up again, and slunk away to the five or six men behind, who had come as if they had known the moment in which the white man was defenceless; he could not retreat or shelter himself in any way; his things were scattered about, and all he could do was to gesticulate as much as possible, while he endeavoured to load his pistols. He succeeded in arresting their attention, till he had put in the charges of two barrels; he fired, but the first would not go off, from being still damp after cleaning. The Australians derided him, even mocking the sound of the pistol lock, and were about to rush upon him, brandishing their clubs. At this moment Tiger came tearing up to his master, and, as usual, the astonishment and alarm of the Australians paralysed them; they dropped their hands, and looked at the horse with astonishment. Cap tain Spencer then reloaded, and this time succeeded; for aiming at a dry bush, close to the people, he covered their naked bodies with its splinters and shattered leaves; the rest took fire, and communicating with other bushes, a train of flames was laid, which soon drove them from their position, and they were obliged to run hard to avoid being burnt. They did not return, and the success of the stratagem was complete. Still on this, as on all other occasions, thankfulness for escape was mingled with regret that he could not effect friendly intercourse with his fellow-creatures. The next day he departed, and came to some villages without inhabitants, the huts of which were of a more substantial form and more compact construction than any he had before seen, seeming to stamp them as permanent abodes. They were surrounded by Yam grounds, whether natural or artificial, he could not tell; deep wells had been dug in several places, which were full of water at that time; and there were marked paths all through the surrounding district, by means of which Tiger was able to pick his way without stumbling into the holes from which the tubers had been taken. At night the howls of the native dogs were to be heard, reminding Captain Spencer of those of Jackals, which they also resembled in colour; and he then remarked that none of those which he had seen had been dark in hue.

Scrub, gravel, and quartz, characterized the soil for the next few days' journey; Grass-trees still showing themselves, and a flight of white Cockatoos guiding the travellers to water; which was reached at nightfall, and by which Captain Spencer again rested; and cutting off the top of some young Grass-trees, and boiling them well with cockatoos, and a little kangaroo fat, he made a delicious mess for supper. "Perdrix aux choux," said he to himself; "and quite as good as any produced by Ude or Beauvilliers. Even Gip eats it; and if I return in safety to India, I shall publish a book entitled, 'Australian Bush Cookery.'"

From the visible diminution of water in the bed of all streams or rivers, Captain Spencer supposed that at a more advanced period of the dry season, all of them would be perfectly dry; it was now with difficulty that enough was found for washing clothes as well as dressing food, and he never contemplated its future absence without a shudder. Near to the spot where Tiger was feeding, he saw what looked like a large, splendid, red Geranium, or rather Pelargonium, eight feet high, with flowers an inch and a half in diameter; and fearful that the horse would trample on or devour it, he hastened to gather and examine the blossoms. By the time he reached the spot, Tiger was stamping and pawing with his fore feet; and, to his horror, he saw a venomous serpent, with brown and red spots on its belly, twisted round the poor beast's legs; he could not chop its tail, because in so doing he might have chopped the horse also; and fearing that the reptile would spring at his nose or mouth, he exclaimed, "Stand, Tiger!" hoping that if he were quiet, the serpent would untwine itself, and go away. Tiger obeyed at the instant, but the flashing of his beautiful eyes proved that he was still in a state of great excitement. His docility, however, saved him, and the serpent left him; ut it was only to attack its new enemy. Captain Spencer stood still, and met the creature with a firm grasp; he had not, however, seized it near enough to the head, for it inserted its fangs into his hand: he was not at first aware that he was bitten, and stamping violently on its tail, he crushed the spine, and it became passive; then severing its head from its body, he went up to his dear horse, and in the joy of having saved him bestowed on him many a fond word and caress. All at once, however, he found his arm and hand swollen and stiff, and looking at the latter, he perceived two tiny red marks. "Aha!" said he, "I fear it is all over with me, for I have no antidote; could I get at the fat of the serpent, perhaps it might save me; but I shake so much, I cannot use my knife:" at these words he dropped upon the ground, the most violent shiverings came on, and an intense cold seemed to seize him from head to foot. These convulsions continued for at least half an hour, during which time the sufferer retained his senses, and he endeavoured to gain strength of mind on thus, as he thought, receiving his summons from this world; he took leave of his faithful companions, and thought with comfort that they could sustain life without his help. They, however, could not tell to any one what his fate had been, and a recurrence to family and friends caused one groan to escape him. Tiger stood by his side, conscious that something was very wrong; Gipsy watched him with close attention, every now and then giving a whine, and looking into his face; Charlie, who had been called to have a final caress, flew to him, saying, "What's the matter, Ned Spencer?" and perceiving that all was not right, remained close by, muttering to himself in an under tone, as he always did when anything disturbed him. Then came on fever and delirium, and a desire to rush about; but weakness prevented his standing: the sufferer swallowed large draughts of water, and overwhelming nausea came upon him, accompanied by violent pains in the limbs; these, however, were as nothing compared to that in the head; and turning upon his face and holding his burning forehead with both hands, he lay upon the ground, and all consciousness left him. He did not know how long he remained in that condition, but it was bright moonlight when he recovered from his sleep, or rather stupor, and he believed that his dear friends had never left him; for Tiger still stood close by, his head hanging down with all the appearance of sorrow in his subdued look; Gip had laid herself by him, and put her paws upon his arm; while Charlie had perched into a bush, and every now and then peered down, with a knowing look, to see what next would happen to his dear "Ned Spencer!" At last the poor wayfarer raised his head, but it immediately fell back. Gipsy licked his face, and when endeavouring to return her caress, the past by degrees returned to his memory, and he was surprised to find himself alive; he sat up, drank some water, and spoke: then did the trio, which had so lovingly and anxiously watched him through his sufferings, show their delight. Gip leaped on him, leaped off again, ran a few yards, returned, and licked him, and then set off once more at full speed. Tiger kicked and frolicked after Gipsy, and shook her well; while Charlie, who was always the most vociferous of the party, screamed, hurrahed, and laughed, till he was almost exhausted.

Before he was able to start again, for it was some days ere the stiffness left his arm, or his strength entirely returned, Captain Spencer received another visit from some natives, who appeared on a neighbouring elevation, using more **extraordinary gesticulations than any he had yet** seen; one of these was to inflate their cheeks to their full extent, and blow at him with all their force; and it was impossible to see their grotesque faces without laughing; this set off Charlie, who uttered his loudest peals of "Ha! ha! ha!" which rendered the men absolutely motionless from astonishment; and then it struck the Englishman, that he had been hitherto looked upon as a sorcerer, and that these poor people were now practising counter incantations. He did all he could to make friends, but they blew harder than ever; and Tiger, at his master's command, displaying his mane and tail, they decamped with a speed which showed that they believed themselves overmatched in witchcraft.

At length the travellers again took their way, and in the first day's march Captain Spencer was startled by what he thought was the cry of a child; Gip also listened anxiously, and then ran about with her nose to the ground; the former thinking that it might be a poor helpless infant dropped in the hasty flight of its parents. Nothing human, however, was met with, and the sound ceased, when Gip put up a bird, something like a Guinea-fowl, but as large as a hen Turkey.* Captain Spencer fired, and brought it down at the dog's feet. On preparing it for eating, he ascertained that it fed on insects, was full of worms, and had a large,

* Leipoa ocellata.

horny gizzard. He had followed the course of the river, and not far from it a curious mound of earth presented itself, about three feet high; but supposing it to be a native grave, he passed it without further examination. He then came to a hut with several entrances, and it appeared to him that it had been constructed by the inhabitants of the place, for concealing themselves when they watched, and wished to surprise the animals that came to the river to drink. He took possession of it for the same purpose, and killed what he at first thought must be Woodcocks, from their manner of running, but which proved to be Quails, some Ducks,* a Crane, a Bittern, and a beautiful Heron, and saw an immense flight of very pretty birds of a dark, dusky green, which alighted, and ran about with their tails stuck up in the most knowing manner. To prepare and profit by this accumulation of good cheer, it was necessary to halt; and when they started again, both master and horse had much additional burden. Greatly puzzled was the former to know which way to go; he now felt assured that the vicinity of the magnetic hills had influenced his compass; his glass showed him increasing tracts of scrub to the west, and he began to fear that he had completely missed his way to Perth; and the only point to which he could now direct his steps and his hopes was Adelaide. The

---

* Anas nævosa.

vision of Swan River, however, was too pleasing to part with all at once, and he still took a southerly direction. "At all events," said he, "that must bring me to the sea again without losing much distance, and once there I may be better able to determine which is the proper course. My preservation hitherto forbids me to despair, and I cannot think that these dear faithful companions are doomed to die in a desert." So speaking, he pushed on with alacrity, and courageously encountered a thick wood, highly scented from the blossoms of the Gum-trees which composed it; but the abundant growth of underwood presented great difficulties. He carried Gip, and cheered Tiger with his voice, which brought them well through it; and as he looked at the tall stems, bare of branches till they reached a great height, he thought of his more picturesque Indian forests.

The most refreshing slumbers restored the travellers, and they proceeded on their journey, not, however, with their usual supply of water; for this had been scarce during some days. None had been allowed in the morning before starting; so Tiger, without any ceremony, directly his load was taken off at night, pushed his nose into one of the cans, and drank its contents, leaving Gip only a little, which she lapped up as it ran over the side of the tin. "Tiger, my boy," said his master, "you must not be in such a hurry again; you were to have had only half that this evening." He denied himself any out of the other can, and cutting off a tuft from a Grass-tree, and folding it closely in its outside leaves, he roasted it in hot ashes, and giving Gip some meat, he and the horse enjoyed a succulent meal, which in some measure allayed his thirst; and thus he avoided the use of water for cooking. The next day they marched at least twenty miles; and the vegetation showed their more southern latitude, for the patches of scrub belonged to the singular family of *Proteæ* They were of the genus called *Banksia*, which is formed of long, narrow, prickly leaves, deeply indented, and brownish green in colour, shooting athwart each other, and forming a mass not less vexatious and difficult than the thorny Acacias. On halting in the evening, before composing himself to sleep, Captain Spencer took only a small quantity of meal-cake, for fear meat should make him thirsty; but Gip was fed as usual. They again started in the morning with a very small allowance of water, a privation which the poor animals took very patiently; and after walking some time through melancholy scrub, they found themselves standing on the edge of table-land, and beyond the steep and rapid descent lay a scene of uncommon beauty.

CHAPTER V.

Bed of a river—Native women—Captain Spencer finds water by digging—Diamond birds—Charlie frightens birds away—Captain Spencer takes yams from women—Gives a horse-shoe in exchange—Conduct of the natives with the horse-shoe—Kangaroo—Howling of native dogs—Captain Spencer eats a dog—Holes of dirty water—Gipsy falls into one of them—Comes out covered with mud—Birds driven away by Charlie—Snake under saddle—A cry of distress—Finds the native whose arm had been broken and lamed by a thorn in the foot—Captain Spencer saves him—Kinchela, name of native—Speaks Malay—Tells his history—Conversation between the Englishman and Australian—Captain Spencer goes to a well—Kinchela cooks—Discourse about Boylya's—Kinchela afraid of Tiger—Opinion of Captain Spencer among natives—Kinchela ignorant of way to Perth—Promises to take Captain Spencer to white men—Asks so earnestly to go with him that no refusal can be given—Grubs in Grass-tree—Frogs—Charlie interferes with Kinchela's lesson in English—Scarcity of clothes.

THE bed of a noble river, which had once watered a fertile plain, presented itself to the eyes of Captain Spencer; how long it had ceased to flow he could not tell; but he thought if in their necessity they followed it towards its source, they should find water, and be able to return to their proper path; for, in spite of his uncertainties, the traveller tenaciously persisted in following the compass towards the spot in which he imagined Perth to be situated. They descended the table and, and perceived some women and children seated in the channel of the stream, and with hands and sticks scraping a hole, as if for the purpose of procuring water. He watched them for some time; and seeing them kneel down, and put their mouths to the hole which they had made, he exclaimed, " Thank God, there is relief for us;" and with a lightened heart he proceeded towards the spot. The river, when full, must have been of considerable breadth; and had, perhaps, even within a few months, overflowed much of the luxuriant valley through which it ran; for there were many signs of former torrents; such as fallen trees, which had been brought from a distance, (nothing like them existing in the neighbourhood,) masses of soil, &c. "How I should like," said he traveller, "to follow the track of this river, and see the forest whence that noble timber came, so much larger than any I have yet encountered! In spite of my thankfulness for having hitherto found enough to subsist upon, I get weary of occupying my whole existence in procuring the wherewithal to eat and drink, and thinking each day of the appetite of the morrow."

On arriving at the shining white sand of the water-course, some little distance from the natives, he began to dig with his shovel, and was not a little surprised to see some beautiful little birds* fly

* Diamond Birds, or Amandina.

in numbers around him, and even perch upon his spade, as if they knew what he was seeking, and were determined to have the first drink. He could not bear to take any of them for food, when they placed such confidence in him; and when the water rose in the hole, which it soon did, he suffered them to satisfy themselves; but Tiger, who seemed to smell the liquid, without waiting to be unloaded, rushed to the spot, and kneeling down, put them to flight, and himself luxuriated in a long draught. Gipsy followed his example, with whom Captain Spencer was a sharer; and then the little creatures again assembled, only to be again dispersed by Charlie, who dashed in among them, screaming out, " Rogues! scoundrels!" as he always did to his feathered brethren, and helping himself, screeched and flapped his wings, as if he were the tyrant king of plumed creatures.

Having been hitherto so unsuccessful with the men of the native tribes, Captain Spencer thought this would be an excellent opportunity of trying to conciliate the women; but as soon as he directed his steps towards them, they all uttered a clamorous cry and ran away. In their haste they abandoned some yams which they had with them, and he took some of them for himself. By way of payment, however, he laid one of Tiger's old shoes in their place. He then retired to a dis-
ce, and with his glass watched their movements.

After some time they cautiously returned to the spot they had left, turned the horse-shoe over and over again with a stick, then they struck it, and at last, as if convinced that it was harmless, one of them took it up, examined it, and looked through the holes where the nails had been. The others imitated her, and seemed to think it incomprehensible. At last, running back to a man who now advanced towards them, and who walked as if he were lame, they, with many energetic gestures, appeared to relate all their adventures to him. He gravely inspected the horse-shoe, looked also through the holes, and then, one of the women giving him a piece of cord out of a bag which she carried upon her back, he, by means of it, fastened it round his neck, and then they all disappeared, probably to their dwelling-place. It was for some little time a subject of debate with the traveller, whether he should go after them, and try to improve any good impression which he might have made, or pursue his way. At last, the uncertainty of being successful, deterred him from straying in that direction; and filling his cans, &c., he in the evening departed. He passed over many low hills, which were fatiguing from their rugged nature, but at the foot of which he was still able to find water by digging.

Leaving the hills behind them, they the next morning entered a Hakea scrub, which Hakea is a Proteaceous bush, much matted together, and having large prickly leaves. There Gipsy killed and dragged to her master an animal which was much too large for her to carry, and which proved to be a smaller kind of kangaroo than he had yet seen. She laid her game at her master's feet, sat down, wagged her tail, looked in his face, and seemed so earnestly to implore him to cook it, that he halted a little sooner than usual; and making a rude imitation of a native oven, contrived to bake it, for he could not afford water for the preparation of his food. He always made a quantity of cakes whenever he filled his cans, not knowing when he should be able to mix the meal again. He cut the Kangaroo in pieces after skinning it, and wrapped it in some of the young twigs of the scrub, covered it well with clods of earth and bushes, and was tolerably successful, finding this a much more nutritious method than boiling. There were probably numbers of the same animal in that part of the country; for at night the native dogs kept up such a screeching and howling, "such a row," as Charlie grumbled to himself, that Captain Spencer could only compare the noise to the yellings of infernal spirits, congregated there to forbid him to advance. The next morning he, without any compunction, shot one of them which he saw crossing the scrub, and carrying it with him, cooked it as he had done the Kangaroo. To his taste it was very good eating, but Gipsy would not touch what perhaps she thought was one of her own kind.

Holes with dirty water, evidently dug by the natives, were occasionally met with, but no signs of streams saluted the thirsty mouths of the travellers, and even these holes appeared to have been filled with the drainings of the surrounding soil. Gipsy and Tiger did not hesitate to drink from them, but it was sometime before their master could prevail on himself to follow their example. He saw Gipsy slip into one; and as she kicked and struggled, he thought she must be choking, and went to her relief. He pulled her out by the hind legs, and could not help laughing at her appearance. Half her body was covered with thick mud; she sneezed, tried to get it off with her paws, but they were also encased in mud; and she then ran into the scrub, and by dint of rubbing and rolling, managed to get rid of the greater portion. Her master hoped, by enlarging the hole, to make the water run more freely into it, but nothing came except mud; and therefore taking two handkerchiefs, he filled them with it, and placing each on the top of a can, he filtered enough for Tiger and himself; Charlie, by dipping his bill into the hole, procured enough for his moderate desires. Captain Spencer found an unexpected advantage in the hole; for as soon as he left it, Pigeons, a beautiful Falco hypoleucus, very like the Gyr Falcon of Europe, some of the Swallow tribe, Finches, Honey-eaters, and others which were new to him, flocked round it to drink, and were afterwards driven away by the hasty arrival of Parrots and Cockatoos, which made Gipsy growl, and Charlie utter his usual abuse; among all of which he, however, secured a whole bagful of birds for future provision.

Green, juicy grass was no longer to be found, except in small patches, and these were very rare; but Tiger wisely accommodated himself to circumstances, and grazing upon the young shoots of scrub, apparently had wisdom enough to be quite satisfied with them. It was almost with reluctance that his master left even the muddy hole, so uncertain was he now of finding water; but filtering as much as his cans and skins would hold, he again continued his journey. The nights were now so much warmer, and there was such a total absence of dew, that the party no longer huddled together under the tarpauling; but Captain Spencer, wrapping himself up in his cloak, generally laid his head upon the saddle instead of upon Tiger; it was with a shudder that he heard a slight rustling as he was about to fall asleep, and instantly starting up, he lifted his pillow, and saw a snake coiled up, which had crept under for shelter. He beat the scrub well all round him, and sat down, intending to sleep in that posture; but slumber had fled; and as he sat in the bright moonlight, which tinged a large extent of country with its bright and silvery hues, he thought he heard a wailing voice at a distance. Gipsy at that same instant put up her head and barked, and in a moment both master and dog were on their feet in order to find the person from whom the cry of distress proceeded. Gip led the way, and not far off lay a young Australian, who now and then uttered a plaintive cry. Captain Spencer knelt beside him, found that his pulse still beat strongly, although he appeared to be very helpless, and he imagined that the sufferer had met with some accident which had disabled him from walking. He therefore began to examine the legs; one of them was very hot, and as he approached the foot he found it was very much swollen; a sudden start and groan from the man, as he gently passed his fingers over one part, convinced him that a thorn was in it, and nothing could be done but to wait till the morning, in order to try and extract it. How to procure temporary relief was the great difficulty, for he scarcely dared waste his scanty portion of water in bathing the part affected, and rubbing would make it worse. While trying to invent some means of cooling it, the poor creature exclaimed, "Yampee, yampee!" Then opening his eyes, he fixed them on the white man, as if not perfectly conscious of what was passing. What these words meant Captain Spencer could not guess; but the swollen tongue and lips, the heat of the skin, and inflamed foot, all betokened thirst, and he congratulated himself that he had still water to give him without absolutely depriving his horse and dog of it. He immediately poured some into his shell; and lifting the native's head so as to lean against his shoulder, he gave him some to drink, and with pleasure saw the relief which it evidently afforded. He laid the man down again, and formed a pillow for him with his cloak; and raising his foot on to the saddle, so that it should not touch anything, he moved all his baggage to the spot, and told Tiger and Charlie to come and lie down there. He then chopped off a piece of the thickest scrub he could find, and fanned his patient with it till he fell asleep. He ventured himself to doze a little as he sat by him; once or twice he gave him water during the night, and at length sufficient light came to enable him to examine the foot more thoroughly. The man still slept, and he took his knife, and sharpening it upon the leathern belt which he wore round his waist, he firmly but gently grasped the leg with one hand, and with the other quickly drew the knife across the swelling. The thorn was instantly discovered; and he drew a pair of small forceps from the handle of the said knife, and extracted a long, sharp spine of Acacia. The native gave a **yell**

CAPTAIN SPENCER HEALS THE NATIVE'S FOOT.

[Page 173]

of pain, and to soothe him Captain Spencer held up the thorn for him to look at. The poor creature nodded his head, and, sick and exhausted, fell back again and slept. His doctor bruised some of the tender leaves of a plant which looked very much like a Mallow, and bound the foot up in them; and as his patient lay, he watched by him, and pleased himself with the hope, that not only had he relieved a suffering fellow-creature, but that perhaps through him he might obtain the good-will of some of his countrymen; a still more comforting suggestion arose, which was, that as these people knew every nook and corner of their country, this man might take him to Perth, and perhaps for the present point out the possibility of procuring water. Of provisions there was an ample supply for a few days, and he was in no hurry. If he had been, it would have made no difference; for nothing would have induced him to leave any one in so helpless a condition as that of the Australian.

When the young man awoke, the word "Yampee" again issued from his lips; and half raising himself, he pointed to the water-can. Captain Spencer supplied him, but at the same time pointing to himself and Gipsy, who was close by, he made signs that he must leave some for them. The man nodded, and fixed his eyes on the Englishman with a look full of gratitude, which suddenly changed to surprise, and he exclaimed, "Ho!

no!" "Ho, no to be sure," said Charlie, and a look of alarm pervaded the features of the native, who remained silent for a minute or two; he then rapidly uttered a long speech, not one word of which was comprehensible to his benefactor, but among the numerous signs which he made, he pointed to a distance, and then to his arm, and Captain Spencer looking at him attentively, thought that his face was familiar to him. Then the adventure of the broken arm recurred to his memory, and in his present patient he recognised the person for whom he had in the north officiated as surgeon. He also remembered that the party had spoken Malay; and as he also could converse in it, a mode of communication with the young man was opened. He immediately addressed him in that language; the face of the native brightened as he comprehended what was said, and in reply, told the Englishman that he belonged to one of the northern tribes, and just after seeing him he had come towards the south in search of nuts and yams, and to catch fish in the rivers; that he and his people had had a quarrel with some of those among whom they had come, and that they had fought. His father and brother had been killed, and several of the other people; in consequence of which he had been kept to supply the place of the dead, and ever since lived in the south. He had been travelling with a party from place to place, as they all did when water and provisions were scarce, and had run this thorn into his foot. His companions had tried to get it out for him, but had only broken and pushed it in still further; and as he could no longer walk with them, they had left him there to die. Captain Spencer asked if they had given him anything to eat or drink when they went away; to which he replied that they themselves had very little, that each was obliged to provide for himself, and that in times of scarcity old and sick persons were often left behind, and died for want of nourishment. He added that he had seen Captain Spencer more than once in his journeys, and frequently, when his people were going to attack him, he told them what the good white man had done for him, and then they left him unmolested.

There was something so cheering even in the society of this savage, that Captain Spencer's spirits, which had never entirely recovered after the depression occasioned by the bite of the serpent, insensibly rose, and he became as hopeful as ever for his eventual safety. He, however, looked forward with pain to the time when he and his human companion must separate. He asked him if there were any water in the neighbourhood, and the native directed him to a hollow at some distance, where he said his people had dug a well, and left it full when they passed, hoping to find some remaining on their return. Calling Tiger to him, the horse neighed, at which the countenance of the Australian betrayed the utmost alarm, and he screamed and hid his face in his hands as the animal trotted up to his master, and laid its nose upon his shoulder. Captain Spencer tried to reconcile him to the docile creature, who would have made friends with him most willingly, but the man shuddered, and said it was a " big, big, dog," and then lowering his voice, added that he was a boyl ya. The repetition of this word struck the Englishman, but he was in a hurry to be off for water; so he put the saddle on the horse's back, laid all his things together, except the cans and skins, under the tarpauling, made the native understand that he was to take care of them till his return, and springing into the saddle, was off in a moment, Tiger occasionally jumping into the air over patches of scrub, and Gipsy also, who emulated his frolics, and Charlie exclaiming, " What a row! hurrah!"

Some limestone ridges were passed, the well was found covered up with stones, the cans and skins, were filled, Tiger had an excellent meal off the green grass which surrounded it, he and Gipsy rolled together, and Charlie laughed; all drank with pleasure, for the water was still tolerably good, and all returned more soberly than they went; the weight of the filled vessels convincing Tiger that his time for play was over. They found that the native had crawled to the tarpauling, and laid his head upon it; and as a small kangaroo had been shot, there was every prospect of the necessaries of life for at least a few days. The native shuddered and crouched as Tiger approached; but dismounting, his master again let him loose, and showed the kangaroo to the man, who instantly exclaimed, " Wallabie!" and said he would cook it. Captain Spencer gave it up to him, and although he did not take off the skin, or cut it up, he suffered him to go on in his own way. The native, who called himself Kinchela, singed off the hair with pieces of burning stick, and constructed an oven with clods of earth much more artistically than the Englishman had done, who supplied him with the materials as he asked for them, and watched him with interest. He heated the oven in the same way, but left the ashes in; he wrapped the kangaroo in the dry herbage which grew close by, covered it carefully with more clods of earth, and then excluded the air entirely with boughs of scrub. When the time came for the meal to be ready the gravy was in it, and the superiority of native cookery was evident. "How associating with our fellow-men takes the conceit out of us!" said Captain Spencer. "I have been fancying myself, of late at least, equal to that Soyer of whom I have read in the English papers, and now the first savage with whom I meet far out-does my best efforts." He was, however, somewhat consoled when he saw with what avidity the savage devoured the yam cakes made English fashion, and was surprised when the man shared the entrails with Gipsy, which he seemed to prefer to the other parts of the kangaroo. Some tops of Grass-trees, which had grown in the hollow, were also cooked in the oven; but before he put them in, Kinchela examined all the leaves separately, and picked something out of them which he put into his mouth. Can he be eating raw insects? thought Captain Spencer. A bag of dried Unios was still left, which when offered to the native he rejected with horror, saying "the boyl-yas would eat him when he was asleep if he took them, and he must sleep to get well."

The repast being finished, and Kinchela appearing to be free from pain, Captain Spencer asked him what he meant by a boyl-ya; on which he shook his head mysteriously, and it was long before he could be prevailed on to answer. At last he said that a boyl-ya was a sorcerer, and turning towards the unconscious Tiger with a look of apprehension, he was again silent. Captain Spencer could not forbear a smile, but not wishing to hurt the man's feelings, he concealed it, and begged to know why the people had called him a sorcerer. Lowering his voice, Kinchela, with some hesitation, said, "that all his people believed him to be one for many reasons: that he travelled alone, which no white man had ever done before; that he looked at something which he held in his hand, and then seemed to know which way to go; that he had a little black dog, not at all like their dingoes (dogs), which made an odd noise, and was also a boyl-ya, for he knew everything its master said; and that he had also a big dog, not like a dog at all, that was a still bigger boyl-ya, that was very fierce, upon which he sometimes flew away in the midst of noise and smoke; that he himself killed every thing by fire, and sometimes pulled the fire out of his body (alluding to the pistols which Captain Spencer carried in his belt); and that when he wanted to cut down grass he only touched it with his big knife, and then it fell. Kinchela spoke of the death of the tall man as known every where, and all supposed he had been killed because he defied the boyl-ya, and wished to destroy him. He said that it was understood in various places that a boyl-ya was going through the country, which some thought would be a blessing and others a curse, and therefore the latter were determined to do him all the mischief they could."

Captain Spencer was highly amused at the character under which he had passed among these people, and also at the scaring influence of Tiger's mane and tail, which, added to his capers, had doubtless confirmed the idea of his flying. He was, however, surprised at the intimate knowledge which was possessed of all his actions, proving how incessantly he must have been watched On mentioning his stay by the side of the lake, Kin chela told him that " the natives avoided him by living on the other side, but that they peeped at him over the tops of the hills, or from the trees in which they hid themselves; that they thought the large tarpauling was a cloud which made him and his attendant spirits invisible, for never before did birds sleep with dogs and man, and talk as Charlie did, which proved what clever sorcerers all of these were, and that the white man's visit and escape from the caves where so many sorcerers lived, had raised their idea of his influence, and showed that he exceeded all others in power."

The foot was healing fast, the water was again low in quantity, and wishing to fetch some more, and yet not leave the Australian, Captain Spencer, hoping that he had convinced the poor man of the harmlessness of himself and companions, proposed that he should ride on Tiger's back and go with him; by which means the recovery of the foot would not be impeded by exercise; but Kinchela's horror was so great at the idea, that it was in vain to try and persuade him; the Englishman therefore returned to the well alone, and procured the proper supply. During his absence Kinchela tried to walk a little way, and had reached some little distance from the place where they had bivouacked. It was then that Captain Spencer thought of sewing the lame foot up in a piece of his most pliant leather; and if with that he could but get him to the place where the well was, he might leave him with every prospect of being able to secure food; he had been going to the north, or they could have travelled together for a short time. He asked him the way to Perth; but the name was wholly unknown to Kinchela, as well as that of Swan River; and it was impossible by any allusion to it, to bring it to his mind; he said he knew there were places where a great many white men lived together, and made a " big smoke;" but he had never been to any of them. The reaching Perth was now entirely abandoned by the traveller; and he inquired if the man knew where the big water was, where the ships lived. Kinchela replied in the affirmative, and pointed towards it, in a direction which was very different to that which the Englishman would have taken, and which perfectly bewildered him. He said that "plenty of white people lived a great way off," and pointed to the east; but he had never seen them; and then Captain Spencer decided on making the sea his principal object; for he could ascertain nothing respecting any other object: every where, the native told him. there was but little water for drinking

Captain Spencer made all preparations for starting; and when he asked Kinchela if he thought he should soon overtake his own tribe, the poor man seemed perfectly astonished, and said he was going with the white man; the white man, however, shook his head; and then Kinchela fell upon his knees, bowed himself to the ground, and clasping his hands together, said. "he would find water for him, catch food for him, do anything for him, and never go away from him; that his father and brother were all dead; he had not any wife, (gin as he called her); and that the white man was like his brother come back to him; and that now he would never go any where but with him." Captain Spencer did not then know the strange ideas which many of the Australians entertain of the reappearance of their dead relations in the form of white men, and therefore could not comprehend the force of the latter part of Kinchela's speech; but he could not treat his solicitations lightly. At the same time he could not bear to drag this poor creature all over the continent, and then leave him among strangers. He tried to explain to him that he lived in the land of the Malays; and after he had seen the white men a great way off, he should go back there across the big water, and never return to Australia; that he had plenty of servants in the Malay's country; and that he might perhaps even go away for ever from them, and live among white men entirely. It was useless to make these representations; Kinchela implored, gesticulated, promised everything he could think of likely to make his presence desirable; but half of what he said was unintelligible, both from its vehemence, and from being partly in his native language; however, the tears which rolled down his cheeks, his sorrow, his supplications could not be mistaken, and Captain Spencer yielded; on which the poor fellow laid his hands upon the white man's shoulders, and put his head upon his breast.

Now it would be necessary to secure a double stock of provisions; and while thinking of this, it darted into Captain Spencer's mind, that perhaps in a moment of frantic hunger, the man might eat his poor Gip; he, however, could not but be pleased on the whole to have a companion which would relieve the dreadful solitude he had often found so oppressive; and he determined, as long as he could, to keep up some sort of mysterious influence, both about the horse and dog, which might render them more secure; and he thought that if he at length reached a settlement, he might easily find some one who would be glad to engage a faithful servant, and so take him off his hands. He told him that he must obey him in all things, which the man seemed perfectly to comprehend; and, although he thought it might be useless, he tried to convince him that Tiger, Gip, and Charlie, were to be as much respected as himself.

Now came the consideration of food; and the wisest thing appeared to be a final visit to the well to increase the supplies; and when Captain Spencer announced his intention, Kinchela said he was quite able to walk, and if he did not do all that was right by the white man, the dogs and the bird, and other boyl-yas, he knew would torment, if not eat him. His master made over to him the two spears which he had secured in his encounter with the natives, and which he had never used. The man seemed to be delighted with the present; examined them, poised them in his hand, and said he would make a throwing-stick when he came to a tree.

The whole party moved to the well, Kinchela limping a little; but he leaned on one of the spears, and his master had patience. A hut of boughs supported by a stick, was erected, the materials for which Captain Spencer chopped down with his hatchet; and as there were some fine Gum-trees of a hard wood near by, he taught Kinchela the use of both that and his knife, for making the throwing-stick and a club; and with the facility thus afforded, the native was delighted. The Grass-trees attracted his attention; but instead of choosing the best-looking, he went to those which appeared to be dry, and giving one a kick, it shook; he then quite knocked it over; and taking a piece of bark from a Gum-tree, he sat down upon the ground, and picked from it more than a hundred caterpillars; he ate one or two as he proceeded; and offered some to his master, who declined them with a feeling of disgust. Kinchela, however, persevered, and wrapping them in the piece of bark, when the oven, which they made on their arrival, was heated, he baked them; and so earnestly entreated Captain Spencer to taste them, that he could not refuse. To his surprise he found that they tasted like nuts; and having once conquered his repugnance, he became as fond of them as the Australian seemed to be. Gipsy also acquired the taste; and Charlie, who had always been extremely busy among the Grass-tress, and never came to one but he sat on the top, screeched, and flapped his wings before he began to eat; seemed to have quite as much pleasure in eating cooked as well as raw caterpillars: saying, as he strutted about, "Very good, very good."

Frogs were caught by the native, and cooked in the same manner; and of these Captain Spencer immediately partook, the Australian having taken out the intestines; he however confined himself solely to the parts which are eaten in France. Cockatoos were shot, and the whole cookery was entirely resigned to the native, who plucked the feathers off, folded the entrails in a piece of by themselves, and baked them separately, reserving them for himself, being now, as well as afterwards, perfectly contented with them for his share, provided they were of sufficient size. His master saw that new sources of food would be opened to him, provided he could conquer preconceived opinions, and take that which the country afforded, and reasoning with himself, he made a determination from that moment, to eat whatever Kinchela provided for him, if the taste were not disagreeable.

The next day, as they sat together after their meal, Kinchela received his first lesson in English, which his master determined to teach him as quickly as possible. Charlie was rather a hindrance, for he also repeated the words, till his master scolded him, and then he repeated the scolding in so ludicrous a manner, that it was impossible to help laughing, and he at length flew away, saying, "Charlie, you rascal, hold your tongue—Ha! ha! ha!" The native was as quick as Charlie, and Captain Spencer was surprised at his daily progress. At night, the bird, before he went to sleep, repeated everything he had learned in the day, and completed the astonishment of the Australian by saying in a sort of patronising tone, "Kinchela, that's right," and Kinchela turned his eyes towards him with fear and astonishment. "Good," thought the Englishman; "he will think Charlie the greatest sorcerer of the four; this shall be encouraged for the poor bird's safety."

Clothes were mended; the two pair of cloth trousers were dwindled into one, and these were much patched; the thread was very low, the shirts had quite disappeared, but the beard, as well as moustaches having been suffered to grow, it hid the deficiency. One cloth jacket alone survived in a serviceable state, and those of linen were in the utmost state of delapidation; stockings had long been gone, but thanks to the moccasins, the shoes which they covered, were still in being. "What shall I do," said Captain Spencer, "if I do not get to some habitable place before long? I may emulate my friend Kinchela in his eating, but certainly not in the absence of his wardrobe; I must kill some more kangaroos, and make a dress of their skins; but how insufferably hot they will be! Well, patience!"

And now the time of starting was arrived, Captain Spencer, as usual, took his knapsack on his back, which was much too light for his comfort or convenience; he also carried his fire arms, his hatchet, and his sword; Kinchela took the spears, and two additional bags which his master had contrived to make from his old clothes, to hold the increased stock of provisions, some pieces of bark and a lighted stick, which he said was much better than for white man to make fire each time; and

Tiger had his usual burden. They at first proceeded by very short journeys, on account of Kinchela's foot being still tender; but before many days were over he walked perfectly well; nevertheless he was always much less able to bear a long march than Captain Spencer.

CHAPTER VII

Kinchela still afraid of Tiger—Zamia trees—Kinchela's first lesson in honesty—Bed of a small lake—Improved cuisine—Australians cannot boil—Fire-stick—Wild fowl—Birds—Kangaroo caught in Kinchela's fashion—Kinchela greedy—Reflections of Captain Spencer—Gums—Manna—Floss Silk—Bee—Kinchela's memory of words—Cold rain—Kinchela catches Opossums—Kinchela makes a cloak—Burnt grass—Catch animals by burning scrub—Kinchela mends spear—Kinchela talks of bad black men—Magellanic clouds—Higher hills—Wallabies—Talperos—Emu—Emu oil—Cross the mountains—Flies—Iguana—Kinchela's fear of a telescope—Beautiful scenery—Flowers—Lake — Ipomea—Everlastings—Nest of Leipoa—Banksias—Finches—Stork—Dragonfly—Beetle—Fly—Grubs—Captain Spencer carries Gipsy everywhere on his knapsack—Native dogs—Wombat—Snake—Kingia—Grevillia—Inga—Eugenia, &c.—Birds and insects—Buteo—Birds—Scenery—Pieces of crystal and agate—Flowers—Mackintosh given to Kinchela—Fungus—Natives frightened away by gun—Python—Arrive at the Ocean.

THE cheerfulness of the travelling party was much increased by the addition of Kinchela, for there was frequent conversation between him and his master; and animals are always cheered by the sound of the human voice. Both Gip and Tiger were accustomed to dark complexions, and were therefore strongly inclined to be familiar with their new companion; more so than he liked, especially as concerned the horse, towards which he still felt an undefinable dread. Even in the midst of cooking or talking, if Tiger whisked his tail, he stopped short and looked at him with terror. The usual practice of Captain Spencer—that of bivouacking in the middle of the day, and marching during the morning and evening hours—was adhered to, unless any unforeseen event occurred to make an alteration of plan desirable. The first morning they were all thus travelling together, they reached some Zamia trees, from which Kinchela was about to gather the clustered cones, but his master stopped him, at the same time saying they were poisonous, because they had made him very ill when he eat them. 'They made white man ill," rejoined Kinchela, "because he not know, and he eats them wet;" he added that he and his party had passed that spot, and buried some in the ground, which would now be fit to eat, and he would take them up. He soon found the spot, and with the sharp point of a stick turned them out of the holes. Captain Spencer examined, and felt that they were perfectly dry; and seeing Kinchela eat them freely, ventured to follow his example. They were very superior in flavour to those which had been recently gathered, and he did not experience any ill effects from them. Tiger and Charlie had their share, with whom they also agreed; and he could only account for this by supposing that the oil which they originally contained had drained from them while they were in the ground. For every one which he had taken from the holes, he made Kinchela substitute a fresh nut, saying, that unless he replaced them, it would be robbing those who had made the deposit. Such reasoning surprised Kinchela, and was his first lesson in the eighth commandment. This seemed to be the southern limit of these trees, some of which were sixteen feet high; and they did not meet with them again.

After some days' journey, with a miserable supply of water, the party reached what once had been a small lake, surrounded by a number of rounded hills, the banks of which were muddy, and the dry bed of which was full of large and deep cracks. The hitherto successful digging was here again tried, and water was reached at a depth of eight feet from the surface. Kinchela, who had hitherto used only his hands on such occasions, was delighted with the shovel, and seemed to think that it would always produce water. The liquid was at first of the most disagreeable flavour; but all except Captain Spencer drank it without disgust. He not only waited till a larger quantity had risen into the hole, but, to the astonishment of the native, he boiled it: indeed, the process of boiling always seemed to be a matter of surprise to him; for as the Australians have no vessels which will stand the fire, they cannot effect this method of heating food; and Kinchela often took up the hot can and looked at it, in doing which he more than once burnt his fingers.

According to Captain Spencer's expectation, he was now introduced to a multitude of novelties for his *cuisine*, and among others was the root of a fern, which he had often seen before, and which, when baked and powdered into meal, was excellent. No more yams were found, but the tubers of rushes, and of a plant something like a reed,* yielded a good supply of farinaceous substance; and Kinchela soon learnt from his master how to make it into cakes, similar to those of oatmeal.

By degrees the Australian became accustomed to the sound of the gun and pistols, but never evinced the least desire to touch them; and his master thought it well that he should continue to feel this repugnance. He always carried the fire-stick, the lighted end of which was wrapped in grass or bark, so that it remained in a smouldering state, and was a most acceptable saving of the powder hitherto used in lighting the fires, or the more laborious process of friction with two pieces of wood. As usual, when water was procured by digging, birds flocked round in an incredibly short space of time, and ample food was thus supplied; several sorts of wild fowl† issued from the reeds; an Eagle also made its appearance, but did not

---

* Potamogeton.   † Teal and Anseranus melanoleuca.

alight, unless it had descended early in the morning. when it was seen at a distance, flying away as if satisfied. The incessant Cockatoos, always announced by Gip's growls, brought some of their young ones, just able to fly, and making a noise like young frogs, to the increase of Gip's anger, and which Charlie provokingly imitated; then came Parrots, Parrakeets, and Pigeons, a bird which made a glucking sound, some Honey-eaters, with cheerful notes and gaily coloured plumage, and another bird, which, after uttering a long, clear whistle, ended with a cry like the smart crack of a postilion's whip; Fly-catchers and a Platycercus added to the number, the latter having a sea-green body and yellow shoulders; and Kinchela's hands were full with catching them in all sorts of ways. He was very skilful in setting snares; and one of his traps was composed of two rods, placed among the grass, and meeting at the top, from which part hung a noose made of twisted fibres of bark, so that the birds, as they ran along, thrust their heads into the loop, which immediately closed round their throats and choked them.

An enormous Kangaroo was started, and Kinchela, anxious to show his powers, entreated Captain Spencer to keep Gip away, and let him kill it without assistance; so to gratify him his master held the dog in his arms to ensure her forbearance. The native then gathered a large bough, which effectually concealed his person, and holding it before him, he cautiously and stealthily advanced towards his victim. The bough, however, rustled a little against the bushes, as he passed some a little higher than the rest, and then the Kangaroo raised its head and looked round. Kinchela stood perfectly motionless till the animal's suspicions were quieted, and thus drew near his prey. He had concealed his spear also behind the bough, and now, taking good aim, plunged it into the poor beast just under its shoulder. It did not fall immediately, but took an enormous leap with the spear sticking in it, which, however, broke as the game reached the ground. Kinchela ran to the spot; but the Kangaroo kicked so violently that he could not come very close, but creeping round, out of reach of the feet, the long toe on which had an enormous nail which might have killed him, he made a sudden dart upon the tail and held it with all his strength; this reduced the energy of the Kangaroo, and it gradually became weakened by loss of blood. It was no sooner dead than Captain Spencer came up to the Australian, and praised him for his skill and courage, at the same time saying, that he should like to have the skin taken off and added to his stock of leather, for Tiger's and his own socks were almost exhausted.

Kinchela was quite excited; but taking up a

sharp piece of stone, which he used much more dexterously than he would have handled a knife, made an incision, by means of which he proceeded to strip the skin from the body, occasionally pushing it with his feet, and often stuffing a piece of flesh into his mouth, warm and quivering as it was. An oven was constructed and heated by Captain Spencer, and as this was going on, and the entrails were removed, they were put into it; but the rapacity with which the native snatched at them, and seemed to grudge Gipsy her share, so completely disgusted his master, that he began to repent the companionship which had at first given him pleasure. He told the native that as they had plenty of other provisions, he would have the flesh of the Kangaroo dried; but Kinchela did not comprehend this, and was evidently disappointed at not eating it directly; his master was therefore obliged to set to work himself, but the Australian quickly comprehended the process: the meat was cut into strips, and hung round the oven on wooden skewers, and when it was sufficiently cooked, it was exposed to the sun for a day, and then stowed away in a bag. The bones were stewed with some of the root-flour, and then Kinchela was satisfied with the supply for the present. He with the stone cut off all the coarser parts of the skin, stretched it on the ground, beat it for a long time, and renewed the process morning and evening till it was quite soft as well as dry.

As Kinchela slept after his ample meal and great exertions, Captain Spencer tried to reason himself out of the disgust which he felt, by considering that this poor wild man was, in his uncivilised condition, scarcely to be called a reasonable being; that his gratitude to himself showed he possessed some of the best feelings of human nature, and he could only expect his savage propensities to be overcome by education, and contact with those of his own species who were superior to himself. "We are all too apt," said he, "to judge of untutored men according to our wishes, and by books, which generally conceal that which would disgust. Even my good Indians would shock polite Europeans, if placed in their drawing-rooms without preparation; but they are refined beings when compared with Kinchela. Their religion too, though repugnant to us, has its softening influence; but neither in Kinchela, nor in any part of the country where I have been, has any trace of religion met my eyes, unless the caves were temples; and even these are relics of times and people passed away:—witchcraft alone supplies its place. But I must do my best with Kinchela, and when I feel annoyed at his gross habits, **must** steadily look to the future, and forbear."

The progress of the travelling party was **slower**

than it had been when Captain Spencer had no human companion, for Kinchela secured so many kinds of food, before unknown to the Englishman, that they seldom started very early in the morning; besides which, the former appeared to be wholly unable to make forced marches. A great article of their consumption was a variety of gums, gathered from different trees, especially that of a bright amber colour proceeding from the Acacias, which was very sweet and good, and which Tiger also delighted to pull off the stems. There were also some not edible, and which Kinchela told his master were used for fastening spear-heads, &c., such as an elastic substance something like Indian-rubber, and others of a more resinous nature; also what very much resembled Gum Tragacanth, from a tree of the Capparis kind. Besides these gums was a substance which both Gipsy and Tiger licked up with great avidity, as well as Kinchela, who complained of their taking possession of it, but who in reality dared not drive the horse away when he saw him devouring it. It was a white, mucilaginous substance, like flakes of snow, lying upon the trunks, and on the ground under the Gum-trees, and which appeared to come from under their outer bark. Captain Spencer could only compare it to Manna, and Kinchela told him that an insect made holes in the bark and let it out, so that it fell to the ground; he was quite greedy after it; but it was of too sickly a taste for his master, who much more enjoyed the sweet drink made for him by the native from the red or yellow flowering cones of the Banksias. They were so full of honey, that they had only to be shaken in water to impart to it their sweet syrup; and other flowers also produced the same, although not in equal abundance. One of these was an Asclepias, with flowers like those of the Hoya, whose pods were full of a substance like white floss silk.

One day, as the party were eating their morning meal previous to their march, Captain Spencer was surprised to see Kinchela suddenly starting up, saying in Malay, "Ah, you fellow! you show me where you live," and he instantly covered a Convolvulus flower with his hand, the trailing stems of which crept along the scrub. He then pulled some of the down from the Asclepias pod which stood near the spot, and wetting a piece of gum in his mouth, he with it fastened the white substance upon a Bee which he had secured. As soon as the insect was released from captivity, it flew away; and Kinchela keeping his eye upon it, followed its course, getting several tumbles on his way from his headlong haste, and attended by Gip, who ran and barked at she knew not what, but thought if there were a hunt, it was her duty to take a part. At last the bee went into a hole in the trunk of a tree, and Kinchela called to his master for the hatchet, with which he chopped away the wood till he exposed the whole nest. The queen issued from it, and consequently all the inhabitants of the hive deserted it, so that the contents became an easy spoil to the wayfarers. They poured the rich, well-flavoured honey into some pieces of bark, and managed to secure it from running out by binding these round with grass, so that it afforded a treat for some days. Gip had suddenly disappeared; but a whine of distress was heard by her master and Kinchela, who sought her in the direction whence the sound proceeded. It proved to be the neighbourhood of a dried-up spring, and the poor thing had fallen into a deep hole, which, being covered with bushes and sticks, had been unperceived by her. It was so deep that she was with difficulty extracted from it by means of a string, which she held with her teeth, and so was pulled up. Kinchela told his master that the pit had been dug by some natives to catch the Kangaroos when they came to drink at the spring, and was one of the many modes by which they entrapped these animals. Something was daily learned from Kinchela with regard to the important article of food; and he in his turn received daily information from the Englishman in the English language, of which he soon learned not only words, but sentences, to which he gave their proper application. It was, however, curious to observe how he retained certain words in his memory and not others, and corrupted the phrases. The latter probably arose from the nature of his own language, for of course it was perfectly original; and from the same source he always called Captain Spencer, Boccolo, which in his own tongue meant chief. There was an endeavour to make him substitute the Sahib of the Indians for it; but he frequently combined the two, and often addressed his master as "Boccolo Sahib."

The season of heat advanced in a manner which surprised Captain Spencer, considering the latitude in which he supposed they were; but in the midst of the dryness, some heavy clouds gathered over head, and there seemed to be every prospect of a heavy shower; it was, however, slight, but the drops which did fall upon his face and hands made him start in consequence of their icy coldness. Kinchela seized upon the skin of the Kangaroo, which still remained unappropriated, and covering his shoulders with it, crouched down in the scrub, refusing to stir till the rain was over. "Boccolo Sahib," said he, coming after his master, who had slowly proceeded, "we stop when we come to big tree, make cloak for Kinchela." How he was to make a cloak out of a gum-tree, which he supposed was meant by big tree, the Boccolo could not imagine, unless it were from the bark; he, however, yielded to his wishes, and arriving at a line of them, he agreed to stop, and more willingly as close by the trees was one of those depressions in which water had lodged and drained from the scrub, and although it was not good, there was enough for all.

Instead of going to sleep at night as usual, Kinchela remained in a listening posture, and hearing a slight rustling among the leaves, he pointed to them. Captain Spencer then saw some small animals which he supposed to be Flying Opossums,* for they flew from the higher to the lower branches; but Kinchela said he did not want them; there were others which were bigger. It was bright moonlight, and sitting perfectly still, with Gip in his arms to keep her quiet, the Englishman saw several of a larger size on the ground, eating the grass. They were about the size of a good-sized cat, had whiskers, and pretty innocent faces, not unlike mice; their eyes were very brilliant, and their ears soft and pretty; their legs were comparatively short, and their claws apparently sharp, with which they were evidently able to grasp small objects; their tails were out of proportion long, seeming to measure from eighteen to twenty inches, and had no hair underneath; their bodies were covered all over with a thick fur of different colours, dark gray, and shades of brown with a golden tinge, and lighter underneath; they

* Phalangista.

twisted their tails round branches of the **neighbouring scrub**, and called and answered each other with a sort of hoarse chuckle. "To-morrow I catch you," said Kinchela, and quietly settled himself to sleep.

Kinchela set to work the next morning, borrowing his master's hatchet, and sharpening a stout stick; he then examined the trunks of the trees, and stopped only at those on which he saw the prints of claws. He blew upon these marks, to see if the sand still stuck upon them where the feet had left it, in which case the opossums must have ascended very recently, and be within the tree, but if it blew away, he went on to another tree. When convinced that an opossum was within the trunk, he cut rather a deep notch, into which he stuck the great toe of his right foot, flung his left arm round the tree, stuck the sharp point of his stick into the bark above him, and lifted himself up; he then cut a notch for his left foot, dragged himself up to that, and thus arrived at the hole, which was a considerable distance from the ground. He routed the opossum* out with his stick; and when it appeared at the mouth of the hole, he caught hold of it in such a manner that it could not bite him with its sharp teeth; and when it was fairly out of the hole he seized it by the tail and dashed it to the ground. He caught a **great**

* Didelphis.

many, but not all with the same ease; for some ran swiftly up the tree directly he began to climb it, and took refuge in the boughs; but he went after them, and shook or knocked them down; others retreated into their holes so far that the stick would not reach them, in which case he descended the tree, and mounted again with some lighted leaves or grass, which he put into the hole, and the smoke soon dislodged the opossum.

More than forty opossums were secured, and they were just sufficient for the cloak. Kinchela performed his office with great dexterity; but as he removed the skins, he stuffed so many pieces of the entrails into his mouth, that Captain Spencer thought he would not be able to eat anything more that day; but it made no difference with the evening meal, and as yet his master perceived he had no adequate idea of the capacity of an Australian's stomach.

The excellent flesh of the opossums was dried, and the making of the cloak employed Kinchela for several days, for he was obliged to beat them a great deal to make them soft; he made thread by twisting fibres of bark together, or by a rude imitation of spinning the fur of the opossum. For a needle he used the shin-bone of a kangaroo ground to a point upon a stone, with which he pierced holes, and then put the thread through, in order to join the skins together. The cloak reached nearly to his knees when it was finished, and he fastened it upon his right shoulder with a wooden skewer; he also made a belt of opossum skin, into which he stuck pieces of sharp stone, a tomahawk of the same material, which had been left with him when he was abandoned, and whatever treasures he thought fit to accumulate.

The individual of the travelling-party who fared the worst was Tiger; for they frequently came upon large tracts where the grass and scrub had been burnt, and no rain had caused the former to spring up again; but the good horse bore his privations patiently and good-humouredly, and the meal and gum which were given to him were very nourishing substances. Still Captain Spencer watched him with anxiety, dreading to see him get out of condition, and was surprised to find with how small a quantity of water, and that of bad quality, they were all in such strong health. He asked Kinchela why these patches were burnt; and he replied, for two reasons, one of which was that it did the grass good, and made it grow well after rain had come upon it; and the other, that when they set the scrub on fire the small animals ran out of it; and he would show him how it was done the next time they wanted to renew their stock of food.

No sooner was the dried meat getting low than Kinchela reminded his master that the burning time was now arrived; and having settled Tiger in a distant spot, they procured some large thick boughs, and going to a distance from the station which they had chosen for the night, they selected a piece of scrub, and stamped and trampled a circle round it, into a still closer and more intricate mass. They then set fire to that which was in the middle, and all three—for Gipsy played her part bravely—contrived to secure Wallabies,* Opossums,† Mice, Rats and Frogs, Lizards and Snakes, which rushed out, and whose escape was impeded by the broken scrub. Gipsy, however, who was very eager in the sport, invariably shrank from the snakes, and was not quite sure that she ought to have anything to do with the lizards. When the flames touched the bruised mass, the two men vigorously beat and extinguished them with their boughs. It was a very fatiguing mode of hunting when only two persons were engaged in it, but very exciting.

The broken spear had never been mended; and now reaching some Grass-trees, which had not long ceased flowering, they saw the tall shafts of hard smooth wood rise from the middle; Kinchela soon secured one of them, and before he slept he fastened the head of the old one on to it with fresh gum. The scarcity of water increased so much, and was such a source of apprehension to Captain

---

* Halmaturus agilis.   † Hypsiprymnus.

Spencer, that he proposed to the native to return northwards to one of the permanent rivers, thinking, that with Kinchela's directions, he might reach it more speedily than if alone, and remain there till the season of drought was over. The man looked very serious, and shook his head, and on being pressed to speak, he said, "No! no! Boccolo Sahib; those very bad fellows; they not think you boyl-ya, and then they eat you up." The Boccolo at first thought Kinchela was trying to frighten him; but on being pressed to speak seriously, Captain Spencer found that there were really some tribes who eat human flesh occasionally, and that Kinchela truly apprehended some such catastrophe. He added that he knew them, but that he would take him to "the big water, where there was good country, good white men, and plenty to eat and drink;" he then pointed, as he had always done, in a southerly direction. His master, who had long abandoned all hope of Swan River, now fancied that King George's Sound must be the point to which his man alluded, and cheerfully acquiesced when that prospect presented itself to him, for he thought that even there he might meet with a vessel which would take him to a port whence he might embark for India.

One evening, as the wanderers sat by their fire, Captain Spencer watched the southern stars, which so plainly tell the distance of Europeans from their home, and Kinchela, who saw the direction in which his eyes were bent, said, "Boccolo, you look at smoke up there?" "What smoke?" asked the Boccolo in his turn. Kinchela pointed to those white specks in the heavens known as the Magellanic clouds, and then gravely assured his master that a black fellow, very well known, had made a fire, and a boyl-ya had taken the smoke up there, where it would always stay. Kinchela "knew it was true." Captain Spencer did not attempt to contradict him, but was much amused at this novel explanation of the phenomenon. He then questioned him, both in Malay and English, concerning the existence of a large sea in the interior of Australia. He replied that he knew of one big sea, and going round that a man would die, and a boy be very old before he had finished; but whether this meant the large sea with which some say the immense and unknown district of the interior is occupied, or whether he alluded to the ocean itself, Captain Spencer could by no means discover.

The travellers were now fast approaching a much higher line of hills than those which they had left far off to their right, and which showed signs of basaltic formation, with here and there a base of granite; the former rising two and three hundred feet, and alternating with sandstone. Little Talperos, as Kinchela called them, the size of a rabbit, but longer in shape, as well as Rock

Wallabies, which were bolder, stronger, and more active than those of the bush, resembling hares in appearance, ran about the rocky soil, which he said lived for months without water; and near whose haunts were many vestiges of native encampments. "Kinchela," said Captain Spencer, "do you see that black fellow stalking about alone there, at the foot of the hills through the high bushes?" "He not black fellow," replied Kinchela, laughing, in which he was loudly echoed by Charlie; and then added, "Gip, Kinchela, and Boccolo catch him." "To him, Gip!" said Captain Spencer, and all started in the pursuit; for he now saw that it was the bird he had so long desired to come in contact with, the Emu. Gip made directly for the game; and her master and Kinchela separated, in order to intercept the Emu in every direction which it might take. Still, with its extraordinary swiftness, it was getting ahead of them, when calling Tiger, Captain Spencer jumped on his back, and galloping round the bird, came before it, having directed Tiger by words and his name. This proceeding rather checked the native's ardour, for he was still frightened when his master mounted the horse; but the poor bird was at last run down, and lay kicking with its strong feet upon the ground. Gipsy kept barking at a short distance; but Kinchela dashed up behind, and broke its wings, for fear it should rise and try to make its escape. Captain Spencer then fired, and put an end to its existence. Kinchela would have dragged it to the place where they had made their fire; but to his infinite satisfaction his master threw it across Tiger's shoulder, and trotted back to their station. All this time Charlie had been a most attentive spectator, and flew about as if he had been mad, flapping his wings, and laughing, and crying "Ho! ho!" like the natives; but he was much too cautious to approach so large a bird. As soon, however, as it was dead, he perched himself behind his master, on Tiger's back, saying, "Well done, boys! Well done, Boccolo! Well done, Ned Spencer! Ha! ha!"

Water issued from the soil where they bivouacked, and which had been chosen from a suspicion that it was the bed of a former torrent; the small supply was pure and well-flavoured; and that night witnessed the baking of the Emu. There was no moon; and Kinchela set fire to the tops of two grass-trees near by, which burnt with a bright flame and delicious perfume, from the fragrance of the resin which they contained. A spacious oven was artistically built; the bird was plucked and skinned; the legs, neck, and head chopped off; the entrails taken out, folded up separately in grass, as well as the head and neck, and placed with the body in the heated circle, and while they were cooking; a fire was made on the ground, the feet were steamed, and were as good as calf's feet. When they were taken from the fire, a tray of bark was set upon stones amidst the ashes, and the skin suspended over it. Oil dripped plentifully into it from the skin, which gave great satisfaction to Kinchela, who rubbed himself all over with it; and wished his master to do so likewise, who of course refused; he also wished to rub Gipsy, but was prevented. When Captain Spencer asked him why he did this, he answered that it was good for the pains in his legs and arms; but of these pains he never yet had complained; and he cast a wistful look at Tiger, as if he would have operated on him, if he had dared. Captain Spencer thought it would be an excellent remedy to have by him, if he could possibly carry it; and when he suggested this to Kinchela, the young man made a sort of bag of the skin, and wrapping it in grass and bark, it travelled safely. The Emu's feathers were not lost; and forming a fillet of grass, Kinchela bound it round his temples, and stuck a bunch of them in front of his head; which, as he was tall and well-made, and had on his opossum cloak, produced a very picturesque effect. His master still wore his plumes, now formed of cockatoo feathers, and renewed them as often as they were dirty, by killing other cockatoos, and mingling the black, the sulphur colour, and scarlet of the different species.

It was now necessary to cross the mountains; and having examined the range with his glass, Captain Spencer chose the lowest and most accessible part, in order to save Tiger as much as possible from fatigue. As they ascended, which they did very slowly, Tiger was tired; and Gip so earnestly entreated to be carried, that her master lifted her up on to his knapsack, very much to the amusement of Kinchela, who looked at the horse, and said, " If big dog wanted to be carried, Kinchela not could carry him." The flies here were again troublesome; and Captain Spencer again had recourse to the handkerchiefs for himself and Tiger; and also put on the ear-cases of the latter. Upon this Kinchela begged to be accommodated in the same manner, to his master's infinite entertainment; and he fastened a red and white handkerchief over him; which was the more ludicrous, as, being too hot to wear his cloak, he had no other clothing than the head-dress and opossum belt; he also asked for coverings for his ears; and was not quite satisfied when he was told that they were only intended for horses. In spite of this, he, however, returned to his old habit of throwing up his chin, and half closing his eyes. Another sort of fly, of a brown colour, was also encountered, and which was extremely troublesome. Captain Spencer thought it indicative of the vicinity of Kangaroos, as he had often seen it on those animals; nor was he mistaken, for there were many on the other side of the heights.

All day did the party clamber, only resting for a short time; and at length, still far from the summit, they stopped upon a ledge, at the back of which was a shallow cave; large enough, however, to hold them all comfortably for the night. Before they settled themselves, they routed from it a large Iguana, with a bluish tint over the head and neck. It was singularly ugly; as, indeed, almost all the Australian lizards are; but Kinchela said it was very good to eat, killed and roasted it; and the supper which it afforded was like the most delicate chicken. On the morrow they again started, and before mid-day stood upon the summit of the range; which seemed to stretch to the north and south, as far as the eye, or even the glass, could carry the sight. On this occasion Captain Spencer tried to reconcile Kinchela to the use of the telescope, which he had hitherto regarded with superstitious horror. He with difficulty persuaded him to look through it at some Kangaroos feeding in the plain below; but as soon as he brought them, as Kinchela thought, close to his eye, the man all but dropped the telescope, and fell flat upon the ground, with his face downwards, to avoid the enchantment; nor could he ever be persuaded to touch it again. His master tried to overcome his fears by pretending to make Gip, Tiger, and even Charlie look through it; but he with tears implored that he might not be exposed to such a piece of sorcery.

It seemed as if all the natural riches of south-western Australia were concentrated in the beautiful spot before them; large districts of wood closed the horizon to the east, formed of lofty timber; the Acacia scrub had many open patches in it; and over its surface the most exquisite plants had frequently spread their trailing stalks, while their scarlet, yellow, crimson, or orange blossoms glowed vividly in the sun; clumps of trees, or single giants, stood in various spots; and a lake of opalic-looking water, with a bed of clay, caused such fertility, that even at the present time, when the herbage was in general brown and withered, there was green grass in its vicinity. It was evidently of much greater extent in the winter; but the basin was probably never dry, for even now the soil was wet and muddy, where water had been. Captain Spencer's first feelings of thankfulness were expressed in fervent ejaculations, and then followed great joy for Tiger's sake. "Dear old fellow!" said he, affectionately caressing him; "there is plenty of water, and some good grass for you, and we will stay here till your coat shines again, and you shall drink and be merry." At these words Charlie rose from the horse's back, saying, "Drink and be merry! hurrah! dear old fellow! Ned Spencer! Boccolo Sahib! Good bye! ha! ha! ha!"

The party occupied much less time in descending than they had done in climbing the heights; they passed beautiful trailing plants; a broad-leaved Capparis, bearing a pear-shaped fruit with prominent lines; Convolvuli; Ipomeæ, with yellow blossoms, and also with large pink flowers, from the seeds of which came a caustic juice, producing blisters on the skin. It surprised Captain Spencer that there were no natives in this beautiful place; but Kinchela said they lived there sometimes, for he saw several huts, and they were probably gone to the big water, as they did every year at this time, to catch fish. As they proceeded to a verdant spot, near to which Kinchela said Kangaroo-grass was growing, they passed some very pretty white and yellow everlasting flowers;* and soon came upon one of those mounds of earth which Captain Spencer had before seen, and taken for a native grave. To his great surprise, however, Kinchela gave a cry of pleasure, and immediately began to scrape away the earth from the centre with his hands. It was five feet high, and forty-five in circumference; and when Kinchela had penetrated a little way into the heap, perhaps about two feet, he with triumph showed two fragile and delicately-coloured pink eggs, which had rested

* Gnaphalium.

on their smallest end, and were of a large size. They and two others were roasted for supper, and although so large, had not the least coarseness of flavour. Close to this, and several other mounds, grew some dwarf Gum-trees, only thirty feet high, which Kinchela said made capital spears, digging and throwing-sticks.

As they ate their roasted eggs, Captain Spencer questioned Kinchela about the manner in which these curious nests were formed; and he told him that the birds scratch the soil up with their feet, and with it a great deal of vegetable matter, which, when it gets rotten, makes the whole heap quite warm; but that the birds, just before the female lays the eggs, turn out the inside to dry; she then deposits the eggs, at the rate of two in one day, and when all are placed, she covers them up, and leaves them to be hatched with the heat of the sun. It was always known when eggs were inside, because then the top of the mounds was round and smooth; and if there were none, there was a deep sinking in the middle. He added, that other birds in other parts of Australia laid their eggs in the same manner, but distributed them in different parts of the heap, whereas these laid them in a small circle round the centre. Captain Spencer found the shells very heavy, weighing, as he thought, eight ounces, and asked what occasioned some marks which he found on some of them.

The man answered that the white Ants penetrated into the mounds, and formed their galleries all round the eggs, so that the young birds found food ready for them immediately on coming out of the shell. A sort of skin covered the latter, which was of a brown colour. When Captain Spencer expressed a wish to see the birds, Kinchela said they must sit quite still and watch, for they were soon frightened; and the next day the native and his master stationed themselves among the mounds, concealing themselves in the bushes. Captain Spencer brought his gun, as well as his pistols, to fire at them, if they should attempt to fly away. At sunset one of the birds came to the mound, and was shot; it was a very heavy, compact bird, as large as a Turkey;* spotted brown and white, with a tuft upon the head, the bare parts of which were of a bright blue; its legs were short, and yet it ran very fast. Kinchela said it roosted on trees, and could live a long time without water. When the young have left the mound, the female, he added, walks about with from eight to ten young ones; they issue two at a time, and directly she hears their cry she runs to take care of them. There is only one pair for each nest; both together accumulate the heap of soil, and the hen lays an egg every morning just before sunrise. When the nest is robbed, she will lay again in the same nest,

* Leipoa ocellata.

but only twice the proper number of eggs in one year; the young birds scratch their way without help, and are then fully fledged, and all have a very strong gizzard.

"We will stay here some time, Kinchela," said Captain Spencer, "and rest ourselves, for there is plenty to see and to do here." "Very good, Boccolo!" was the reply; "then Kinchela make you new cloak," pointing to the mackintosh, the lower edge of which was hanging in ribands; and he started in search of more Opossums. Numbers of Banksias studded the plain with their honeyed blossoms, and bees were as plentiful as flies, but they did not sting. The pretty Finches also abounded in the same shrubs, made their nests, and warbled their cheerful notes. Near to the more barren parts of the mountains, but among the trees, a curious noise was heard in the evening, which lasted far into the night. Kinchela said it was not a Cadli, or wild Dog, but a big dog of another kind, which ate trees, and did not leave one branch till all the leaves were gone, and then it went to another. He and his master captured one, and it proved to be what the latter had seen described under the name of Koala, or Sloth, and had a sharp nose and coarse fur. Kinchela thought it would be good eating; but with plenty of food of other kinds about him, his master did not fancy its appearance; he, however, made use of its skin.

as he had done of the kangaroo's, and continued to collect skins while in this place. He caught many animals, and more especially the rock Kangaroos, which always sit with their tail between their legs. He was more anxious to secure them at this period, on account of the quantity of bark, which was yielded by numerous Acacias, for tanning their skins.

Charlie feasted on the abundance of insects; and the good bird, because Captain Spencer had frequently called to him to bring various specimens for examination, now of his own accord constantly flew to him with some of his prey in his beak. Among them was one of the Dragon-fly species,* the lower wings of which were very extraordinary-looking, like a long thread with two enlargements at the end; then he brought a Thynnus, looking like a wasp; another which Kinchela called a Barde,† and a Phoracanthus, with very long, spinous, and remarkable antennæ, which hovered about the gum-trees. To his annoyance the Englishman himself caught a beetle,‡ with a St. Andrew's cross on its wing-cases, which, when he touched it, sent forth a filthy odour. One or two others had the same property, but he abstained from again touching any of that form, except with a twig. A fly, with a sharp head and golden eyes,§

* Neuroptera Hattei.   † Bardistus.
‡ Mictis profanea.   § Chœrocoris paganus.

made fierce attacks upon them; and a small caterpillar, with sharp spines, strong enough to run into the finger, attracted the traveller's notice. A Smaragdina had a gorgeous red thorax; and yellow and brown Locusts seemed to be particularly acceptable to Charlie.

Kinchela one morning was busy preparing some slender twigs, from eight to ten feet long, which he bent into a hook at one end, and with which he proceeded to the gum-trees. There his master saw him insert these twigs into holes in the ground, and after a little manœuvring drag up what he called Laabkas, which proved to be fine fat grubs; and as Captain Spencer had eaten those of the grass-trees, he did not hesitate to partake of them, and found them of excellent flavour. Kinchela said they were the first part of some curious moths, which the Boccolo would see by and by.

Gipsy enjoyed the stay by the lake less than any of the party, on account of the presence of many snakes; for she had never forgotten her adventure in the other plain, and also of the number of native dogs, which would have snapped her up in a minute. She could not be left with the baggage on account of the latter, and dared not run on the ground for fear of the former; Captain Spencer, therefore, always put her on his knapsack when he went on his excursions, and Gip thus accompanied him every where on his back. The dogs howled horribly at night; and the Englishman asked Kinchela, who was always timid after night-fall, if he did not think they were boyl-yas; the man shook his head, and whispered that these were not boyl-yas, for they were in the trees, where he could at that moment hear them, alluding to the creaking of the boughs. Kinchela ran down some of the dogs, finishing their fate by throwing a stick at them. He brought the first to the bivouac to cook, and had it all to himself, for his master refused any share in the feast; he took out the entrails, filled the inside with grass, fastened the aperture together with wooden skewers, and put it into the oven. Nothing annoyed him more than to be obliged to cook any animal without its skin, the hair of which was always singed off. He said that when black fellows caught puppies, they took one or two to tame and live with them, but always ate a great many. The dogs, however, had two still more powerful causes of destruction—the snakes and themselves; for they ate each other in times when other food was scanty.

The Wombat* was an inhabitant of this plain, with its short nose and thick body; and Kinchela drove these animals to their holes in the sides of the mountains, closed the mouths with stones, lighted a fire, and suffocated them; causing Captain Spencer to think what a fierce warfare man,

* Pnascolomys.

who does not till the ground, carries on with other animated parts of creation. The native treated the elegant little Jerboas in a very summary manner; for he merely broke away the under jaw, bit off the tail, and then making a hole in the sand, which he heated, he put the animal into it, and when it was cooked he ate it as it was, fur, skin, entrails, and bones. Captain Spencer longed to teach Charlie to call him a greedy fellow, but was very cautious in this respect; for as Kinchela now understood a great deal of English, he was afraid of creating some enmity between them, if Charlie told disagreeable truths.

Kinchela called one of the snakes Tookyte,* and told his master if it bit him he would lie down for three days, and then get well, and it was very good to eat. He also showed him a Death Adder, which he said made people die in a few minutes, without their knowing that they had been bitten.

Some of the Grass-trees seen by the travellers had been seventeen feet high; but in this spot was another kind, even larger in stature,† and which looked like a palm with simple leaves; it had the rough, cylindrical bark of the Xanthorrhea, but its leaves were narrower. A large Hakea, of a different species to that which formed the scrub, had drooping leaves a foot and a half long, and was twenty-five feet high. A Grevillea was de-

* Raja. † Kingia.

veloped into a small tree, with very long, riband-like leaves of a silvery grey; and one of the same genus had beautiful red blossoms, and two flat seeds, surrounded by a narrow, transparent membrane. A large Fig-tree, sixty feet high, with rich foliage, had bunches of fruit of small size and excellent flavour; but it was almost impossible to eat them, because they were so full of flies and ants, the two great pests of the country. The Inga moniliformis, with its articulated pods, yielded a rich perfume, which fragrance was somewhat of a rarity among the flowers of Australia; and a noble Eugenia, with large, white blossoms, wide, leathery, shining leaves, green bark, and a hard trunk, stood forty feet high. Its scarlet and ribbed fruit was on the tree at the same time, a constant occurrence in such climates, and was six inches in circumference. If suffered to hang till it dropped, it was good to eat; but if gathered, was pungent, though always aromatic. The wind whistled through the articulated branches of the drooping Casuarinas on the borders of the lake, like the tones of an Eolian harp, and their blossoms looked like crimson fringe. One of the Hibiscus tribe afforded some string to Kinchela; and a Proteaceous tree, with silvery leaves, had seeds surrounded by a broad, transparent membrane.

Black Swans, with their bright red beaks, floated upon the lake; some beautiful Falcons took their share of the smaller and exquisite birds which frequented this lovely place. One of them* had gray plumage, yellow legs, and very brilliant eyes; another was sooty black,† of exquisite shape, and rapid flight; and a Kingfisher,‡ seemed to live on lizards, beetles, and grasshoppers. One of the Honey eaters, when opened for cooking, had its crop full of the remains of beetles; and its head was covered with a yellow pollen, proceeding from a flower very like a Mallow, which was a great resort of those insects in the heat of the day, when the petals closed over them.

The Australian told Captain Spencer a curious history of a Buteo,§ which he caught; saying that it was so bold, it would drive an Emu from her nest when sitting, and would take a stone between its feet, drop it on the eggs, and then eat the contents of the broken shells. It had great powers of vision; and Captain Spencer having left a dead Wallabie in a grass-tree as he passed, intending to take it up as he returned from a distance, found that the bird had devoured every part except the skin, and saw it fly away as he approached. One of the Swallow family was killed, which the traveller had once seen in England;|| some Gymnorrhiæ fed on fruits and insects, and sang in numerous choral notes. The Falcunculus built its nest

* Falco hypoleucus. † F. subniger.
‡ Halcyon sanctus. § Buteo melanosternon.
|| Acanthylis caudacuta.

on the branches of gum-trees, which were at least fifty feet high; it was the shape of a cup, was made of bark, lined with grass, and contained from four to five shining white eggs speckled with olive. Here also did the Bower-birds again form their play-grounds; and their cup-shaped nests were made of sticks, lined with grass and feathers. The Calyptorhynchi were rivals to Kinchela in their fondness for grubs; and they went about in small flocks, with a heavy flight, and a low, crying note, very different from that of their noisy brethren of the parrot tribe. Some ducks' nests were discovered in the trees; and there seemed to be no end to the natural wealth of this favoured region. It was, however, time to depart from it, and move to the south, before the greater drought should distress them still more in their after-progress.

On the last evening of his stay, Captain Spencer placed himself a little way up the mountain-range, from whence the ground gradually sloped away to the fruitful plain; the thick woods, the stillness of which was only interrupted by the rustling of the Opossums, as they ran up and down the trees; the moon shining brightly on the lake, the waters of which reflected a soft opalescent light; the clear and well-defined outline of the immense distance, in that dry climate: the large occasional flocks of wild-fowl which passed over his head, and splashed into the lake, making tiny and glittering waves around them; the foreground darkened by the shadow of the mountains, lighted up in one spot by two brilliant natural torches, which had been kindled by Kinchela, who was seated on the ground enjoying the most peaceful repose—formed a scene which was never forgotten by the wanderer in any of the fair or busy scenes of his after-existence.

The travellers made active preparations for starting: Tiger and Gipsy resumed their sober habits; Charlie confined his flights to their immediate vicinity; as much water as could be carried was secured; and Kinchela had loaded himself with pieces of crystal and agate, which he had found on the mountains, together with all sorts of fancied treasures. He endeavoured to stuff them all into the opossum-belt round his waist; but one after another dropped out again, till he bit his beard with impatience. "Why do you not make a bag for those things?" asked his master; "there is plenty of skin, and you had better do so tonight, then you can carry them with all convenience." Kinchela gave rather an indignant toss of the head, and replied, "Black fellow not carry bag with stones; Gin carry bag;" by which Captain Spencer understood that his dignity was offended by the suggestion; but as he did not choose to burden Tiger unnecessarily, he did not tell him to add these valued possessions to his load. At length, taking off his belt, the native folded them up in it, and seemed to think little of the additional weight. They passed on amidst beautiful flowers, among which various Papilionaceæ, the Bossiæa virigata, with its yellow and crimson blossoms; the Kennedia Maryatta, like a large coral tree; the Eriostemon, with pannicles of pink and white, five-rayed stars; and the splendid Choryzema, were the most conspicuous; and never did beautiful Australia look more beautiful than when they bade farewell to the lake and plain. Scrub, fatiguing, obstinate, tearing, pricking, provoking scrub succeeded, and the bivouac the next night took place in a very different scene to that of the preceding.

On the completion of the opossum-cloak, Captain Spencer had bestowed his old mackintosh on Kinchela, who then folded up his own, and in imitation of his master carried it on his back, when throwing the mackintosh outside he caused himself to look infinitely ridiculous, as he was evidently oppressed by the additional covering. Day after day passed, during which time, a large, misshapen, brownish mass, issuing from some gum-trees, had delighted the native; for he gathered as much of it as he could stuff into the bags whence food had been taken, and at night he roasted it over the fire. It was a fungus, and excellent to the taste, without producing any ill effects. "Plenty black fellows come here," said Kinchela; "some coming now;" and Captain Spencer turned his head to look. "Are they good fellows?" asked he. "No, Boccolo," was the answer; "they come to take away; make them afraid, seem as if you sleep." The travellers pretended to be ignorant of the approach of the two men, who were evidently a detachment from a larger party, sent to discover the proceedings of the strangers. When, however, they were close by, Captain Spencer let Gipsy out of his arms, and shouted to her and Tiger, "Up, boys, after them!" The two animals rushed upon them, which made them retreat with the most grotesque haste, and then Captain Spencer fired over their heads. Such vigorous proceedings prevented any further molestation; but Kinchela said he knew there had been a large party, for he heard the sounds of their feet; and he laughed and chuckled with intense delight at the alarm which had been produced. In this his master could detect the feeling of superiority which association with civilized man constantly produces in a savage, and leads him to triumph when the inferiority of the latter is manifested.

On coming to a rocky district, Gip uttered a cry, which her master well knew betokened some danger; and rushing back to him, she leaped at once into his arms, which were always ready to receive her; and Kinchela immediately after exclaimed, " Wakeh !" and pointed to a huge Python, at least twelve feet long, of a beautiful greenish-brown, with yellowish-white spots, sluggishly uncoiling itself, and making for a tree which stood near by. Before it could reach its hiding-place, however, Kinchela sprang forward, seized it behind the head, and in one moment wrung its neck; he then flung it across his shoulders, much to the horror of Gip, who did not look up or leave her master till the Python had been skinned, cut up like an eel, and roasted, thereby yielding an excellent supper. A certain degree of dampness seemed to fall upon the party that night, which betokened their vicinity to the sea, and which chilled Kinchela (who wrapped himself in his mackintosh with the air of a general officer at least). The next day, before the sun was high, they stood on the edge of a lofty cliff, which overlooked the great Antarctic Ocean.

CHAPTER VIII.

Captain Spencer makes a signal to a vessel—Boat comes ashore—Captain of the vessel comes in the boat—Offers assistance—Captain Spencer and his companions go on board the French whaling ship, the Marie—Life on board the Marie—Native feast off a stranded whale—Natives pay a visit to the Marie—Kinchela spoiled—Charlie learns French—Captain Spencer leaves the Marie—Scrub—Tiger very happy—Cranberry—Kangaroo—Kinchela has a fit of gluttony—Cliffs—Return to the sea-shore—Fishes—Musical Teredo—Salsolæ—Eryngium—Fruit—Plants, &c.—Reptiles—Birds—Crabs—Kinchela ill-humoured.

THERE was something most exhilarating in the prospect of the broad and dancing waves spread out before the travellers, and the feeling of home which they ever bring to the minds of Englishmen who have wandered over their surface, even in spite of the sorrow or suffering which may be associated with the recollection. After gazing before him for some time, Captain Spencer thought he should now only have to coast along the shore till he reached Adelaide, which he knew must lie to the east of his present position. It was evident that both Perth and King George's Sound must have been missed; and as he looked right and left of him, he felt convinced that he was in the Bight of Australia. That look presented him with a sight even more grateful than the sparkling ocean, for white brethren were near. A large vessel rode at anchor at some distance from the shore, but as she had no ensign up, he could not tell to what nation she belonged. He took a spear from Kinacla, tied a handkerchief on the top of it, hoisted it as high as he could, and immediately after fired his gun. Anxiously did he await the answer to his signal; the fire was returned from the ship, and in a few moments a boat was despatched from her to the shore. As she came near, Captain Spencer and his party descended the cliff by a winding path, to await her approach; he forgetting the extraordinary appearance which he must make with his grass hat, cockatoo plume, bronzed complexion, long hair and beard, and patched garments. The boat lay-to when within speaking distance, and one of the crew hailed the travellers in broken English, an air of surprise pervading the whole party. Captain Spencer advanced to the brink of the waves, saying that he was an officer in the East India Company's service, who had been wrecked on the northern coast, with his horse and dog, and had found his way through the country to the place where he then was, which he concluded was the southern shore, and had picked up the native on his way. The boat after this ran upon the beach, and a fine young man, evidently superior in rank to the others, jumped out of her, and, touching his cap, said he was Alexis Royer, commander of the Marie, the whaling ship now lying in the offing; and although he could not speak English well, he had understood what the officer had said, and begged to assure him that all the assistance which he could afford was perfectly at his service. Captain Spencer, who spoke French fluently, gave him a rapid outline of his adventures; and the Frenchman entreated of him to come on board the whaler with him, assuring him she was his own property, and what she contained should be devoted to his accommodation. He added, that they were some distance from King George's Sound; for he entirely avoided entering any English ports, because, while touching at Bahia on his way, there was so strong a rumour of war being declared between France and England, that he feared, if not a capture, a vexatious detention. This, however, need not make him a personal enemy to Captain Spencer; and he begged for the honour of a visit from him in the only residence which he could offer for his accommodation. The Englishman looked at Kinchela and Tiger; and, reading his thoughts, Captain Royer then assured him there was plenty of room for his horse and servant, and from the stores of the vessel he would be able to replenish himself in all the necessaries for the remainder of his journey. The offer was very tempting; it must be sincere, for compliments do not often pass on such occasions, and in such places; and the wanderer yielded to the prospect of enjoyment which it afforded. He frankly accepted the proposal, and told Kinchela they were all going on the sea. The man seemed at first to shrink from it; but, after a moment's hesitation, he said, "Boccolo go, Kinchela go." Just as they were about to step into the boat, Captain Spencer said, "I have yet another companion, whom I must not leave behind; but as he will not take much room, I hope you will allow me to bring him also." "Certainly," said Captain Royer, wondering if it were a pet kangaroo. The Englishman then called "Charlie! Charlie!" and uttered the peculiar whistle to which he had accustomed the bird; and in a minute he flew rapidly from the cliff, and perched on his master's shoulder, saying, "I'm coming; here's Charlie!" "I should have been sorry," said the Frenchman, smiling, "to have left out such an interesting portion of your company;" and they entered the boat, Tiger creating much astonishment by the dexterous manner in which he not only stepped on board, but contentedly resigned himself to the hoisting up by the side of the vessel. As to Kinchela, the sea was smooth, and he was delighted; much more so, however, when he was invited to partake of a good dinner.

The conversation of the French captain and his chief officer, the accommodations of the Marie, the knowledge of time, and the civilized occupations of those about him, made a happy break in the hard-faring, rude life of the soldier; and he was surprised to find how short a period had been consumed in coming from the scene of his misfortune, for it seemed to him an age since he had begun to traverse the continent; and he was also surprised at having made so much more easting than could have entered his calculations. He now found, that in about another month, according to the ideas of one accustomed to the regularity of Indian seasons, the rain would come, and then he might not be able to travel. Captain Royer, in his uncertainty as to the relative position of their two countries, could not take him to Adelaide, had he been so inclined, and therefore he determined to start again after a week of indulgence; besides which, he felt that it would be dangerous to linger among those decencies of life, which a well-ordered vessel of any nation presents, and that the longer he staid in agreeable society, the less should he be inclined to launch again into the wilderness. His kind host insisted on his accepting a new suit of clothes from his own wardrobe; and being tall and slight, they fitted well enough to be perfectly comfortable. There was no spare flesh on Captain Spencer's bones, but muscles were hardened and developed, so that he well filled the loose garments of the sailor; the delight of wearing shirts was inconceivable; the luxury of soap, for which he had so long been obliged to substitute sand, was indescribable; and well-trimmed hair, and a portion of the beard properly taken away, instead of being cut with a knife, made him feel, as well as look, quite another man; the more particularly as the carefully-reserved cap was taken from the knapsack, and worn instead of the grass hat. When Kinchela saw his master thus equipped, he seemed lost in astonishment, and burst into loud exclamations. Gip jumped with delight; but Charlie was very grave, as if he did not quite understand the metamorphosis, and seemed particularly glad when the voice reassured him that it was indeed his master. Tiger took everything most philosophically; he munched the hay which was given him from the different packages on board, drank sparingly of water, occasionally gave Gip a shake, and received the visits of Charlie, who often sat upon his back, with apparent pleasure, to the infinite amusement of the sailors, who said all the beasts were charming, even the *Capitaine*.

The next day Captain Spencer was taken to land to see the garden which had been formed under the brow of one of the cliffs, by the side of a small stream of fresh water, which proceeded from a fissure in the rock. It was a rich piece of sloping ground, as if the good soil from the top of the cliff had been washed on to it, and it was planted with a variety of European vegetables, which were calculated not only to give enjoyment, but to contribute to health during the many weeks the Marie was likely to continue in that spot. When they heard of all the animals which were to be killed inland, many evinced a desire to procure fresh meat; but Captain Spencer could not help observing how much better the French vessel was found in what are called preserved meats, than those of his own country, by which means the whole crew were fed with fresh rations once in every week. It was during this excursion to the shore, that Captain Spencer saw the remarkable appearance of network on the face of the cliffs, which has been reported by many navigators, and which he at first supposed had arisen from the interlacing of fossilized branches, or roots of trees, but which, on examination, he now found to arise from some peculiar cause in the formation of the sand and lime of which they were composed, and connected with the washing of rains. Beautifully coloured shells lay upon the shore, which he gathered for the collection of Captain Royer.

It was proposed to the Englishman to take away with him a few of the Madagascar sheep from

Captain Royer's stock, which would make a certain store of provisions; but he refused, thinking that with only Kinchela to take care of them, they might prove an incumbrance, and it was better to depend on themselves for food. Some pieces of beef and pork, however, were hung up to dry, that they might have some sort of supply. As to Kinchela, he did not give one thought to the future; he could not understand a word which was said to him by the Frenchman, but the abundance of the present moment was a source of sufficient happiness; and the men, finding him to be insatiable, amused themselves by cramming him until he was almost unable to attend in the cabin, where his master requested he might be admitted at the hours of repast, that he might form some notion of knives, forks, spoons, and other et-ceteras. No spirits were given, by the especial order of both captains.

The whalers rose before dawn every morning, and went out in the boats to a considerable distance, in order to look for whales, which one of the men, who had been experienced in the northern fisheries, said were of a different species to those known in Europe; the parties, however, were not successful during the visit of the travellers, for the season was but little advanced. They returned very early one morning, and reported that a large whale had been cast ashore, probably killed by some of its ocean brethren, and that a numerous party of natives had gathered round it, and were busy eating and devouring every morsel through which they could get their teeth; that the beacon-fires which had been lighted above, they supposed were signals, for they had seen several other parties arrive, and they must have been at work all night. It was on the other side of a promontory, which hid them from the ship; and as it was a curious sight, they thought Captain Royer and the English captain would like to witness it, and had therefore returned. They could land on the near side of the bluff, and ascending the heights, unknown to the Australians, look down upon them without their being conscious of the vicinity of white men.

The two gentlemen armed themselves, and started, and a small gun was put into the boat, with which their retreat might be covered in case of a hostile attack. Gip was reconciled to be left behind, by ordering her to lie upon and guard some of her master's clothes; while Kinchela, tossing his head, thought himself too well off to eat whale.

The party proceeded, and lying flat down on the cliffs, as Captain Spencer had done on a former occasion, they beheld a very large body of natives assembled with their wives and children, most of them apparently in high spirits and good humour.

Some were rubbing themselves, their wives and children, all over with the blubber; others were employed in dividing the huge morsels of flesh severed from the bones into smaller pieces, and handing these to the women to broil upon the large fires which they had kindled around them, and who crammed pieces into their mouths, and those of their children, which they pinched off from the quantity given by the men. The whale was already becoming putrid; but they seemed regardless of this, and set aside large lumps to be carried away, when they went inland. They had made their entrance into the body, whence issued graceful looking young girls reeking with oil, and reeling from over-eating. A few were lying upon the ground, quite overcome by their excesses; and two or three others, ill-tempered from indigestion, struck their wives and quarrelled with their companions; and many started with loads to be carried to a distance, which left a train of bad odour as they passed along. "It is as well to see such a sight," said Captain Spencer, "as exemplifying the manners of the people; but I have no desire to behold it a second time; if you have seen enough, let us go." Captain Royer gladly assented, saying, "Think what it must be to come near those people for the next month." They returned, and the Englishman tried to forget his disgust in the perusal of the newspapers brought out by the Marie, and which led him back to European history. Some of the natives afterwards paid a visit to the ship on their rafts; and their presence induced Captain Spencer to prolong his stay for a few days, that they might leave the neighbourhood before he ventured into it; they were surprised at seeing Kinchela, who understood what they said, and were very curious to know why he was there, and where he was going; but he very prudently gave them as little information as possible. Large quantities of fat, or lard, were melted for these people by way of a treat, and they drank some with avidity, and rubbed themselves and children with the rest. When they were going away, they said there was no water, even in deep holes, except occasionally on the coast; but rain would come before long, and fill the country again. They paddled ashore, and in a very few days no traces of natives were to be seen, except the ashes of their fires and the skeleton of the whale.

Two woollen shirts were given to Kinchela, Tiger's saddle was newly stuffed and repaired, and the blacksmith of the Marie offered to make him new shoes; but his master thought it better he should go on without them, as extra sets would be cumbersome to carry, and one set would probably not last for the rest of the journey. The shattered tarpauling was replaced by a large, new piece; the tin cans were well examined, and as they gave signs of wearing out, were exchanged for new ones; and everything that could be thought of, as afforded by the vessel, was pressed upon the traveller. Captain Spencer had several pieces of gold, (Indian currency,) and these he offered in payment for some gaily coloured handkerchiefs, and knives, which he selected as presents for the natives; but Captain Royer said everything in the ship was his own, and therefore Captain Spencer need not hesitate in making use of them, or anything else. A pair of scissors to cut the beard and whiskers, completed the generous Frenchman's thoughtful attentions. Kinchela's ambition was further gratified by a leathern belt, which he put outside his shirt, and in which he stuck the knife which had been given to him; but a difficulty arose as to how he was to convey the other shirt, and the valuable pieces of crystal; the sailors wanted to throw the latter away, but he looked in such an agony when they took them up, that they asked his master why he set so much store by them. Captain Spencer repeated their question to Kinchela, on which he, in a solemn whisper, and with a piteous look, requested him to tell them that they were to keep off the boyl-yas. The shout with which they received the explanation seemed to frighten, more than create vexation. He settled his difficulties by wrapping them in his spare shirt, and tying them round his body next his skin. Captain Royer accepted the opossum-cloak in exchange for one of his own, and his mate received that of Kinchela; the address of Captain Spencer's agent in India, and that of the Frenchman in his own country, were carefully noted, that intelligence of their mutual adventures might be given to each other, and the parting hour arrived. Captain Royer offered to exchange watches, because his guest's had ceased to be of service; but the latter declined this accommodation, saying he had now so long been without, that a time-keeper was not necessary. The fire-arms were cleaned, the ammunition put into new water-proof bags, and Gip, Tiger, and Charlie, received many farewell caresses from their good friends. The Englishman shook hands with all the men, in which he was gravely imitated by Kinchela; he thanked them for all their kindness, and hoped they never would look upon him, though an Englishman, as an enemy. The boat was ready, and the travelling party entered it, Captain Royer accompanying them. On the shore his feelings overcame him, and although he knew it to be wholly un-English, he with tears in his eyes put his arms round his friend's neck, and kissed each cheek without the power to say farewell. The land travellers ascended the cliff, and the seamen fired a gun, which sent a booming adieu across the waters.

Rocky land caused Captain Spencer to leave the close vicinity of the sea, and he plunged into the sea of scrub instead, the intricacies of which seemed only to deepen the regret he felt at quitting his generous friend; he noted the hour and the day in a precious little almanac given to him by the Frenchman, and in his memory treasured the last twelve days with ineffaceable gratitude. A sandy country succeeded the scrub, thickly strewn with a plant which Captain Spencer at first, from its appearance, imagined to be heath, but it was an Epacris, not quite so difficult to traverse as the Atriplex, but still fatiguing to those who had been so long at rest. Plenty of Grass-trees grew amongst it, and it was amusing to see how Kinchela now disdained them. The only one of the party in whose opinion the change was pleasant was Tiger, to whom the absence of exercise had been anything but enjoyment. No wonder then that he frolicked, even with his load on his back; and so frisky was he, that when unburdened at night, he took it into his head to run after Kinchela, which completely undid the little progress he had made towards familiarity on board ship, and the man again feared to trust himself in the vicinity of so marvellous a creature. Charlie took the change as a matter of course; and having added French to his accomplishments, said, as he flew away to get his supper, "Bon voyage, Monsieur de Mallet."*

The next day the party came to a chain of pools, at which they slaked their thirst, and disturbed several Wallabies from the surrounding grass; they picked their way across the rocky bed, and then arrived at a region of Gum-trees, Banksias, and Kingias; and following the course of the channel with the eye, they saw afar off some sloping banks of moist herbage, towards which Tiger rushed in rather an outrageous manner; but after taking a few mouthfuls of it, he trotted back to his master, and thrusting his nose into his neck, seemed to ask forgiveness for his frolic. The next remarkable feature of the country was a salt-water river, where oysters and cockles were so plentiful, that they stopped there to collect some. Kinchela, however, would not eat the former; and when asked why, he said it was "Kobong," and he must not. He could not clearly explain this; but his master understood that it was some native law. Kinchela said he never had eaten what was Kobong but once, and that was the first Emu which had been killed, because he was so very hungry; none but old men and old gins ought to eat it, and he hoped the boyl-yas would not eat him in consequence; that was one reason why he was so care-

* Alluding to a French farce in which is a traveller of that name, and which supplied this cant phrase to the sailors.

ful to keep his crystals. His master could not help smiling, in spite of the melancholy reflection that a whole nation of human beings had no other religion, as far as he could understand, and in place of it such puerile or absurd superstitions.

After passing a poor and unfertile district on the other side of the salt river, the travellers found themselves in a deep ravine, where there was a fair portion of grass, but high, rocky cliffs were on the further side, formed chiefly of mica slate, about which hovered many beautiful Pigeons, making a whirring noise. Here they came to the pretty little plant called Drosera, and the large Fishing Eagle flew over their heads, wending its way to the sea. Some brackish water lay in this ravine, and a huge grayish Horse-fly abounded near them, with an immense proboscis, and not only worried Tiger exceedingly, but penetrated through the clothing of the two men. A kind of Cranberry* crept along the ground, the acid berries of which being quite ripe, were very agreeable to eat. A beautiful Butterfly constantly flew past them, covered with red and yellow spots.† The brackish water became a lake further on in the ravine, where Captain Spencer shot a Swan and two Ducks; he did not aim at the Pelicans; and then they came upon a gum scrub,‡ where there were

* Astroloma Eumifusum. † Aganippe.
‡ Eucalyptus dumosa.

so many fallen trees, that poor Tiger became breathless in scrambling over them; for it was impossible to leap with a load on his back. Night fell before they could get half through it; and cutting down some bushes to make a fire, they found a soft, short herbage underneath; and, tired as he was, Captain Spencer cleared a space sufficient to yield a plentiful meal for Tiger. He was turned into it, and supped while the others partook of the game which had been killed. Kinchela emulated his prowess on board the Marie, and was sitting in a half sleeping state over the embers of the fire, when by the bright moonlight he saw a large kangaroo.* The animal seemed to be so perfectly unconscious of the presence of strangers, that they easily crept softly behind a tree at some little distance, and waited for its approach. Gip was held, to keep her from it; and as all were tired, and ammunition was plentiful, Captain Spencer said he would shoot it; and the discharge of one barrel brought it to the ground.

Whether it arose from a longing for his native food, or whether it was a fit of genuine gluttony, awakened as this propensity had been of late, it was impossible to say; but Kinchela now said he was very hungry and tired, and must eat a great deal. His master, rather provoked by his greediness, replied that he might eat the whole kangaroo

* Macropus halmaturus.

if he pleased, and laid himself down. The Australian took out the inside of the kangaroo, and cut off the two hind legs; he renewed the fire, cooked them, and devoured them; he then laid himself down again. In about two hours his master heard him fidgetting, and asked what was the matter; he replied that he was hungry, and he then ate the fore-legs and the tail. Captain Spencer slept till morning; and great was his astonishment then to find that not a vestige of the kangaroo was left, except the bones; Kinchela had eaten the whole, including the skin, from which he had singed the hair. When he was told to get up and light a fire, he was cross; said he was in pain, that he walked too much, and had a burning throat; but he nevertheless swallowed a piece of swan. Not doubting the cause of his illness, and telling him to lie down again and go to sleep, Captain Spencer quietly resigned himself to the delay this occasioned; for it was useless to attempt to go on till Kinchela had recovered the effects of his excess. He rather blamed himself for giving him leave to eat a whole kangaroo; and made a vow that he would never again offer him any such license. He cleared another space for Tiger, and wandered about, when his attention was attracted by the beautiful red blossom of the Clianthus formosa; by a creeping plant like a large, bright scarlet Vetch, with a purple centre; and Tiger found a blue, succulent Geranium in an old watercourse, which he ate with avidity. A stunted tree, with a small fruit, looking like a russet apple, hanging in bunches at the end of the lesser branches, afforded, within the rough rind, a large stone surrounded by a pulpy substance; and a white fluid issued from the branches when they were broken. A flight of birds like Land-rails flew over his head, and were succeeded by hundreds of Hawks, which sent Charlie back, calling out, "Great rogues, Ned Spencer!" Pretty Everlastings* grew in the driest places; while the fragrant Jasmine hung its festoons over the bushes.

At length Kinchela recovered; and his master tried to make him sensible of his fault by pointing out the consequences; but all he could get from him was, that he had been very happy; and they again started, in order to mount the cliffs. On crossing to them, they met with a softish white substance, which Captain Spencer had often seen before, and which Kinchela now told him was white paint. On examining it he ascertained that it was pipe-clay, which seemed to abound in every part of the country.

On the level ground, at the top of the cliffs, the soil was very sterile; and the party again turned to the sea, in the hope of finding water, which trickled from the cliffs; and after passing along

* Gnaphalium spiculatum.

their high and precipitate edges, they found a **path** used by the natives, at the end of which was a well dug by them in the sand, with more than usual skill; instead of being a mere hole, it was quite round, two feet in diameter, dug straight down, and from fourteen to fifteen feet deep; it had a good supply of water, and was fed by drippings from the rock; when they took the stones from the mouth, however, the Englishman recoiled from it with disgust, for a large brown Snake was living in it. Kinchela, nevertheless, tossed it out, killed it, and then drank with eagerness; but his master caught the rock-drippings for his own refreshment. On the shore they found plenty of Periwinkles,* which not being Kobong, were eaten by Kinchela, who, with his spear, very cleverly managed to catch several of the fishes which frequent those seas; Captain Spencer helped with his hook and line; and they remained there a day or two to take advantage of the supply. The Barracoota, and a Platycephalus, were speared by Kinchela; and his master caught a fish which resembled a Whiting in appearance.† A spotted Sole‡ was secured by the native with his toes, as he walked in a small, shallow bay, as well as the sluggish Jewfish;§ but he abhorred the Ostracion, the Stingray,‖ and a sort of green Skate.¶ Besides these,

---

* Turbo. † Sillago punctata.
‡ Platessa. § Cheilodactylus corponemus.
‖ Urolophus. ¶ Platyrhina.

was a very clear, delicate fish with transparent fins,* which was good eating. There were two species of Shark which the Englishman had not before seen; and Mackerel was so plentiful, that a store was dried and carried away. Gip lived on fish as well as her master; but after this rest, during which Tiger ate meal, the cans were filled, and they departed along shore, till a bold headland forced them to go up again. Just as they were about to turn off, they were suddenly arrested by a sound of soft, low music. They listened; looked for the person who produced it; no one was to be seen. It seemed to come from a large log of wood lying on the shore; and Captain Spencer, on examining it, found it full of the boring worm called Teredo; and there could be no doubt that from it came the vibration which produced the tones. They were so pleasing, that the Englishman was unwilling to leave them.

The cliffs had presented sand and limestone, with indications of iron in the former, and granite in the latter; in the first were some fossil shells, of which Captain Spencer vainly endeavoured to ascertain the genus. As they went on, they met with salt pools; and digging near them, found brackish, but drinkable water; and salsolaceous plants† began to appear. The pretty, pink-flowered Mesembryanthemum existed in large patches,

---

* Cristiceps.   † Nitraria Australis.

and as the tips of the leaves were turning red, Kinchela said the fruit was ripe; and gathering a quantity of it, they stopped a day to dry it in the sun, that it might form a relish for future meals. Tiger delighted in it, leaves as well as fruit.

Fires of native encampments were seen at a distance; but Kinchela said he did not know "those fellows," and they had "mock ears and wooden foreheads; and it was better not to go near them." Whole acres of fragrant Clematis and bright Grevillea flung themselves across the scrub; and in sandy places the Eryngium showed itself. When they came to a swampy plain, a bulbous root, which Kinchela called Balillah, was abundant; and so good to eat, that they took some on with them. A beautiful Fusanus, twelve feet high, appeared again; and surrounding the fruit of it with flour-and-water paste, in the manner of a turnover, Captain Spencer made so good an imitation of a tart, that Kinchela was delighted. A berry, called by the native Eutopko, grew on a low, creeping, tap-rooted plant among the salsolaceous plains; which were, no doubt, swamps in wet weather, with bushes of Polygonum. Its leaves were soft, like velvet; and the berry of it was so small, that Kinchela cut a tray of bark from a stunted Gum-tree at a little distance, and lifting the plant over it, shook the fruit off the stalks. This being done, he next shook the tray, that the dirt might fly off; and in this manner collected a supply of it for days. Other berries, of an acid flavour, were met with; but some which looked beautiful were bitter and nauseous. Large and beautiful Correas appeared. There was a Cassia, with pods a foot and a half long, and seeds surrounded by a spongy tissue; but Captain Spencer knew the nature of Cassias too well to venture to taste the seeds. Kinchela, however, swallowed them with impunity. Then came a profusion of Pitcher-plants; the pitchers of which contained a quantity of discoloured water, and drowned ants and other insects, which Charlie ate with pleasure, tearing off the lids or opercula with his beak.

There were plenty of reptiles; and one Snake had swallowed a bird, which stuck out like a lump in its body; Kinchela said that it climbed trees and robbed birds' nests. Some black Ants bit them severely; and then Captain Spencer advised Kinchela to save the skin of the next kangaroo which they killed, to make socks of; but he was not in the least abashed at the recollection of his gluttony. Of one of the Snakes the Australian had an intense horror; its head was a shining black, the back was of a rich, deep brown and orange, and he said a man must die if bitten by it; if Boccolo killed it, he could not eat it, but if he killed it himself, it was very good for him; he accordingly demolished it by smashing its skull with a stone, and his master was surprised that he appeared to be ignorant of the Indian method of disabling the reptile by crushing or severing the tail. He examined the fangs, found that there were two on each side, and that they turned inwards.

Numbers of Wallabies lived among the Mesembryanthemums; Bitterns* and Cranes were heard at night; while the Mosquitoes kept them awake; Gulls flew round them; and what Kinchela called a Bidgerigung,† passed from the north in a straight line, was of a bright yellow and black, and had blue spots on each cheek; with it was the Parrakeet,‡ which always keeps its crest erect, of gray, white, and sulphur-coloured plumage, and in the centre of a yellow patch on each cheek was a scarlet spot.

Wombats, the size of Badgers, and tasting like young pork, with the usual supply of animal food, were to be had for the killing; and they marched on, Kinchela being narrowly watched for fear he should again commit any excess. The opossum-skins were never destroyed by cooking the animal in them, but were left gradually to accumulate, till enough were saved to replace the cloaks left on board the Marie.

Whole districts of Melaleuca seemed to be a favourite resort of the said Opossums; and it was

---

* **Ardetta flavicollis.** † Melopsittacus undulatus.
‡ Nymphicus.

amusing to see how eagerly Gip mounted these trees in pursuit of them, if they were in the least out of the perpendicular, often preceding Kinchela; and how knowingly she looked at him when she knew he alone could climb the upright trunk.

The travellers still descended occasionally to the shore, where they caught crabs, which fought vigorously with one claw, while with the others they endeavoured to get away, and when the ground permitted made a pirouette and disappeared. Gip could not help pursuing them, but was much afraid of her nose; and her frequent astonishment at their sudden disappearance was quite laughable. Charlie's favourite language was still French, which made Kinchela very angry.

Here they saw Penguins and Seals, the latter of which Kinchela wanted to kill and eat; but his master would not suffer him to do so. They one day came to so plentiful a supply of Rock Cod, and water ran so freely from the rocks, that they made a halt, and, as usual, Kinchela ate till he could not move. Captain Spencer knew he would have done so with the seals, and the quality of that food would have made him perfectly unbearable. When he had recovered a little, his master, while he attended to drying the fish, despatched him and Tiger to the land above; the one to get animal, and the other vegetable food. Kinchela went unwillingly, however, and the horse returned first, trotting up to his master, and neighing with fun in a very significant manner. Captain Spencer did not quite understand this, but went on with his occupation. In about an hour after, Kinchela came back, looking very much out of humour; and when he saw Tiger, he muttered something to himself, and throwing a load of game upon the ground, sank down by it in a fit of sulkiness. Captain Spencer thought it better not to notice him, and turning his back, went on with his occupation. In about half an hour the native exclaimed, "Kinchela bring plenty to eat, Boccolo Sahib not look." This was quite a new feature in the man's character, and showed how he had been spoiled by the sailors; so, turning to him, his master endeavoured to reason with him; but all the time he was speaking, the native cast furtive glances at Tiger, and he saw there was something passing in the man's mind which he did not express. At last, on trying to penetrate the mystery, he found that Kinchela had tried to make Tiger carry the load for him; but when he was going to place it on his back, the animal started and ran away, and, added the man, "he is a very bad dog." "This is something gained," thought Captain Spencer; "he no longer thinks Tiger a sorcerer;" and then he endeavoured to convince Kinchela that the horse did not know he was to obey any body except his master. "Gip does what Kinchela says," was the reply; "and Gip is a dog; Tiger is a dog, why not know as well as Gip?" "He is getting on," said the Englishman to himself; "he begins to reason, and it is better not to attempt too much at once; I shall leave him to indulge in the belief that Tiger is a dog." And he ended the dialogue by ordering him to cook and prepare the animals which he had speared, or knocked on the head.

It was with the greatest difficulty that Captain Spencer prevented Kinchela from again eating too much, and as it was he fell back and slept. "He wants a little starvation," said his master to himself; "he behaved better in times of suffering; but we know not how soon he may have to learn a fresh lesson." They travelled on the next day, ascending the cliffs, and descending to the shore, where they were more likely to meet with native wells. Here they found some beautiful shells, Patellæ and Phasianellæ, and the cliffs were often composed of gray granite. The changes of temperature were frequent; and in one hour there would be a difference of several degrees. One evening they were assailed by a heavy sea-fog, which caused them to shiver and feel very uncomfortable. Captain Spencer covered them all and himself with the cloaks and tarpauling, and Charlie, like all pretenders, misapplied his knowledge sadly as he crept under the covering, and said, "J'ai chaud, Ned Spencer." After this Kinchela seemed to be incessantly fatigued; the horse and dog no longer made excursions of their own, but followed soberly in their master's tracks; moreover, Gip often asked to be carried. Captain Spencer himself felt an indescribable languor creeping over him; and thinking that that damp night, and the continued reflection of warm air from the cliffs had engendered a certain portion of fever, he deemed it advisable to leave the immediate vicinity of the sea, and go more inland for the sake of a dryer atmosphere. His compass, he flattered himself, was regular in its movements, and that there would be no difficulty in keeping the proper direction for Adelaide. He immediately chose the first accessible part of the cliff, by which Tiger mounted with his load; and all things secured, they started early in the morning, and were saluted on their arrival above by the odour of the Clematis, and a number of Gum-trees in the distance.

CHAPTER IX.

Spinifex—Bark of Gum-tree—Excrescence on tree—Well—Rhagodia—Water scarce—Water from Gum-trees—Hot wind—Dew—Salt lake—Salsola—Mirage—Gum-tree roots—Emigrating birds—Cold wind and frost—Hakea—Curious stones—Absence of animal and vegetable life—Sand, quartz, iron—Scorching sun—No water, no food—Distress of Captain Spencer—Dog and horse suffer much—Tiger appears to die—Sorrow of Captain Spencer—Kinchela lies down to die—Captain Spencer gives himself up for lost, and becomes insensible—A shower in the night somewhat revives him—A Pigeon shows the way to some water—Captain Spencer rouses himself and reaches the place, drinks, and takes some to his companions—All go to the well—Kinchela and Gipsy eat Kangaroo skin and fall asleep—While sitting with his face between his hands, Captain Spencer's hat is taken off—Sees Tiger with it in his mouth—Joy—Rest three days—Mountains—Country improves—Copious rain—Old Man.

POOR Tiger was henceforth obliged to content himself with dry and withered grass, for the Xanthorrhœæ and Kingii were getting very scarce; and nothing seemed to offer itself as a likely substitute. The young shoots of trees were occasionally boiled for him when there was water; but those of the Gum-trees turned black on being so treated; and then his master feared to give them to him. Digging holes in the sand of dried beds generally yielded some liquid; but never, unless it was a large pool, did Captain Spencer enjoy the luxury of water ablution; on one occasion, however, he was disappointed even of this; for, just as he had walked in up to the knees, he saw the water full of small brown leeches; so that he was forced to make his escape as quickly as possible, with bleeding legs. Sand-rubbing, in the Arab fashion, was therefore resumed; and dry enough it was to scrub very hard; and there was no moisture in his skin to soften it, as is generally the case when drought is coming on in this country. When the diggings began to fail, he felt great alarm; and whole tracts of Spinifex increased poor Tiger's difficulties. Gip profited much by the smaller animals in it; and Kinchela, who was fast recovering his former good temper and activity, still kept up his spirits. He told his master that he could get him plenty of meal; and he gathered the seeds of the withered grass,* which was almost too dry for the horse, separated them from the husks and pounded them; or he took the bark of the Gum-trees, and roasted and crushed that, which was a little bitter, nevertheless palatable. "It will make us strong," said Captain Spencer. "Yes," replied the man, "black fellow eat nothing else for long time." On the following day there was

* Panicum lævinode.

no water to moisten the meal, and Kinchela found a tree with large excrescences; he tapped each, and listened; stuck his knife into one, and from it issued a quantity of fluid, which answered the purpose; it was rather bitter; nevertheless Tiger drank it; but he seemed to consider that that master who had hitherto supplied all his wants, no longer obeyed his request for drink. Two days had passed without liquid of any sort; but towards evening a flight of black Cockatoos and other birds passed over their heads from the north, and descended to the ground at a little distance. "Boc colo, see those birds," said the native; "they always go down and find water; we find some too." He and his master started with cans and skins; and on arriving where the Cockatoos had alighted in numbers, they perceived a native well, carefully covered over with stones. Gip was only too happy to help frighten away the Cockatoos; and Charlie fought with two or three who were more bold than the others; so that they were all kept at bay, while Captain Spencer removed the stones. The water was green and muddy, but Tiger and Gip were glad of it; then came Kinchela's turn to be served, and but a cupfull remained for their master. Some of the birds were killed for eating, and the rest took flight with loud screeches. The stones were replaced; and it was hoped that water would drain in before morning. A mere drop was obtained, in which Charlie was allowed to dip his bill once or twice; the rest was bestowed on the four-footed beasts. "All's right," said the good bird, as the well was finally closed; and Kinchela came in for praise on the score of forbearance; his master being always particularly careful to do this when he could; and never excited the sensitive jealousy, which he, in common with many other savages, possessed; not confining it to the human race, but extending it to all objects of preference **or affection.**

The route was more and more difficult; and the travellers proceeded slowly through a monotonous but hard sort of scrub, formed of Rhagodia, in which they saw many Pigeons, which had crept under the bushes, apparently in the course of their migration from the north, and some of which they secured. That night they all lay down to rest without a drop of moisture for their parched throats; and Tiger crept close up to his master, and laid his head upon his shoulder, as if he knew the serious alarm which that master felt for his dear horse, and wished to console him. In the morning Kinchela begged him to take his glass and mount a hill at some little distance, and "look for much tree." Captain Spencer obeyed, and did see a long range of Gum-trees, the news of which was **joyfully** received by the native; and he entreated **his** master to let them all go there and look for water. Tiger was stiff and languid; but he roused himself at words which he had seldom disobeyed, and slowly followed to the trees. On arriving they proved to be Eucalypti; and asking for the spade, Kinchela quickly ran from one to the other, as if to select the best. He stopped at one that was large and healthy, to all appearance; he dug at a few feet distance from the trunk, and came to some of the lateral roots; he laid them bare; and breaking one on the side next the tree, he lifted up the root, and his master helped him to take several feet of it out of the soil; he then divided it into pieces from six to eight inches long; shook one into the can, and water came out of it, spreading like a fan; the others he placed in the cans, and the liquid freely ran from them. The moment he saw the drops issue, Captain Spencer seized one of the pieces and held it in Tiger's mouth, every part of which was moistened; and he ended by munching the root with great satisfaction. Gip had a piece thrown to her with an order to eat it; and she with delight lay down on the ground with it between her paws, and sucked out the refreshing fluid. In a quarter of an hour a quart had exuded from the different pieces of root, and then Tiger had a long drink; and as he enjoyed it, he turned his large expressive eyes on his master with a look of affectionate gratitude. "Boccolo take spade and stop here," said Kinchela; "get plenty of water to go on;" and this was not to spare himself, for he dug at the same time with a sharp-pointed stick. On going to younger trees he took up some of their roots, peeled off the bark, put them in hot ashes till they were crisp, pounded them between two stones, and made them into excellent meal, which reminded the European of the taste of malt. Then did he entirely rejoice in the presence of Kinchela, which, when disgusted with his gluttony, he had occasionally regretted; for these resources must have remained hidden from a stranger; and even when Kinchela again trespassed beyond the bounds of moderation, the recollection of the Gum-trees procured his forgiveness. The discovery revived his cheerful anticipations, and gaily did he start again with full cans and skins; for he hoped they should be able to travel from one set of trees to another, and never again know privation.

How fallacious the hopes of Captain Spencer were, was proved by the increasing scarcity of the Eucalypti; the same sufferings recurred, and were again endured with patience. Tiger was the chief anxiety; and there were times when the poor beast laid himself down, that he scarcely seemed to care whether he ever got up again. Now and then Charlie also seemed to suffer, and appeared exhausted, as if he had flown far in search of water, and had not found it; then he would say, his master having once uttered the epithet on such an occasion, " Here's Charlie, poor fellow! Boccolo Sahib, Ned Spencer, poor fellow! poor fellow!" He must, however, frequently have been able to drink when they were destitute of the life-supporting liquid.

In order to keep the wheaten flour brought from the Marie in better condition, it had been made into thin cakes, and not touched as long as any other could be procured. One day, by way of experiment, Captain Spencer gave a piece to Tiger, and to his great pleasure the animal ate it with avidity; and as it engendered much less thirst, than the raw meal, and was much more nutritious, it was solely reserved for the horse. This precaution was of great service; for it seemed to recruit his strength, and was much lighter than the heavy mashes with which he had lately been fed; he walked much better; and though he did not recover his gaiety, he resumed much of his usual action.

They came to a large open scrub, without a sign of a hill or a tree; and Captain Spencer looked round him with a heavy foreboding. A hot withering wind blew from the interior. "This cannot have come across a sea," said he to himself. The ground was so scorchingly hot, that the horse, when he stood still, pawed the ground to find a place under the surface which would be cooler for his feet. Timber had been there, but it was now fallen, and was dead; the scrub was dry and brittle, and sharp pieces of flint lay upon the soil. Knowing that natives much frequented these places, for the sake of the Wallabies, Opossums, and small Kangaroos in them, when he had resigned his portion of water to the others, and covered the baggage with tarpauling, Captain Spencer determined that Gip should lie on the open ground, that she might be alive to the least sound which might foretel danger. All, however, was perfectly quiet, and the party slept soundly till about an hour before sunrise; then Kinchela started up and awakened his master, exclaiming, "Up, Boccolo, up, get water! when sun comes, all gone!" At this welcome sound, Captain Spencer was on his feet in an instant; and following the instructions of Kinchela, he, with a wisp of dried grass, swept large drops of dew from off the bushes and long grass, into the cans, and was surprised to see how rapidly it accumulated, and the quantity which they collected. "Quick, Boccolo! quick!" said Kinchela, "sun coming:" and he was right; directly the sun shone above the horizon, the dew disappeared as if by magic. This discovery again seemed to take a load from the Englishman's heart, and he cheerfully thought, these are the secrets of the desert, and this is how wild men are able to travel through these arid regions, and pass over hundreds of miles without finding a pool or a spring. He, however, soon came to a still more desert region, and entirely passed the limits of that belt of vegetation which surrounds the barren waste in the interior of this mysterious land, and which seemed to be very narrow on the southern side. As he walked on that day, Kinchela suddenly caught him by the arm, and dragged him on one side; for on the spot where he would next have trod, lay an Adder, more than two feet long, and beautifully marked. It was quite quiet, and Gip had passed wide of it, and so escaped alarm. Kinchela told him that it was its way to be quiet; but if he had touched it, it would have sprung upon him, and if bitten, he must have died immediately.

The dog and horse were renovated by the collection of dew, and then came the consideration whether they should or should not advance into the sandy hills, which now lay before them, and were most unpromising, rising like dead brick walls in the field of the telescope. They appeared to be of vast extent, and no dew was left; would it be better to traverse them at once, or wait the chance of another dew, for these blessings were not of nightly occurrence? They decided on going on; and a second dew did come, where there was neither grass nor bushes on which it could rest; and then it struck Captain Spencer that he might catch it by spreading out the tarpauling, and laying over it the handkerchiefs and linen, which had been given to him by Captain Royer; the latter of which he had not worn while travelling. This was put in practice every night, and they were more than once saturated with dew, were wrung into the cans, and afforded a mouthful or two to those who most wanted drink.

The travellers were now encircled by a region of sand-ridges, without a blade of grass, or a small animal for Gip's dinner, and late at night they sank down, overcome with thirst and fatigue. In the night, Captain Spencer was restless and feverish, and almost mechanically rose to examine the linen outside the tarpauling; he drew one of the handkerchiefs to his mouth, sucked it, and was refreshed. An ample supply was afforded in the morning, and they all started with tolerable comfort; it was, however, the last time that the blessing was vouchsafed. They mounted a ridge of sand, which lay before them, and to their great surprise, a broad sheet of water, extending nearly north and south, lay before them; not fresh, however, for the deep indigo-blue of its colour too plainly indicated its saline nature. The telescope told, that far to the north it inclined towards the east. "Did it reach the sea on the south?" asked Captain Spencer of the native,—"was it a large arm of the ocean, or a lake?" Kinchela did not know, but pointing to the north, said, "Very bad country up there; nothing to eat, nothing to drink; Kinchela (for he generally put himself first), Boccolo, Gip, go back to find big-tree, make boat, and go away far, far; but big dog not can go in boat." By this his master supposed he meant a canoe of the Eucalyptus bark, and knew well that Tiger, with all his cleverness, could not cross in so fragile a conveyance; and he assured the native, that if it were to save his life, he would not leave Tiger behind; but he might go if he pleased. Kinchela shook his head, and said, "Not can go.' Fortunately the lake was frequented by wild fowl of various species, which afforded a supply of food. Fresh water was the difficulty, and digging in the neighbourhood only produced brine. It was fortunate that none of the party were aware at that time that they had at least three hundred miles to go before they could get rid of that lake, and a terrific desert to cross on the way; for although Kinchela had some idea of it, he could not measure the extent of the evils which awaited them. With such a certainty in prospect, Captain Spencer would probably have turned back to the west, and once more endeavoured to reach one of the settlements of that coast. He now, however, was as anxious to proceed rapidly as he had before been inclined to take matters leisurely. He determined, from that time, with Kinchela and Gip, to subsist entirely on animal food, as the prospect of refilling their meal-bags was so distant, and Tiger must have all which was left.

Only when obliged to halt, in consequence of the intense heat, did the travellers rest in the middle of the day; and now Captain Spencer thought it right to proceed on the Sunday, for since he had possessed the almanac, he had kept the Sabbath as a day of rest. Whenever they came to a fresh sand-ridge, if not obliged to cross it, he mounted on to the top, glass in hand; and on one occasion far away to the west, he saw a belt of trees, the sort easily recognized by their peculiar green. The travellers gladly diverged from their route, and proceeded towards it, where the water and food afforded by the roots again saved the poor horse. It was easy to trace their way back again by the marks of their footsteps, so that they had no unnecessary wandering in that dreadful region, the soil of which was so impregnated with salt, that it lay in shining crystals under their feet. The only vegetation consisted of patches of a salsolaceous plant like samphire, which Tiger at first eagerly cropped; but the sensible animal finding that it made him more thirsty, soon refused to touch it, green and fresh as it looked. Occasionally a stunted bush of Goodeniæ was found among it, but it was nearly withered.

Several days passed in this manner, and again Captain Spencer thought he saw a row of trees looking like the useful Eucalypti; he rejoiced for poor Tiger's sake; but it was only a deceitful mirage, and their situation could not be satisfactorily ascertained; they were possibly those which they had last visited, and when the reflection of them appeared in the sky, all hope was gone. Worn out and footsore, he could scarcely unload the poor horse, who that night instantly sank upon the ground. Alarmed at this exhaustion, his master shook off his own fatigue, and called Kinchela to help to rub the poor beast's legs. No answer was made to the summons, and the man was not to be seen. "What can have become of him!" said Captain Spencer; "and Gip missing too! what has happened?" He called, he whistled, but only Charlie came with his usual cheerful note, and information of his arrival; but this induced his master to look for the others in the direction whence he flew. Then he saw them, like small specks upon the sand, but evidently returning Kinchela, more accustomed than he to the appearance of Australian scenery, had succeeded in finding the trees, and taking Gip with him, was returning laden with roots, the broken ends of which he had stopped from flowing by lumps of sand. A piece was instantly put into the horse's mouth, who munched that and others till he could swallow them. Some of the liquid proceeding from them was then poured into his mouth, and he was refreshed. Gip now so perfectly understood all which happened, that she had already helped herself, and was as gay as ever. Kinchela, who rose in energy, activity, and willingness in all cases of emergency, proposed to his master to wait where he was till he had been two or three times to the trees to ensure fresh supplies; and contriving to raise the tarpauling upon the spears, and put a heap of sand at his back, he assented to the plan. In addition to the water and roots, Kinchela procured some Acacia seeds from the scrub, which were beaten into a meal, which he liked very much, and ate while his master devoured the roots.

Again the travellers started, keeping rather wide of the lake, for close to it the sand was so heavy that the labour of walking was increased threefold; but they remained as much as possible on the top of the high ridges which ran parallel to it. Countless numbers of migrating birds, all from the north and north-west, replenished the provision-bags, being evidently on their way to some more fertile region; for all the Psittaceous or Parrot tribe are known to confine their habitations to rich and well watered districts. Among them were the Psittacus Novæ Hollandiæ, or New Holland Parrot, and the Shell Parrakeets, looking like flights of Starlings. Occasional showers of sand, probably raised by a current of wind, annoyed and almost blinded the travellers. Several times small whirlwinds raised smoke-like columns of sand, and frequently made the Englishman hope that native fires were near, and that there he should find water.

One night a cold wind surprised Captain Spencer, also coming from the north, whence the hot and withering sirocco had hitherto proceeded: it was impossible to account for this, as well as other sudden variations; and to his astonishment, a more remarkable phenomenon made its appearance in the shape of a frost, as an accompaniment to the cold breeze. For some little time, however, the mornings and evenings had been much cooler, and even opossum-cloaks had been acceptable during the hours of slumber. These sudden changes of temperature were, nevertheless, refreshing, and enabled them to go through the additional fatigue occasioned by deep fissures in the soil, which obliged them frequently to go round, for they were generally too wide and deep to leap over; they, however, showed that the basis of the country was sandstone, with a bed of clay, on which were heaped the ridges of sand, and which to a certain degree bound them together. Again did the heat return as suddenly as it had left them, and clouds frequently gave hopes of a thunder-storm; but the heated air which rose from below dispersed the clouds, and they were disappointed. At a distance lay lagoons, which Kinchela was sent to inspect; but he invariably returned, saying they were salt; and some being dried up, left a glittering white residue of this mineral. The mud which he now and then brought back from the borders of the pools, seemed also to contain gypsum.

At length the water of the lake gradually shrank in its wide bed, which had now much more decidedly taken an eastern direction; then it lay in pools, leaving a residue of sand and clay between them, which was much too soft to bear their footsteps. A region of Hakea scrubs, interspersed with Mimosa, Gum, and Melaleucas, offered some resources, and they halted for a few additional hours; Captain Spencer anxiously watching the frequently gathering clouds, all of which, however, gave but deceitful hopes. In this spot they came upon a solitary pool of fresh water, when least expected, which gladdened the eyes and throats of the suffering wanderers, and formed another of those strange inconsistencies with which Australia abounds. They slept by it, filled their vessels, and left it to wade through a thick scrub of fatiguing and prickly Spinifex,—during which Gip again rode on the knapsack. It was interspersed with occasional patches of small stones, a little convex on one side, looking like biscuits, in which Captain Spencer detected lime mixed with the sand; and others, in which lay round balls of iron and sand;

some like marbles, and others like cannon-balls with rings round them; some were clustered together like grape-shot; and all were probably formed by the action of water. This monotonous region was in some degree relieved by the presence of plants, such as Polygonum, Angophora, and patches of dried-up grass, from which Tiger vainly endeavoured to derive nourishment. Then appeared stunted Gum-trees, which were really useful, though their roots were nearly dry; then succeeded a plain, which became more intersected by dry water-courses, seeming to tell that in the winter the whole place was filled with torrents of water Salsola bushes looked tempting, but were a dangerous indulgence, and Captain Spencer was pleased to see that Tiger resisted them; his own life was one of continued forbearance, that he might prolong that of others; and he afterwards thought that, to his extreme moderation in drinking, he owed much of his power of sustaining positive drought.

At the end of a long journey, continued with but little intermission during the whole day, Captain Spencer remarked that no birds, no trees, no living thing had been lately seen; for even the scrub had disappeared, and the horizon was bounded by some sand-hills which appeared to lie directly in their path. " Beyond these," said he, " is surely the head of the lake, and there we shall find something better." Arousing the party earlier than usual, he having been too anxious to sleep, and swallowing a mouthful from their now scanty stores, he gave the dumb beasts—for Charlie now asked for one or two dips of his bill—the last drop of water ere they started; Tiger stiff and sore-footed. On they went, silently and slowly, and with difficulty did the poor horse ascend the hill, his master almost pushing him up the steepest parts. Kinchela was in advance, and when he reached the summit, he suddenly stopped, and exclaimed: "Oh! Boccolo, bad place!" and truly did the prospect appal even the stout heart of the Englishman. Before them lay a large tract as wide as the eye could scan, the whole surface of which was covered with large and small stones, on which nothing grew, and near which nothing appeared to live. These stones were chiefly composed of quartz and sand; and occasional undulations showed that water might lodge there in the winter season, but all had now evaporated. Also frequent masses of almost pure iron made the compass unsteady. The sun scorched this sandy plain, and so heated the stones, that Tiger and Gipsy were almost afraid to put their feet down upon them, and frequently Captain Spencer could not hold them. The often-repeated question again rose to his lips, of what was to be done? the telescope everywhere disclosed the same features: no water, but little food, no apparent termination to the sterile ocean before, behind, and all around them. To go back the traveller knew was a certainty of days without relief; to go forwards, he feared would be the same; and, leaning his head upon Tiger's neck, the strong man was for a moment overcome. Kinchela looked wistfully and sadly at the scene. Gip inquired most meaningly by her countenance what was the matter; and Tiger stood patiently with his head bent towards the ground. But the faith and trust which had hitherto supported the English soldier were not wanting in this hour of extremity, and a silent and fervent prayer was lifted to Heaven for further succour. Then followed the consideration of how human means could be made serviceable in overcoming this fearful difficulty. Some strips of dried meat were still left; and making some of the largest into balls, he pushed them down Tiger's throat, gave one to Gipsy, another to Kinchela, and then took one himself. "On we must go," said he to the native, "and not stop till we fall." He fastened the skin coverings on Tiger's hoofs; his load, from the absence of provisions, could scarcely be lighter, and, in fact, could not be an incumbrance to him. Kinchela drew his belt tighter round him, and walked on with quiet resignation; his master kept by the horse's side to cheer him with kind words and caresses. Miles were passed over; Tiger now and then, with his thin legs, stumbling over a larger stone than usual, and giving his owner an additional fear that he would fall and cut his knees. Then Gip came to a standstill, whined, and lifted up one of her fore-feet to be looked at; and when Captain Spencer examined it, he found that it and all the others were blistered and cut; and she was of course lifted on to his shoulders, for which she showed her gratitude by licking the back of his neck; and he was quite startled when he felt how hot her tongue was, bringing to his mind hydrophobia and other evils.

After hours of unremitting toil and suffering, nature seemed as if she could do no more; the sun was sinking, the horse could with difficulty drag his limbs along, and Kinchela had several times laid himself down, saying he could not go any further; on which, taking one of the spears, Captain Spencer threatened to strike him with it, if he did not proceed. Tiger's foot-coverings were cut to pieces, and his hoofs almost worn to the quick, so that he limped instead of walked, and his master thought they must all lie down and die. Charlie had altogether disappeared, and it was hoped that his wings had enabled him to soar high enough to descry relief. When night came, however, the stones were smaller, sand was mixed with them, then ridges of bright red sand came, and beyond them, ridges of the same sand were seen in the distance. Captain Spencer made almost superhuman efforts to reach them; he went straight towards them, spoke incessantly to Tiger with words of love and approbation; he almost lifted him up the sides, hoping to see something beyond which should impart hope; but ridge succeeded ridge, a dizziness came over the soldier's eyes, his head became confused, and he fell with Tiger by his side, loaded as he was, and the whole party lay prostrate on the sand.

The cool breeze at night was refreshing, and Captain Spencer thought it his duty, as he awakened from a long sleep, to try and eat what remained of the dried meat, if his swollen throat would allow him to swallow; he took the bags from Tiger, and altogether unloaded him; the bags were empty, for the Australian had appropriated the last morsels. A flash of indignation at his selfishness crimsoned the worn cheek of the soldier, but he reflected on the pressing calls of hunger, and forbore even to reproach. Then, indeed, his heart completely failed, thick darkness seemed to come over him, and he lay down, thinking he should rise no more. After a while Tiger dragged himself closer to his master, put his nose on his shoulder, heaved a long sigh, a convulsive shudder ran through his frame, and he lay motionless. "Dead, Tiger, my dear faithful friend!" said his master, throwing his arm round him; "this is almost too much to bear. Gip, darling, are you gone too?" but Gip uncurled herself, walked round poor Tiger, licked him, looked at her master, and again lay down.

In the morning, Captain Spencer, following Kinchela's example, tightened his belt, and turning round to call him, saw him devouring one of the water-skins. "Come," said he, "we must carry all we can." He slung the tins across his own shoulders, and the skins also, for fear the man should eat them, giving him the cloaks, spade, &c., taking care, however, to make his own burden the heaviest; and with Gip in her usual place, he prepared to start. He cast a look of agony on the beautiful and motionless form of that faithful creature, who, in days of happiness, had borne him in the race, in the hunt, and before the admiring looks of rank and beauty; who had travelled many hundred miles by his side, never rebelled, never strayed, and had more than once been instrumental in saving his life. Tears coursed each other down his cheeks as he turned away, feeling as if he ought not to leave him, although his own existence, and that of the remaining party, depended on his advance.

They traversed ridge after ridge, till the Australian said: "Boccolo, Kinchela die!" Gipsy was unable to raise her head, and then, her master taking her in his arms, lay down, saying, "We must follow poor Tiger." He dosed, with visions of waterfalls, streams, verdant plains, crowding upon his sight and mind, and he became insensible, with the sound of water trickling in his ears. He did not know how long he lay in that unconscious state, but it was morning when he opened his eyes, and recollected all that had happened. He was wet all over, everything about him was damp, and he was sure that either a storm or heavy dew had fallen; still he felt as if he could not raise his head, and he lay still for some time, when one of the beautiful pigeons of the country flew over his head; at some little distance she descended to the ground behind a sand-hill, stayed for half a minute, and then rose and continued her course. "Bird of God," he exclaimed, "thou hast saved us!" Hope gave him fresh energy; he laid Gip upon the ground, and crawled to the spot where the pigeon had alighted. He there beheld a large pool of water with green grass, and some stunted Box-trees growing round it; he seized a can, supported himself with one of the spears, dipped it in, took a long draught, and felt a new man; he was then strong enough to return to his companions; he poured some water down each of their throats,—Gip recovered the first, and shaking herself, licked her master's hands. Kinchela rose and proceeded to the pool. Captain Spencer returned to it; but in the midst of his thankfulness he dashed the tears from his eyes by passing the back of his hand across them, and in spite of his deep gratitude, exclaimed: " Too late for my poor Tiger!"

The travellers sat down by the water, and a piece of the kangaroo-skin being left, it was stewed for Kinchela and Gipsy; and Captain Spencer took the provision-bags, scraped them, turned out the corners, and beat them, by which means he accumulated a small heap of flour which he made into a cake, and satisfied his hunger, which in fact was not very great. The native then lay down, and fell into a most refreshing slumber. His master sat with his head leaning upon his knees, and also slept; but he was shortly after awakened by his hat being suddenly lifted off his head: he started, saw Kinchela and Gip still fast asleep, looked around, and beheld his beloved horse standing close beside him with his hat in his mouth, and Charlie on his back, who said, " All's right, Ned Spencer!" He was for a moment struck with the idea that his senses were disturbed, and it was not really Tiger who stood there; but the next he dipped the can in the water, held it to the horse's mouth, and the needful cordial was quickly imbibed. He never could account for this resuscitation; but he believed that while they lay insensible the night after Tiger appeared to die, there had been a storm copious enough to revive the poor animal, who had afterwards risen and followed his track. The warm embrace which followed, the noisy delight of Gipsy, and the astonishment of Kinchela, mingled with joy and dread, all told how welcome the lost one was to the whole party; and as to Tiger himself, he had a great inclination to dance upon his hind legs, but he was not yet quite equal to such a performance. "If I am ever so hungry," said Captain Spencer to himself, "I never will destroy another pigeon." In the evening, Gip and Kinchela started in search of food, and brought back some Jerboas. Tiger revelled in the grass, Charlie had plenty of insects, among which were Ant-lions;* and they all became "giants refreshed."

After a rest of three days, the party again went on their way, Captain Spencer hoping that his worst trials were over; he bent his steps to the south-east; Jerboas and two Crows in his bags, two feeds of grass for Tiger, which he had with great labour cut, some pounded bark for meal, and as much water as they could carry, of which Kinchela drank such a quantity before starting that he could scarcely walk; his master and dumb servants refreshed more wisely and moderately. They had not proceeded far when Captain Spencer again perceived the blue waters of the lake at a great

* Myrmeleon.

distance, and beyond them a range of lofty mountains. A dark green plain also met his eye, which told him that the ground there was covered with Salsolæ, and in it were dry lagoons of salt. As they proceeded, some violent blasts of wind now and then assailed them, which were precursors of rain, and which covered them with sand; they, however, stopped under a hill, turned their backs to them, and waited till they were over. "I have not seen a trace of the inland sea," said he to himself; "but I have been too much occupied by the difficulties of my route, to take much notice of anything which was unnecessary for our advance or preservation. It is evident that there is a great depression through which water has passed from north-east to south-west. A well-equipped party perhaps might penetrate the mystery, but not without camels, I should think."

The country was evidently improving; small pools of water, either permanent, or filled with surface-draining after recent rain, were met with; the liquid was not always good, but to them it was acceptable. Atriplex and Acacias appeared, and now and then a patch of newly springing grass. They bivouacked by a small brackish lake, ornamented by Acacias, and in this they caught some silvery, Perch-like fishes, about six inches long, which were greatly relished by Kinchela. While here the clouds again gathered, and a heavy storm approached; Captain Spencer prepared to receive it, protected his fire-arms, spread out the tarpauling, with its edges turned up, to catch the fresh water, and Kinchela took off his shirt. This was too good a plan to be despised, and Captain Spencer adopted it, hiding his own clothing under the tarpauling. Torrents of large drops fell, Tiger and Gip held out their tongues, and even Charlie hopped about and shook his wings, saying, "What a row! hurrah!" for he was gradually forgetting his French. This copious shower both seemed to infuse new vigour into all, and give fresh life to the whole country, for the pools of water were more frequent as they went on, and Kinchela said, "Plenty rain come now, Boccolo." He was right; and now it became a matter of anxiety to get into some place of shelter before they had too much water—before the plains were turned into swamps, rivers into floods, and they into aguish, shivering travellers.

For the present, however, these bursts of rain softened the ground for Tiger's feet, which being again wrapped up in skin, the hoofs grew, and he proceeded with great alacrity in the cooler atmosphere.

Natives here began to appear; and the first they met was a solitary old man, who seemed to be very much alarmed at the rencontre. He looked as if he too had been travelling across the stony desert, he was so emaciated, and he would have run away as they advanced; Captain Spencer, however, stopped, and desired Kinchela to speak to him; he could not or would not understand, but he made signs that he was very hungry; they offered him a bird, and this kindness inspired him with confidence. He remained with them for two days, during which time a Wombat was speared by Kinchela, for Captain Spencer would not use his firearms for fear of frightening the old man away. He had his share of that spoil, and when they parted he had some given to him for his journey. Captain Spencer tried to make him understand that he might go on with them, but he pointed to another direction. He was wholly without clothing, had only a spear and a stick in his hand; he had no means of carrying a store of provisions, how then would he travel, how obtain sustenance? When his master imparted these thoughts to Kinchela, the native laughed, and said, "Black fellow not go far, Boccolo. He have gins not far off; he hide his gins from Boccolo, and gins get him food. But perhaps old man a boyl-ya (here he lowered his voice, and boyl-yas can get everything; but Kinchela not like to talk about boyl-yas, for they make black fellow ill when he talks." Captain Spencer smiled, for he had always found, when Kinchela could not explain anything, he made a convenient use of boyl-yas.

CHAPTER X.

Plenty of food—Yellow bean—Rough ground—Emus—Fishing—Natives—Painted man—Birds—Man and his wife—Captain Spencer rescues nets from flames—Rivers—Kinchela recognizes the country—Finds a dead Kangaroo—Kinchela not allowed to take it—Building rat—Cold—Encampment of natives—Kinchela's friends—Captain Spencer well received by them for his sake—Captain Spencer consents to stay the winter with them—The natives build him a house—Supply him with provisions—Two men, Warrup and Ugat, superior to the rest—Opinion of Tiger—Description of natives—A new tribe arrives—Their reception—Captain Spencer taken for the ghost of a relation—Corrobbery—Dance of hill tribe—Warrup and Ugat talk of native customs to their guest—New sorts of food—Native manufactures.

To those who had been so long half-starved, the increasing supplies of food created a lightness of heart and strength which enabled them to travel at good speed. The country assumed that park-like appearance which is so refreshing, because it is shady, yet sufficiently open to afford a circulation of air. Oat-grass again presented itself, and was eagerly taken advantage of by the travellers; also plenty of birds, especially Crows, varied their animal fare. Dried up places, like old water-courses, still presented themselves, and Captain Spencer could scarcely think that they were all filled during the winter, unless, indeed, that talked of mysterious sea occasionally poured its waters over the land. Pieces and indications of different ores and metals attracted attention; but it was impossible to stop and examine them minutely, on account of the haste supposed to be necessary for gaining shelter from the heavy rains which they expected. Still this heavy rain kept off, and the storms were local, for they met with surface-pools, when they themselves had not experienced any fall of water. The Yellow Bean* reappeared in quantities, which was a welcome change of diet both to man and horse; besides which some long silky grass† was not only eaten by the latter, but when he came to it he looked so earnestly in his master's face, that he was unloaded, and permission given to him to take a roll in it; the more necessary as his weary master had not of late been able to give him his accustomed cleaning. Glimpses of mountains were occasionally seen, which looked more lofty than any yet met with; and in their own path, they came upon hills of sandstone, cemented with iron, from which so many lumps and boulders had rolled down, that Tiger's socks were in requisition. These boulders often disclosed gypsum, and opalised wood; and the tops

* Dolichos. † Kangaroo grass, or Anthistiria.

of the hills looked as if they were of totally different formation to that at their base, so that when the latter rose, they had not disturbed the superincumbent strata. Fossil limestone now and then cropped out, chiefly containing shells. Again did they come across Emus; but as Kinchela was not old enough to eat them, his master did not expend time or strength in their capture. A Banhinia, twenty feet high, had the fruit of two seasons still hanging from the ends of its branches, and the large flat seeds were roasted and eaten.

Rhagodia formed the scrub of large flat plains, which refraction sometimes magnified into trees; low sand-hills were ascended and descended, and on the plain below were tall Gum-trees, the roots of which were no longer necessary to their existence.

At length, after passing through many "a tangled maze," the party halted close to a pond, the waters of which were somewhat brackish, the grass round it was coarse and wiry, but they had with them a supply of a better kind for Tiger, and Captain Spencer tried the experiment of fishing. No sooner had he baited his hook and thrown it in, than the same sort of shining white fish appeared which he had before caught, and a numerous capture gave them a feast; others were split and roasted, and Kinchela would have devoured them all at once, but his master insisted on his forbearance, and he dried a number for the supply of their future journey.

During the march of the ensuing day, the travellers fell in with some natives, who stood and stared at them, as if paralyzed with astonishment, and whether they did or did not understand Kinchela, they would not speak; then they came upon two huts made of boughs, in which were some children at play, who ran and hid themselves at their approach; and after these a man came over a hill who was highly painted with various colours, and who, being equipped with spear, shield, and club, looked as if he were going to war. He did not evince any surprise at the strangers, but motioned to them to go away from the neighbourhood of their huts. Captain Spencer then offered him some fishes, which he eagerly accepted, and ate immediately. The wayfarers then passed on, without further attempts at conciliation, supposing some tribe to be near, and the Englishman had no inclination for an encounter with superior numbers. The man stood gazing after them for some time, evidently watching the direction they took. They made a longer march than usual to get beyond his reach, and during the night kept watch alternately.

The path continued through open woods, and then an impervious jungle obliged them to alter their course. Beautiful birds of the parrot kind were again seen, and very small Parrakeets of exquisite colours seemed permanently to inhabit these forests. Among the numerous feathered creatures were Hawks with signs of evil intentions, and Charlie flew up to his protector with rapidity, calling out, "Rogues and scoundrels!" and he was so closely pursued by two of them, that Kinchela knocked them down with his stick, and Captain Spencer dispersed the rest by firing among them. The noise of the gun was heard afar, and, as the travellers turned round the foot of some low hills, they saw a man and his wife, who were so frightened that they threw down all they had with them, such as stones for grinding grass-seeds, skin-bags, containing roots, grass-baskets, some nets for catching birds, made of bark fibres, and the usual fire-stick. The latter set the grass on fire, and the bags, nets, &c., would all have been consumed, had not Captain Spencer rescued them from the flames, which fortunately were driven by the wind away from the spot where he was. He held them up to the natives, but they would not take them, and he therefore deposited them in a tree, and went on, passing through a lovely country, where flowers of great beauty, among which was a splendid yellow Ipomæa—showed that they had had rain. Green grass was under their feet, and they walked till evening, when they reached a beautiful river, winding through a ravine of cliffs, presenting an appearance of fertility and freshness which could only be produced by the existence of a permanent stream, and promising a much more hospitable country, in every sense of the word, than any they had seen since they left the Marie.

The cliffs of the river gradually became lower as the party advanced; they crossed the land where the river took a large sweep, and by so doing lessened their labour; then they perceived that they were standing on the border of one stream which joined another; the tributary was so much overflown that large trees were considerably immersed in it, and they were obliged to keep at some distance as they proceeded, to avoid the swamp, in some parts of which they sank till the water was above their ankles. This was refreshing enough for a time, but it was not good for a long continuance, or for sleeping; it however convinced Captain Spencer of the locality of the rains, or rather that rain was more tardy in visiting the arid region which they had crossed, than this part of the country; and he now began to think he should not reach Adelaide before the winter arrived, for he was obliged to turn to the north, and thus leave the settlement behind him. It became, therefore, necessary to think where he should pass the winter, for it would be impossible to gain the southern settlements anywhere, and he mused on the possibility of attaining eastern Australia. "So much the better if I do go there," said he to himself; "I shall be longer here, but I shall get back to Bombay from Sydney sooner than elsewhere. At all events, I shall now be obliged to stop, for we can never travel through the floods; and what is more, I shall have jungle-fever worse than in India, because more exposed." The faith and trust of Captain Spencer, however, was now equal to any difficulty; and He who protects those "who travel by land or by water," and who had preserved this little party in almost a miraculous manner, watched over them with His unceasing beneficence.

The wanderers lost sight of trees, and a beautiful pasture district succeeded. Here Kinchela, on looking around him, seemed to revive from the subdued state into which he had fallen since the time of their great sufferings, and uttered a cry of joy. "Kinchela knows this place, Boccolo!" he exclaimed; "he take you to see white men, far, far away," and he started at a pace which looked as if he intended to traverse the whole distance that night. He drew himself up to his full height, and his whip-cord sinews seemed all at once to regain their full vigour. They came upon signs of former encampments of natives, and Kinchela examined them carefully, muttering several names to himself, and then went on with continued confidence. At last he stopped, as if a sudden thought had struck him, and said, "Boccolo, me take you to good man, where you stop when it rains." His master nodded assent, and felt that if he could gain some native friendly tribe, he might be able to find food and shelter for himself and his companions as long as was necessary.

The water had been stopped by a large dam thrown across it, which had probably caused the flooding below; they crossed it, and Kinchela stepped on as guide, with an air of confidence in his own knowledge of their locality. They were not delayed by the necessity of filling their skins or cans, which now travelled empty on Tiger's sides, and they had a store of eatables; they crossed scrubs of Fusanus, Hakea, Acacia, and other plants, and trod upon a conglomerate soil, mingled with metallic indications. The country was here and there beautifully wooded, and verdant hills were near; they, however, kept in the plains for miles, in which the Gum-tree alone seemed to take up its abode; but they were able to push forward at an accelerated pace, on account of the comparative coolness of the weather. At last, one evening, as the sun was declining, they reached what Captain Spencer concluded to be the main river, of which they had crossed a tributary. The whole scene was gilded by the glorious rays of the departing luminary; beautiful drooping trees shaded its banks, young green reeds and grass rejoiced Tiger, who, as soon as they stopped for the night and was unloaded, plunged at once into a rich pasture, of which the juicy Sow-thistle and Mallows increased the value. They took their station close to a hollow Gum-tree, lighted their fire, and while they were busy with their preparations for a stew, the painted man came up, laid opossums, flag-roots, and pounded grass-seeds at Captain Spencer's feet, and retired, but not without casting a look of surprise at the tin can on the fire. It appeared as if he had followed them on purpose to give this supply, in return for saving the nets from being burned.

The next morning the travellers proceeded along by the side of the river, and found a kangaroo which had just been killed, from which the hunters had probably fled at their approach. Kinchela would have taken it up, but his master prevented him, telling him, as on a former occasion, that it did not belong to them; and after they had left it behind at some distance, he turned his head, and perceived several of the natives assembled round the kangaroo, now looking at it, then following them with their eyes, and pointing at them with much gesticulation, tossing about their arms like the sails of a windmill. The soil now consisted of a tenacious clay; the river was sluggish, hardly filling its bed; and the only alteration in the features of the country were several ridges, on which

Pine-trees seemed to grow. The whole scene was extremely picturesque; beyond the flats were hills beautifully wooded, and the ground was tossed up into strange and confused outlines. Captain Spencer lay down with the full expectation of much greater beauty on the morrow; but his rest was early disturbed by a loud, rushing noise, and suddenly starting up, he perceived the lazy, insignificant stream converted into a foaming, impetuous river, not as yet, however, reaching the level of its banks. He did not know how soon, with this rapid increase, it might pass even beyond them; and fearing they were too near, he awoke his companions, collected all he had, and moved on. As they left the river, the country was not equally rich, and they met with Salsola, Atriplex, and other sorts of scrub, only now and then seeing a scrub of much beauty, which had not before made its appearance. On a sudden Gip, who was before, stopped short, looked at her master as she lifted one of her paws, and then she went round a large nest made of sticks, with her nose and eyes examining every part. She began to demolish it, which caused its frightened inhabitants to rush out, to whom of course she gave chase, and her master went close up to look at the structure. The sticks varied in length from three inches to three feet, and in thickness from a quill to that of a large finger. They were so systematically arranged, that it was difficult to pull them asunder; the whole nest was four feet in diameter at the base, and three feet high, looking like a great bee-hive. It had five entrances at the bottom, nearly equi-distant from each other, with passages from them, leading to a central hole in the ground, in which stores of food were kept. There were two beds of grass in the centre, in which were some very pretty and tiny young Rats; and passages from these interior nests ran diagonally to the ground, or rather stick flooring of the principal nest, and they communicated with each other. Gip brought in one of the grown-up owners,* which measured six inches from the tip of the nose to the tail; its fur was light brown in colour, of a fine, soft texture, and the hind feet were very large in proportion to those in front. It quite grieved the Englishman to have disturbed so clever and pretty a building, and, in his vexation, he suffered Kinchela and Gip to eat the rat; but he prevented the dog from destroying any more of the skilful architects.

The weather had now become positively cold, and Kinchela so far conquered his fear of Tiger as to creep up close to him at night; and in the day he appeared to be very alert, with a constant expectation of something, the nature of which he would not communicate. The storms became more frequent, and the ground was constantly wet to lie

* Bandicoot, or Mus-conditor.

upon, so that Captain Spencer seriously thought, if he did not speedily find some natural shelter, he would dig a cave in one of the hills or banks of the vicinity, where he could remain till the worst of the winter was over; but it was necessary to be very careful in choosing a site where they should meet with the principal necessaries of existence. They came to a low range of heights covered with grass, and near them was a belt of Gum-trees, stretching across the country in an oblique direction, and he thought they might contrive a dwelling there, which should be partially formed of their boughs. He mounted these hills to reconnoitre with his glass, and there he found that the river lay beyond; and between it and some banks, which protected them from inundation, was a large assemblage of huts, with their native owners.

The women shrieked at the appearance of the travellers, and the men stood for a moment as if paralyzed with astonishment; they awoke from this, apparently to consult with each other on the reception which was to be given to the strangers. Many raised their spears, but Captain Spencer quickly cut a branch from a low bush close by, and held it up as a token of peace, and this seemed to induce them at least to pause. Kinchela stood with his hand over his eyes, anxiously surveying one of the groups, and, after a minute's hesitation, he with a cry of joy bounded down the hill, and exclaiming in the language of these people, dashed through the multitude. He was soon recognized, and all was tumult and curiosity. Captain Spencer quietly stood and awaited the issue, with Tiger, Gip, and Charlie; and then he saw those around Kinchela make way for one of their number, who came out of a hut; he and Kinchela sat down directly opposite to each other, laid their hands upon each other's shoulders, leaned their heads upon each other's breasts, and cried violently, while the other natives stood by in silence. This continued for a short time, then the two rose, and Kinchela spoke for some time. His master gathered from his gestures that he was telling the history of their first and second meeting, for he pointed to his arm, then to his foot, and acted the scene of finding him almost dead from hunger and thirst; then he pointed towards the stony desert, discoursed about Tiger, at whom they looked very solemn, nor did he forget the dog and the bird, and then there was a general consultation. As all this was going on, some persons arrived from the west, whom Captain Spencer recognized as those to whom the nets had belonged, and also the painted native to whom he had given the fishes. They took their part, earnestly made a speech, and the result was a sort of deputation from the tribe, preceded by Kinchela. through whom, as interpreter, they asked him to stay among them during the bad weather. They added, that they would build a house for him and his companions; then pointing to their wives, said they should cook and provide for his support; and as he had taken so much care of their friend Kinchela, who had once lived a long time with them, they would take care of him, till the rains and storms were over; after which they would tell him which was the shortest way to get back to "white fellows."

There was but little time for consideration, and making up his mind immediately, Captain Spencer consented to the proposal, provided the house were big enough for Tiger also, and that they would take as much care of his companions as himself. They readily assented, and his compliance put them all in motion; they begged him to rest where he was for a time, they brought him some food as an earnest of their intentions, told him that as he had not taken the kangaroo some of them had killed, they would now give him some; and then they set to work upon his habitation. They repaired to the Gum-trees in the neighbourhood, cut some branches from them with their stone tomahawks, chopped them into logs, piled the logs one upon another with much skill, covered the pile with grass, the grass with large pieces of bark, and so rendered the hut impervious to rain. They said they had not till now had rain for a very long time, and they should have plenty, which was the first intimation Captain Spencer had of the irregularity of the seasons in that part of Australia; for it appeared to him, as far as he could understand from Kinchela's interpretation, that they had not had any of consequence for two years.

The house was round in shape, higher than any of the others, so that even Tiger could stand upright in it, and the entrance was so proportioned as to require but little stooping. The ground inside was perfectly smooth, all the stumps and stones having been removed; and in one corner was a bed of dry leaves and grass, to which Tiger thought he had as much right as his master, and often contrived to push him off, and take possession during the night. Kinchela was to sleep at the entrance, and Gip and Charlie in their usual places. It was erected at some distance from all the others; and, when finished, at night the people led him with songs to it, by the back of their own encampment; and Kinchela requested that he would always go and return that way, and not pass through the village. The people had not taken as much pains with their own habitations, which presented a variety of forms, some being only semicircular, others large enough for two families, with several entrances. Some of the single men had joined together in making a hut for themselves, in parties of eight; they said plenty of people were come, and many more would come, for tribes united when the river overflowed its banks, in order to catch fish, and they would come back to their old houses, which were made to last a long time. When they wanted them for a little time, they made them as the traveller had seen in other parts; and from what he now heard, he felt convinced that he must have passed many encampments without knowing of their existence, so artfully were they concealed with bushes, grass, and boughs, and which were deserted in consequence of his approach.

The evening meal over, Kinchela told his master that " Boccolos wanted to see him." By the word Boccolos, Captain Spencer supposed he meant the chiefs of the tribe; he afterwards learned that they have no chiefs, but merely pay unusual respect to those who have shown superiority in any way; even personal stature and strength securing for the owners a sort of weight in matters of importance, which did not amount to authority. The two men came, father and son, who were of sedate appearance, the latter being the painted man whom the travellers had met, and who he now learned had not equipped himself for war, but for fetching a new wife; for " black fellows liked to look handsome before their gins." He had been to Adelaide, where he had picked up a few words of English; but Kinchela was now such an adept, and Captain Spencer had learned so many words of him, that between the interpretation of his servant, and his own knowledge, he contrived always to understand these two men, who became his principal friends and paid him frequent visits. On this occasion they had come to say, that as the rain would soon be here, when they could not so well leave, they would now make a Corobbery for his sake, and they must prepare for it; they hoped he would excuse their going out to hunt Emus and Kangaroos for him, but the women should get all that was necessary. The guest of course acknowledged the honour in a becoming manner, and the natives would have gone away, but he asked them to stay and talk to him; they complied, but begged to be seated far from Tiger, for they owned that they thought the big dog was a sorcerer, and they hoped he would not work them any harm; they had some very great sorcerers in their tribe, but they looked upon Tiger as still greater. Captain Spencer gravely promised, that, as Tiger always minded what he said, he would take care that they should be safe from him. He could, by the light of the fire outside the hut, near which they sat, distinguish their countenances; and he could not but remark that they were like all others whom he had seen, barring the trifling differences which exist between man and man; each had lost two front teeth, but the front teeth which were left and the eye-teeth were of the same shape. The old man, whose name was Warrup, had a fish bone through his nose; their movements were graceful; their manners easy, almost polished; and the son, who was called Ugat, proud of his English, frequently smiled and said, " Very good, very good;" which, however, caught Charlie's ear, who repeated it inside the hut, adding to it his heartiest " Ha! ha! ha!" This unexpected sound evidently made both the men uncomfortable; and Warrup asked Kinchela in a low tone, if the white fellow had another sorcerer with him, or whether it was the big dog which had spoken. Captain Spencer comprehended the inquiry, and took that opportunity of explaining the powers of his bird; and told them they possessed many in their country which might be taught to speak in the same manner. They seemed better satisfied after this, and added, "that they knew birds already which would mock everything they said; and that one nearer to where white man lived always laughed very much."*

The heads of these men were well developed, and the proportions of the brain apparently good; their thick necks betokened great strength; their feet and hands were small and well-made, and their heels were like those of Europeans; but the calves of their legs were very small, as in all others, except a very few instances. Their carriage was

* The laughing Jackass.

upright and dignified, and their chests wide, which, with their backs, were covered with thick scars. Captain Spencer asked them how they procured the paint with which they decorated themselves; and they replied that most of it was dug from the earth, and used either raw or baked; and that to produce a bright red, they mixed a yellow clay with red ochre, both of which had passed through the fire; that they also collected yellow from flowers, and a fungus; that the black was finely-powdered charcoal; the blue was extracted from a plant; that the earths were not to be found everywhere, but they bartered with other natives for it. The white was always to be had, it being the pipe-clay which Captain Spencer had so frequently seen throughout the country. They added that the ground on which the village stood was their own, and had always been so since it was made, and that each tribe in every part had its peculiar hunting-grounds, though disputes often arose about the boundaries, and led to war. When white men, however, appeared, they did not mind these boundaries, and took all, drove kangaroos away, and by and by they should all starve. The conversation was ended by Kinchela falling fast asleep; and the men arose, saying, " that a friendly tribe had sent them some long, narrow nets, made of rushes, and had taken them away that morning; therefore they supposed they would come to-mor row, and they hoped the Englishman would witness their arrival."

The next morning Captain Spencer went with Gip and Tiger to have a bathe in the river; and on his return, he left the latter to feed on the delicious grass which had rapidly sprung up since the first rains, and which looked exactly like bearded wheat. In a short time he saw men, women, and children gathered round him, looking at him with curiosity and awe. He was afraid that he would undo any favourable impression he might otherwise make, if he should take it into his head to dance on his hind legs into the midst of them; and he therefore called out to him, " Quiet, good horse." Tiger put up his pretty head and neighed a reply, at the same time whisking his long white tail. This, however, was enough; they instantly took to their heels, and many of them with more haste than good speed; so that they tripped each other up, and rolled away like so many barrels, which made Captain Spencer shout with laughter. They were never completely reconciled to the big dog; though some degree of alarm subsided on further acquaintance. When he himself galloped off on Tiger's back, they believed him to be a sorcerer of unlimited power.

The oldest and the principal men seated themselves cross-legged to receive their friends, who had brought some strangers with them; they were shown, or, as would be said in civilized life, introduced, with an account of their birth and country; after which all the males of the two tribes saluted each other by putting their hands on each other's shoulders, and bending their heads forwards, so as to touch each other's breasts. When, however, as in the case of Kinchela, communication was made of deaths which had occurred since they last met, they wept violently, and sitting down, went through the same forms as with him. The females remained behind, laden with bags, baskets, firesticks, mats, and children; they were silent; but those of the river tribe came and led them away to their huts, where there was plenty of talking, both loud and fast, although their voices were soft. Their gossiping continued the greater part of the night; and according to Kinchela's account, they told all about one another; and probably a little scandal went forward. These people came from the interior hills; the men carried all their warlike weapons, but they were feeble and diminutive.

To Captain Spencer's astonishment, while he was standing at the door of his hut that same afternoon, a procession of the females of the new tribe, headed by two women, came towards him. Tears were streaming down the cheeks of both; and the eldest, walking close up to him, said, "Yes, yes, it is he;" for Kinchela was close within the hut, and told him what they meant; then she threw her arms round the Englishman's body, and rested her head upon his breast; she was old, ugly, and filthy; and the other, nearly as dirty, knelt crying at his feet. The first proceeded to kiss him on each cheek, wept again, and called him the ghost of her son, who had been killed by the thrust of a spear. Even with the aid of Kinchela's explanations, Captain Spencer felt quite bewildered, and would rather have encountered an attack of a host of waddies; then came a young woman, who declared she was his sister; and she was followed by the whole number, who uttered exclamations of delight; father, brother, then encircled him with their arms, put their right hand against his right knee, and their breasts against his. "A goodly tribe of relations!" thought he, as he gravely bore this infliction; the children were then brought to him; but they at first kicked and screamed with fright at the white man; but when they saw that he received them kindly, there was a strife between them who should reach him first; and two or three put their fingers in their mouths, and then rubbed his skin with them, to see if he were painted. After this ceremony was ended, and the newly-claimed had promised to stay a little time among his self-elected relatives, he asked Kinchela for further explanation; and the man told him that black fellows believed the spirits of their dead went into the bodies of white men, and often returned to their own country, because they loved it so much; and that they knew them by the likeness which they always retained to their former selves. "Very flattering," thought Captain Spencer, who was by no means unconscious of his large share of personal beauty. "Then how is it," said he to his man, "that these returned spirits do not also know their relations?" Kinchela said "he could not tell that, but this ignorance always caused great surprise;" he added, that some believed all black fellows, when they died, went up to the clouds, where they had plenty to eat and drink; in which state they were often let down again by a rope; and his own brother had returned in that manner.

The whole of the next day the natives were busy preparing for the Corobbery in the evening, by making up numerous cockatoo and emu feathers, and painting themselves with all their colours. The women rolled up some kangaroo-skins as tightly as possible, which they beat with their hands, till they sounded like drums; others beat flat sticks together; in fact, all the music was performed by them, and would have been insupportable had it not been for the admirable time which they kept. They in a very few instances shared the dances of the men; but they had some among themselves, from which the men were excluded.

The Corobbery began by imitations of the sounds

and actions of different animals, especially the kangaroo, which they pretended to chase; they then went through various evolutions with their spears and shields, and emu feathers on their heads; then they performed a series of the most intricate figures by way of dancing, holding their waddies, or clubs, and boughs of trees. On this occasion the women danced at the corners, changed places often, by passing at the back of the large group, and frequently uttering the most abominable yells, which were most distressing to their guest, after the long comparative solitude to which he had of late been accustomed. Tiger peeped out to see what was the matter; Charlie said, "What a row!" and returned into the hut to sleep; while Gipsy, although in her master's arms, barked furiously. Even if quieted for a time, she burst forth again; and Captain Spencer assured his entertainers this was a mark of her approbation. The effect of this dance could never be forgotten, heightened as it was by an immense fire, which being constantly fed with fresh boughs, sent forth incessant flames. The legs of some were covered with broad white stripes; and they had a peculiar method of shaking them, which made them appear as if they were constantly turning round; others had boughs tied upon their legs; and, after dancing some time, suddenly stopped, stamping their feet with loud grunts, and rustling of the boughs; then they would pause suddenly with a deep guttural exclamation, and again start off, or drop all at once from a standing to a squatting posture, and hop away with outstretched arms and legs. The full dress of the females was an opossum-cloak, a band of white swan-down round the head, and a bunch of cockatoo feathers in front; their movements were not always as decorous as those of the men, and long before the Corobbery was ended, the person in whose honour it was performed was heartily weary of the whole scene; and he heard with dismay that, on the ensuing day, the recently-arrived tribe were anxious to display their accomplishments to the stranger, with whom they fancied themselves connected. It was necessary to conceal his annoyance, however, if he would not disturb the friendly feelings now existing.

The hill-tribe were adorned much in the same style as their friends; but besides feathers on their heads, they carried them in their hands, tied on to the top of short sticks, and the women danced in a line parallel to that of the men. After various evolutions, they advanced with a man in the centre, who bore a rude representation of a human figure at the top of a pole, formed of grass and reeds, covered with kangaroo-skins, painted all over with small white circles, the head made of feathers, and the arms represented by sticks. After dancing with this they roared, and again advanced, with two standards, each composed of a pole, on which nine branches were left. At the end of the branches was a plume of hawk, owl, or emu feathers, tied on with white swan-down, or white painted bark, which was continued down the pole. These retreated, then many came forth with their spears, danced for some time, came closer to their friends, who sprang up to meet them, stuck two or three in the shoulders, and the ceremonies were ended. Tired and heated, Captain Spencer retired to his hut, but not to sleep, for he was kept awake by the songs which were sung around him; and, in fact, in honour of him, these people having improvisatory powers. The songs were continued far into the night; one was a very sad lament, and Kinchela afterwards told him they were mourning for the dead; another, slow and wild, was concerning a sorcerer; and there were comic dialogues, which created great laughter.

During the heavy rains which ensued, the principal amusement of the traveller was the conversation of Warrup or Ugat. They delighted in speaking of themselves and their customs, did not take any interest in descriptions of civilized communities; but when Captain Spencer told them of his own black men in India, they were much pleased. It was difficult to come to any conclusion concerning their religious belief; but, as far as he could understand, they were aware of the soul being distinct from the body; which souls, some believed, lived in trees all day, came down at night to eat caterpillars and animals, but not vegetable food, and remained the size of a boy eight years old. Their notions of creation were equally vague; they said that a father and three male children lived in the clouds; the father, very powerful, who made the world, fixed names to everything, put the tribes into their own districts, gave them their languages, and brought them from some place in the east, over the water, and that souls go to live with these four. These natives thought that there was a large serpent, which lived in high, rocky mountains, and which made all things by one stroke of its tail. They declared that every body believed in an evil spirit, which haunts dark caverns, wells, and gloomy plains; that its name is Jinga, and that they are afraid of him at night.

The gun of Captain Spencer was a constant source of apprehension, and kept up the notion of his being a sorcerer. Having been told by Kinchela that he knelt and prayed every day to the Great Spirit (which his master had said to him), they thought he was then working his spells. His relations treated him with great deference, and most particularly attended to all his requirements; generally speaking, however, he and Kinchela procured their own provisions. Gipsy would have led a happy life, if the dogs of the camp had not persecuted her, either with their enmity or their friendship; but at last her master invented a collar of kangaroo-skin, into which he inserted some of the strong thorns of the Acacia, and this, with her furious barking and sharp bites, after a while, kept them away, for they were great cowards. Charlie was perfectly independent; but he would often electrify Kinchela as he flew over the village, by saying, "I see you, Kinchela;" and the man began to believe that the bird was acquainted with all his actions.

The new sorts of food brought to Captain Spencer by his friends were different species of fungi, and emu eggs, which, however, he could not eat, as they, and those of the Leipoa, were stale; the natives themselves cared but little in what condition an egg might be, they ate it all the same. They brought him an abundance of small animals not much larger than mice,* which burrow in the sand, and which they say will go for months without water. They had beautiful, full black eyes, their long tail had a brush at the end, their fur was light red in colour, and they generally hopped on their hind legs, and carried their tail horizontally. Gip most delighted in moths, and grew quite fat. Little or no hunting took place, because there was a general feeling that the river

* Hapalotus Mitchellii.

would suddenly rise to a great height, and then every one must be ready. Preparations, therefore, were constantly making for fishing and catching wild fowl, and Captain Spencer watched their rude manufactures with interest. They did not, however, show much ingenuity; and the various hard woods of the country were their best resources in the way of tools. They made a cement with resin, gum, and wax. In forming a canoe, they choose a large Gum-tree which has a protuberance in the bark, open it with their tomahawks, strip the bark off very easily with a stone in large pieces, bind it into the form of a canoe, and stop up the ends with clay. This was their only boat, and yet, fragile as it was, in it they contrived to place a fire, and fish for hours. Their netting-needles were only a pointed stick like a pencil, round which the string was wound, and they did not use any mesh. The strongest nets were made of the tendons of animals, of opossum fur, spun with or without fibrous plants; mallows, grass, and rushes, supplied materials for mats and baskets, well-rubbed skins for bags; and they had rude wooden shovels; they cut their food with flint fastened into sticks, and their teeth and great toes were serviceable to them in all operations. The drinking-cups of some of the tribes were the skulls of those whom they had best loved.

CHAPTER XI.

River overflows—Different modes of fishing—Cooking—Frogs—Cray-fish—Tortoises—Birds—Wind—Hatchet missing, and restored—Description of sorcerers—Sorcerers come to cure a boy—Restrictions concerning food—Native laws and customs—Women—Quarrel and combat—Boomerang—Large Kangaroo hunt—Tribe goes away and steals a young woman—Preparations for war—War-song—Departure in pursuit of the enemy—Captain Spencer follows—Encounter of the tribes—Captain Spencer fires, frightens, and pursues the guilty tribe—The young woman found bleeding to death—Taken home to be eaten—Captain Spencer goes away.

At length the important moment arrived: the river was suddenly converted into a broad sheet of water, evidently the consequence of a rush from higher ground; and the noise of its foaming and tumbling was accompanied by the clamours of the natives. Other tribes had joined them, and all was bustle and turmoil. They suffered the first violence to abate, then they formed weirs with mats and nets across convenient places; and taking a quantity of water in their mouths, before they placed the weirs, they squirted it upon them just before setting, to ensure luck. Some then took small nets in their hands, and walking into the inundated parts, dexterously placed them under the fishes, thus securing their prey, and biting the fish to kill it, threw it to their wives. Some of the latter, however, were also in the water, groping and catching the fishes with their hands. Captain Spencer joined the spearing party, for he had practised much during his travels, and become very expert with this weapon. All that he caught he distributed among the children, which made him extremely popular.

In a few days the water subsided, and then parties of divers were formed, who, joining in a line of thirty or forty, dipped down in succession; but the most interesting portion of the fishery was carried on at night. A bed of wet bark and mud was placed in the bottom of a canoe, and sticks of resinous wood, sometimes brought from a great distance, taken on board. These were piled upon the wet mud in the shape of a cone, and lighted in the stern of the canoe, in which were two men, the one to attend to the fire, and the other to guide the canoe, and to fish with a spear. The latter part requires great skill, as the canoe is so unsteady. A fish rises, the spearman strikes it, drags it to the side, leaps into the river and secures his prize, which is thrown into the canoe, and he follows, in order to make a fresh capture. Nothing can be more picturesque than a fleet of these canoes; for the fires, which burn with a peculiarly clear flame, light up the whole river, and disclose the beautiful drooping trees on its banks, and the dark forms of the natives in graceful attitudes, now throwing the spear, and now struggling with their prey in the water. The women also dive with great facility and strength, and go in large parties.

Among the fishes which were caught there was not much variety, being mostly of the perch or carp kind.* One, however, had very large scales, on each of which was a pink spot; and another was remarkable for some singular bones, placed vertically in the fish, connecting the spines of the back-fin to the back itself, and in shape resembling small pieces of tobacco-pipe. Some were of enormous size, which Captain Spencer felt certain must have weighed more than sixty pounds. Every other day was a day of feasting; for then they ate what they had caught, and Kinchela no longer stood in the light of a solitary instance of gluttony. They never seemed to think of laying by a store for future support; they said they always had plenty on their grounds; and their visitor then tried to influence the last-arrived natives from the interior, who looked weak, emaciated, and melancholy; but he did not meet with any success. He tried to enforce his precepts by example, and attempted to dry fish outside his hut for his future journey; but they were invariably stolen. Some of these fish were merely thrown upon hot ashes and broiled;

* Gristes.

but when their captors desired to take pains, they wrapped them in a piece of bark, which was folded like the paper used by civilized cooks for cutlets, and fastened with grass; they were then slowly baked in the ashes, and served in the bark. Among those so treated were some which resembled white-bait, both in size and flavour.

Fishes were not the only edible animals caught in or by the side of the river, for there were loads of delicious Frogs and excellent Cray-fish; which, when the floods subsided, came out of holes in the ground. The women waded for them in the swamps in long, close rows, walking backwards, and groping with their hands. The moment they seized hold of one of the Cray-fish, they tore off its large claws, and put it into a bag, which was hung round their necks; they called them Ukodko,* and captured thousands. The rats were also driven out of their holes by the floods, and captured with equal avidity, but were not equally acceptable to the European.

One morning before he left his hut, Captain Spencer heard a great deal of laughing outside, and going to the entrance, he saw four young men, who had brought him twenty-seven tortoises, and laid them at his door to surprise him. One of the tortoises weighed half a pound; and he rewarded

* Astacus

the good-natured donors by such presents as he could command.

At last Captain Spencer became tired with all this fishing, and the cold and wet of the surrounding neighbourhood, and he was longing to start again. The state of the country, however, was an insurmountable obstacle; and all the diversity he could obtain was to ride to some distance from the river, and to his surprise and pleasure he always found Kinchela ready to go with him; for he did not, even in the midst of temptation, commit his former enormities. During these excursions they saw very few birds which they had not seen before, and these were chiefly wild fowl, which came to feast upon the fish. On arriving near some trees, Kinchela made a sign to his master to be very cautious; so he dismounted, and telling Tiger and Gip to be quiet, the two men, by great manœuvring, came near enough to see an immense number of those beautiful Cockatoos which have rose-coloured tippets, and scarlet and yellow crests;* they were evidently holding a council of some sort, and had placed sentinels all round them on the boughs, which constantly stood on tiptoes, as if to watch against danger. Besides these was a brown-headed Swallow,† which had built nests of clay in rows, one above another, in the shape of bottles. A Pied Warbler‡ was very common, which sang

* Cacatua Leadbeaterii. † Chelidon linel. ‡ Acrocephalus Australis.

the greater part of the night, and its tones reminded the Englishman of those of the Nightingale. A small, speckled Dove of great beauty, with lilac plumage, white delicate spots, and a red skin round its eyes, often excited his admiration;* and another species surprised him by the power which it had of sending its voice to a distance, as if it were a large bird, singing far away.† Some very pretty little creatures assembled in numbers, and stood in a circle with their heads inwards.

On returning to the village from one of his rides, Captain Spencer heard a melancholy sort of chant kept up by a number of persons; and on asking Kinchela what it meant, he was told that the people were singing for the wind to jump up, that the water might be rough, and better enable them to catch the Wild Ducks, Widgeons, &c., which were now so numerous. When the wind did "jump up," the natives proceeded to the river, each having a noose fastened to a long rod; with this in their hands, they entered the water, a bunch of grass or reeds on their heads, and slowly advancing with a peculiar whistle they approached the birds, and slipping the noose round their necks, pulled them down without alarming the others.

Captain Spencer's hatchet was missing, and he was convinced it had been stolen, for he recollected to have brought it home in safety on the previous

* Geopelia curvata.   † Geopelia tranquilla.

day. The whole village appeared to be in a state of stupefaction from the excesses of the previous night; but he determined to make an instant inquiry, and proceeded to the dwelling of his favourite Ugat, whom he found quite as lively as usual, for he was not one of the great eaters, and said he never engaged in such feasts. He cheerfully arose, went to his equally temperate father, and by various kickings, questionings, and shakings, the two succeeded in finding out what boys had been seen about the hut while Tiger was feeding away from it, for they were sure none would enter while he was there. They then nodded their heads, and went straight to one of the huts where parents and all were asleep; they had some difficulty in rousing them, but when they were awake, Ugat laid hands on a youth of about fifteen, and desired him to give up the white man's hatchet. The boy at first denied the theft; but on being told that it was known he had slipped in unperceived and taken it, and that it was useless to deny it, the rogue cried, and Warrup walked into the hut and discovered it, although concealed in a heap of rubbish at one corner. It was of course restored; and when their guest asked the natives how they ascertained which was the culprit, they said that when they knew who had been seen near his dwelling, they singled him out, because he had large **eyes**, which look every where, and are never still, and it is not good to trust a black fellow like that. The father requested Captain Spencer to name the punishment; and he ordered that the offender should not be allowed to eat any fish or fowl for three days.

When Captain Spencer found that Warrup and Ugat did not eat as the rest did, he invited them to talk to him; and he and Kinchela then started for a walk, and with the restored hatchet cut a quantity of honey from a tree, together with a waxy substance, which tasted like gingerbread, some of both of which he gave to several children on his return, purposely leaving out the thief, who was also present. "What is the reason," said he to Kinchela, as they sat under a tree together, "that your people carry fire-sticks about at night, when they do not want to make a fire?" "Because they try to keep away bad spirits," replied the native; "they always sitting up in the trees, unless when they go about in canoe on the river; they have crooked legs, but they teach the people to sing." "Tell me something about boyl-yas," continued his master. "Ugh!" returned Kinchela; "it makes me so ill; they can do all things; one come to-morrow to cure poor boy. Boccolo see him; poor boy got bad legs." "Well," continued Captain Spencer, "that need not prevent you from telling me about him now." "Let me come close, then," resumed Kinchela: "boyl-ya got bone in his leg, which dead man put there, and he can kill with that. Ugh!" "He dare not kill you when I and Tiger are so near; besides which, you know you have stones to keep him away." "Oh, Boccolo! boyl-ya sit down close, hear Kinchela—be very angry. I shall not tell you any more; he come along in sky when you sleep. Ugh! it makes my head ache; he kill us both; eat us up like fire." "Does boyl-ya then eat men?" "Yes, Boccolo; all boyl-yas eat man once; but he not bites, not eat bones; he sits on man's grave; but if black fellow be sick, he charm, charm, charm! He walk away there! Ugh! I shall not tell you any more."

Warrup and Ugat that evening confirmed all that Kinchela had said, and told Captain Spencer that besides the common boyl-yas, there was one which inhabits water only, and makes people die gradually, especially women; also one which gives the nightmare, which the Englishman thought a very natural disorder for them to have; and that the only way to get rid of him, was to jump up, twirl a lighted stick round the head while they cursed him, and then throw it at him, for he wants a light, and when he gets it will go away. They added, that shining stones were good things to keep away spirits, but women must not see them; and when they took their leave, they begged of Captain Spencer to witness the power of the sorcerers the next day. The patient had erysipelas in the leg, supposed to have been given him by the water spirit; and he was carried to a distance from the village, put upon the ground, and his friends sat in two rows looking on, but not near to him. Three sorcerers appeared, coming in the figure of a triangle, with bunches of fresh reeds in their hands, which they frequently shook as they galopaded up to the boy, with the right foot foremost, singing a low dirge, which was answered by the natives, who thumped upon the ground. When they reached the patient, the foremost fell on his knees and took hold of the bad leg, while his two companions continued to sing and dance; he then retired, and each of the others took his place, and touched the leg; then they all three danced together, preserving the triangular figure, the boy in the middle. After this they blew from their mouths, spat, made all sorts of horrid noises, pressed the sore leg for the spirit to give signs of going away, and after carrying on this farce for some time, they pretended to extract a sharp stone from the diseased part, which was driven into the ground too deep for any one to see. The friends of the boy then took him away, and the sorcerers danced in a triangle round the spot, and galopaded all the way to the river, to drive the evil spirit into the water.

In further conversations with his friends, Captain Spencer learned the restrictions concerning food; and found many of them to be confined to certain ages, beginning at nine or ten years, and taken off when advanced in life. They told him that a father has absolute power over his wives' children, and that families always know where the absent members may be, although dispersed, and that messages are sent, or signal-fires made, to call them back in cases of danger; that matters of dispute are discussed in a general assembly of the tribe, when those who speak may go on till they are exhausted; that all are left to die when they are helpless, even parents; that children are often killed to get rid of the trouble of rearing them, that the first three or four are almost always destroyed, and that the children of white fathers are invariably murdered. That every family adopts a kobong or tiendé, in the shape of some peculiar animal; and they dare not kill and eat it, unless in the first instance they give it a chance of escape; that names are bestowed on account of peculiarities, such as the Father of Seeing, for a man who always looks about him; that children are named after their mother, and that no woman can marry a nearer relation than her cousin, and even that very seldom. That a man may have as many wives as he pleases, and treat them as he likes, and that there is no marriage-ceremony. That the bodies of old women are often tossed into trees, because they are not worth the trouble of burial;

and sand is put into the tattoo wounds, when first made, to render them hard, and the scars projecting.

The tattooing, they said, varied according to the country and the tribe; at twelve or fourteen, boys are partially tattooed; and at about twenty, the shoulders, arms, and chest, are cut with sharp shells, which causes great suffering, and is often resisted, although it is supposed to be a great addition to beauty. Warrup had a mark like a horse-shoe upon his shoulder. The modes of burial differ even in the same family. There were other ways of curing disease than sorcery, they said, for they bled with a piece of crystal or bone; which bone, if burnt, will cause the death of enemies: they use bandages for wounds, and bark splinters for fractures. They suck the bites of snakes, if plenty of water be near with which they can wash the mouth. There are many natives deformed and blind, the first caused by eating charmed food; but such persons are always respected.

In their intercourse with each other, as far as he could see, the natives of the interior of Australia appeared to be honest and trustful, generous in dividing spoil, giving the largest share to old persons; but their good qualities were much diminished where women were concerned. This portion of every community was in a painfully degraded state. They were in all cases more diminutive than men, seldom attaining even five feet; their heads were not so well formed, but their hands and feet were small, and delicately shaped. They are made to work hard from earliest childhood, while the other sex bask in indolence. They are perfect slaves to their husbands, and nevertheless possess a certain degree of influence over them. If any privation is to be undergone, it is they who are to bear it, even before the children, who are much indulged; they collect and prepare the food, dig, make huts, bring wood for fire, and carry all the burdens. The women's bag contains all their useful implements; while their husbands sit by the fire, they are allowed to shiver in the wet and cold, and in extreme heat they are to be seen toiling with their loads, and their sole relief a bunch of wet grass on the head. They paint themselves with green and red, ornament themselves with feathers, necklaces of kangaroo teeth, and stems of plants, and are fond of decoration; they are often promised in marriage during early infancy; when they become orphans or widows, they belong to the nearest male relations; and if a girl be unusually handsome, she will be covered with scars of spear wounds, made by those who have wished to have her for a wife, or the marks of injuries done to her by her jealous companions. Both sexes, if you are without protection, are willing to afford help, and will go miles out of their way to show you your proper direction.

It is very rarely that any great meeting of tribes takes place without a quarrel. They are generally attacked by indigestion, in consequence of excess; and indigestion but too often engenders ill-humour. They are at all times boastful; and several disputes arose during their assemblage by the riverside, which Warrup allayed by his influence; but on one occasion two men of different tribes were so determined to come to blows, that matters were obliged to take their course. They agreed to attack each other first with spears, and then with waddies or clubs; and a regular ring was to be made for the combatants the next afternoon. One of them, however, lost his courage in the morning, and was inclined to let the affair drop; but the women were mixed up with it, and his mother tried to persuade him, for the honour of the tribe, to meet his antagonist; she made him a long speech, which she ended by saying, that the eyes of all the young women were upon him. Inconsistent as it was with the subdued condition of the females, this was conclusive, and the fight took place. The men were showily painted and decorated, and the graceful attitudes into which they threw themselves when they avoided each other's thrusts, was a fine exhibition of the human form. At length, amid their wild cries they suddenly came to a stop, at each offered his leg to the other and received a spear wound in the thigh. This ended the spearing part, and then came the club combat; each stooped to the other alternately, and received his blow; and Captain Spencer found it difficult to divest himself of the belief that there was some trick in it; the blows were so tremendous that it seemed impossible for any skull to bear them, but several were sustained, and then one fell insensible to the ground, as the other staggered and also fell. Both men were carried away, but were walking about the next morning as if nothing had happened.

Whenever Captain Spencer talked of going, there was some reason urged on the part of Warrup and Ugat for detaining him still longer. He had not seen all their games, he had not seen a large kangaroo-hunt; but he soon became so seriously determined, that they at last hurried their sights on in quick succession; they promised to let him witness the throwing of the boomerang or kiley; and before they began they had a game played with a bunch of emu's feathers tied to a short stick, which was shaken in defiance, and the sport consisted of efforts to take it from its possessor. It was interesting from the display of swiftness, wrestling, jumping, and manœuvring which it evinced. The boomerang is a thin, curved piece of wood, from two to three feet long, and two inches broad, one side of which is slightly rounded, and the other flat. Those intended for war are the largest, and are less curved, because they are only intended to fly in a straight direction; but they are dangerous weapons from the unerring precision with which they are thrown. Ugat, who was the most skilful in the tribe, stood up to show his powers to the Englishman; and he sent his round so as to make a circumference of two hundred and fifty yards from left to right, when it fell at his feet. For about fifty yards it flew as rapidly as an arrow, and continued with diminishing speed till it came to the ground. With a stroke even more vigorous, it hovered like a bird in the air, with a hurtling sound, and taking a downward course, the tip touched the earth three times with a twang like that of a harp-string; it then continued its circular course till it returned to the thrower. Captain Spencer was very much struck with this singular weapon, the principle of which he could not at all explain; he was told that nothing but practice from childhood would enable any one to use it well; that directly they poised it, the skilful could tell whether it would fly or not, and that the slightest swerving from it would prevent its flight. The next man who threw it cast it too forcibly, and when its progress was consequently arrested, his companions shouted with laughter. The downward throw was also a failure;

for it passed the spot where it ought to have rebounded, towered up fifty feet, and then came down quickly. At night some old boomerangs were lighted at one end, thrown all at the same time in different directions, and the effect was beautiful, like that of birds flying about with fiery tails. They are much used in killing Cockatoos. A quieter game was that of cat's cradle, in which these rude natives could have set all the European players at defiance.*

The Kangaroo hunt was then organized, and Captain Spencer, mounted on Tiger, was ready first; so having to wait for them, he rode to the river, and was surprised to see how its peculiar plants had flourished since he had last been there: the Geraniums were in full blossom, and the splendid and remarkable Doryanthes excelsa, with its long, broad, aloe-like leaves, was in all its splendour. The hunting-party took their way to the spot where they were sure of meeting with Kangaroos: it was no longer the stealthy, artful attack of the native, whose wives and children lie flat on the ground, scarcely daring to breathe while he gets near to his game; it was not the following of a single man upon its track for three successive days, till the animal, worried and tired, lies down, careless whether it live or die; but it was a regular battue. A plain in which the Kangaroos were feeding was encircled by wood, and the older men

THE KANGAROO HUNT. [Page 221]

assigned stations to the younger, so as to surround the animals before they were conscious that enemies were approaching. They gradually narrowed the circle till one became alarmed, and bounded away; but before it had proceeded far, it was stopped by the most terrific and hideous shouts; it returned to its companions, and they were paralysed with fear; the natives then dashed on them with their spears, and effected a great slaughter. The prey belongs to him whose spear has first touched it, however slight the wound may be; and if, according to their laws, he is too young to eat it, it is given to his nearest male relation who is of the proper age. The cries used in this hunt are peculiar for every stage of it, and the first is a harsh utterance of the syllable *kau*. Many were the feasts held that night, and large was the quantity eaten; but the Englishman was not forgotten in the distribution of the best parts, beautifully cooked.

A few nights after the hunt, Captain Spencer was awoke by a great commotion in the camp, talking, quarreling, and movement in every direction: he sent Kinchela to know the reason, and he returned, saying, that his tribe had departed suddenly in the night, and stolen a young woman, and now it was found out; that the river tribe had often been at enmity with it, and made up their quarrels, but were now determined on following them as soon as they could get ready, and punish them for all their misdemeanors, without waiting till they could make a demand for the young woman to be returned. Now, thought the Englishman, I shall be able to get away; but he was mistaken. His friends asked him to go to war with them, for white men knew how to fight. Although a fighting man by profession, Captain Spencer was not so enamoured of it as to wish to fight except for his own country, or in self-defence; and besides this, the crafty sort of warfare of savages little suited his ideas of fair play. He tried to make them understand this; but they said although he had not used his gun while among them, for fear of frightening them, they knew he could kill every body with it; and they begged him to go to war with them, and shoot every one of their enemies. He dismissed the deputation, by saying that he would think over the matter, and let them know his determination in a day or two.

Nothing now was to be heard but the chipping of spear-heads, or seen, but fires where provision for the march was preparing, and lumps of paint or bunches of feathers passing from hut to hut. All these employments were mixed with songs of threats and hatred; and Captain Spencer plainly heard in one of the dwellings nearest to his own, a man singing to himself,—

> "I'll spear his liver,
> I'll spear his lungs,
> I'll spear his heart,
> I'll spear his thigh, ho!"

Then his wives took up the burden, and enumerated other parts of the body to be speared; and as they are very much influenced by their songs, it was easy to see that something serious was likely to occur. Captain Spencer then thought it best to consult Warrup and Ugat; and sending for them, he made them in some measure comprehend what he felt. They, however, entreated him to go with them, and pointed out a way by which he might save rather than spill blood. It was at length arranged between them, that the tribe should start first, he follow, and remain at a distance; and when they had thrown their spears, he should fire over the enemy, but not into them, unless such a proceeding should be necessary.

The warriors, fully equipped, departed at early dawn; and their feathers, their shining spears, their painted bodies, and their chants, dying away in the distance, produced a most imposing effect. The Englishman slowly followed on Tiger, with Kinchela, Gip, and Charlie; he would willingly have dispensed with the presence of the two latter, but where he was, they thought they must be also. He came up with the parties as they stood fronting each other, in a most hostile attitude; he gave the signal of his arrival in one of the native calls which he had learned, and remained behind; the spears were thrown, and some wounded: but before a second attack was made, Captain Spencer fired his first rifle-ball over the heads of the guilty tribe. The flash of the gun, the smoke, the whizzing of the ball over their heads, electrified the enemy, and made most of the friends tremble; and before the former could recover from their panic, a second ball sent them all flying, except the Englishman's own friends, who stood in awful silence. Then galloping after the fugitives, Charlie screaming over his head, "Ho! ho! what a row!" he fired both barrels of one pistol, and the rout was complete: they all disappeared, exclaiming, "Irru! irru!" On returning from the pursuit, and laughing at the effect which he had produced, he saw the body of a female lying on the ground; she had been speared, and was insensible from loss of blood, though not dead. He rode up to Ugat and told him, and she proved to be the missing woman; who, by the by, had been a willing fugitive, and was now struck, either by those who had taken her away, or by some of her friends. Captain Spencer proposed to staunch her wounds; but her relations refused, and carried her with them as she was. The injuries on the side of her tribe were very slight, yet they proceeded slowly with their burden. Warrup and Ugat therefore offered to take their friend home by a shorter path, and at a quicker pace; they seemed gloomy and unhappy, but thanked him very warmly for his interference, which they said had saved many lives; and when they, late at night, had seen him to his hut, they yet lingered, as if they had something distressing to tell him. He pressed them to say what was the matter; but they shook their heads, and answered that he had wished to go away, and they had wished to keep him a long time, but now they thought he had better go directly; they would bring him plenty of provisions, and Kinchela would tell him their reason when he was gone far. He was only too glad to profit by this change, and immediately made all his preparations; they were soon completed, and he snatched a short interval for sleep. Just before dawn his friends appeared with the supplies, which were lodged in the skins as usual; there was no fear of a scarcity of water, and the country was rich in resources of all kinds. The good creatures presented him with two ample opossum-cloaks, made by their wives, and a large bunch of feathers. To Kinchela they gave a cloak of kangaroo skin, with many instructions which way to proceed: there was no fear of falling in with the hostile tribe, as they had taken quite a contrary direction. Captain Spencer in return gave to each of them some gaily-coloured handkerchiefs for themselves and their wives, and two clasp knives, with which they seemed quite delighted. They walked with him for a few miles, repeated their directions to Kinchela, and placing their hands on the Englishman's shoulders, and touching his breast with their head, they took their leave with tears streaming down their cheeks.

It was now broad daylight; and though Kinchela was a little sorry to leave his comfortable quarters, the three dumb creatures seeming to be aware that they were going to resume their former habits, hailed their departure with infinite joy; the shaking of Gip was not forgotten; and Charlie, with plenty of native words in his vocabulary, which made a most ludicrous addition to his French and English, wound up his vociferations with "Very good, very good! ho! ho! hurra!" At night, after he had chosen a convenient station, Captain Spencer asked Kinchela to tell him why Warrup and Ugat had wished him to go away. He replied, that they had given him leave to tell, now he was far off—that the people were going to eat that young woman, and his friends did not like him to be there while they did so. "Then it is true," said Captain Spencer, "that people in this country eat men?" "Sometimes, Boccolo," replied Kinchela; "and one of the women who used often to come to our hut, carried the skull of a child in her bag which had been eaten some time ago." The Englishman shuddered, but perfectly appreciated the good feeling of Warrup and Ugat, which made them desire to spare him so revolting a spectacle.

Kinchela, who had visited this part of the country some years before, being in perfect possession of the route, they did not keep close to the river, but avoided its tortuous course, and merely came now and then upon its banks. Ponds, pools of water, small lakes and streams presented themselves, and signs of natives were frequent. This rendered it necessary to resume all their former vigilance; and they took it in turns to sleep during the night. After a long day's march, they bivouacked under a clump of trees on the top of a hill, Captain Spencer being always anxious to avoid low situations, or those which were much enclosed, for fear of surprise. Kinchela went to collect fire-wood, and gather a plant which he said was good for supper, and which very much resembled cress, while his master unloaded Tiger. The man returned very speedily, saying that on the side of the hill, in a plain, there were some natives about to bury one of their people, and he could show Captain Spencer a place from whence he could watch their proceedings, without being seen himself. The travellers accordingly stationed themselves, then Gip and Tiger were told to keep quiet, and the former to watch the things. The grave was already dug, and the body was wrapped in skins, and bound round with cords; the women and relatives uttered loud lamentations, scratched their noses and cheeks, tore their thighs, their breasts, and their backs with shells and pieces of flint, from which the blood flowed freely. The men at first stood outside with their weapons in their hands, then they closed round the grave, and the lamentations of the women were more vociferous than ever. A man went to the head of the corpse, and another to the feet; they cut the cords; the arms, which were crossed, were laid down by the sides; a gash was made by a sorcerer—the intestines pulled out, a piece cut off—the woman screamed louder and louder—a handful of green boughs was waved over the fire, and thrust into the body—the severed part of the entrails wrapped in fresh leaves, and put into a bag—the rest put back to their place with more leaves, and the body was again tied up. One relation violently jumped up, and screamed, seeming as if he were going to spear some one; but he was prevented, and the severed piece of intestine shown to him, as a proof that the deceased had died a natural death. A skin was spread at the bottom of the grave, and covered with boughs; the body placed east and west upon these; more boughs were thrown upon it, the earth was pushed in with the feet, then raised into a mound, and the whole covered with bark and netting. The shrieks were redoubled, and the party dispersed. Kinchela said that the women would come back alone in a little time, and cut themselves and cry afresh. The men had shorn their hair and beards, painted their heads and breasts with pipe-clay, and even put hot ashes on their heads to produce a singeing effect. The lamentations were continued at intervals during the night; but as they never mention the names of the dead, Kinchela could not ascertain who was gone, although he knew the tribe. His master asked him who the women were with caps on their heads made of pipe-clay; and he said they were the widows of the deceased.

CHAPTER XII.

Return to the river—Beautiful scrub—Bauhinia—Marjoram—Ornithorynchus—Natives become more frequent—Watching necessary—Another native funeral—Beautiful country—Casuarinæ—Chirping bird—Sorrel—Wood-ducks—Spiny Anteater—Women carrying dead bodies—Old woman—Flowers—Herd of wild horses—Blue mountains—Overlander—Cattle cross the river—Meeting of Captain Spencer and Mr. St. John—Captain Spencer entertains the Overlander—Conversation between the two gentlemen—Astonishment at Charlie—Mines of Adelaide—Murray river—Arrive at the river Darling—Character of natives—Mr. St. John gives introductions to Captain Spencer—The friends part with regret.

"KINCHELA," said Captain Spencer, as they started before sunrise, "we must go back to the river; for our roots and meal are getting low, so let us turn about." They proceeded through a rich scrub of the pendent Acacia,* the broad, green leaves of which drooped, and the blossoms of the richest yellow prevailed over all that part of the country. The trees had every day become more beautiful; it was not the season for their fruits, but their flowers were profuse. A Bauhinia, twenty feet high, was covered with white bunches; and a small bush, looking and tasting like Marjoram, gave the Englishman home recollections.

* Acacia pendula.

Salsolæ and Solani were plentiful in patches; and a shrub, looking like the Hawthorn, shed a delicious perfume. Kinchela took the shovel, Captain Spencer unloaded Tiger, and was walking up with the bags, when the man exclaimed, "Ho! ho!"— "Ho! ho!" said Charlie, "what's the matter?" and flew with the utmost curiosity, and perched himself on the boughs of one of the drooping trees close by, hoping to find food in the newly turned-up earth, which was disturbed by the shovel. "Kinchela have him," said he, holding up an animal which he had dug out of its hole, and which his master instantly, from its extraordinary appearance, recognized as the far-famed and much disputed Ornithorynchus paradoxus, which he had so much wished to see, and which Ugat had told him was so difficult to catch, from its quickness in burrowing the moment danger approached. It expired in a few minutes; and near it were two young ones, which had been deriving nourishment from the mother. "Does this beast lay eggs?" said Captain Spencer to his man. "Ho! ho! ho!" cried Kinchela, and went into a fit of laughter, which was echoed by Charlie, who added, "Hurra! hurra!" but to the astonishment of all the party, from the trees near by came another laugh, noisy and half-chattering, which was taken up by others; and for some minutes there was such an intense noise, that the Englishman thought they were about to be attacked by a numerous body of natives; but Kinchela laughed again, and said—"Not man, Boccolo, bird;* look at him in tree. He laugh in morning, laugh when sun goes; he eats snakes, lizards, plenty things." "I heard the same noise in North-western Australia," said Captain Spencer; "but not as loud or ridiculous as this." "That bird bigger," returned Kinchela; "small ones go everywhere." The skins of all the Ornithorynchi were carefully preserved, and they were the only incumbrances which the Englishman allowed himself to take; he did not know that specimens of this curious, duck-billed animal, with its mole-like propensities, were then common in his native country; at all events, they were rare in India, and were preserved for the doctor. Kinchela and Gip ate the bodies, but they were not tempting to their master.

The supply of roots made, the party turned away from the immediate vicinity of the river, and journeyed through a country which presented every beautiful variety of scene except lofty mountains; these were replaced by rocky hills, sometimes rising in abrupt precipices, sometimes looking like a mass of enormous fragments, piled one upon another; and then lower hills of sand-stone formed a series of undulating plains, or were covered with the loftiest trees. Upon the latter were

* Dacelo corvina, or Laughing Jackass.

many Pines,* with their tall, straight trunks, and crowns of leaves, each one looking as if it were fit for the mast of a ship. The Melaleuca and Leptospermum were also abundant, and Gum-trees of numerous kinds, often of enormous height, rose in various directions, while small streams and rich grass made Tiger perfectly happy. So rich a country was of course more thickly inhabited; and frequently small parties were met with, whose vicinity demanded the most careful vigilance, on account of their pilfering propensities. Captain Spencer had seen the Thugism of India, and therefore was well able to take precautions against marauders. Gipsy was invaluable, and seemed to understand that she must always be on the alert, and yet not fly into a fit of anger. It was curious to see how her manner of proceeding was altered since she came into Australia; and she was now as wary and quiet as she was before noisy and impetuous. The night they last turned from the river, she gave a short, stifled bark, which, however, was sufficient to rouse her master, who, without moving, whispered to her, "Good dog," and both watched without appearing to do so. Captain Spencer thought he saw something moving in the tree above him, and as he pretended to be asleep, that something was soon discovered to be a boy; for he dropped down, and for a minute or two stood close

* Callitris.

to the body of the tree; he then threw himself flat upon the ground, and was slipping himself along towards the baggage, when Captain Spencer whispered, " To him, Gip!" The dog seized his leg, and her master his arm, while he fired his pistol over his head, and gave him a good shaking. This noise awakened the heavy-sleeping Kinchela, whose practised eye soon detected a considerable body of natives running away; and as the Englishman only wished to alarm, he suffered the boy to run after them.

There was no accounting for the fact, but equally without reason, some of the natives were ferocious, and required the utmost courage and activity to keep them off, while others were anxious to conciliate and be friendly; some begged for everything which they saw, and even tried to take the baggage from before the owner's eyes, while others seemed not to expect or wish for anything whatever. Among these last, were a set of men who, from their koolimans, or vessels of bark for carrying water and provisions, gave them some kangaroo meat and roots, and asked them to come and see a dispute settled. They followed the natives to a hollow, where a large party was encamped; and one man seated in the midst, with his head hanging on his breast, was continually uttering a mournful cry. A pause ensued, and the cry was answered by some women: he rose and advanced, repeating his lamentations, and his companions also rose, and formed a circle round him. The men who had caused the death of the mourner's friend stood still with their spears in their hands; the son of the dead man was behind, and was the accuser; and the widows of the dead were with him wailing and crying. The avenger in the middle asked for a spear, but no one gave it to him; he then took one from the hands of his friends, and paced furiously up and down before the enemies, threatening, crying, and brandishing his weapon. After he had sufficiently excited himself, he lifted his spear, and each of the accused, to the number of five, held out his left arm, without shrinking. He thrust them all with his spear, after which he hung his head, and renewed his wailings and gesticulations for a time, and finished the affair by ordering all present to go to their different encampments. Captain Spencer gave a handkerchief to the man who had invited him to witness the ceremony; and refusing all solicitations to make a longer stay among them, he too pursued his route.

As the travellers advanced, they came upon several tributaries, which fell into the main river; but helpless as he was in regard to guidance—for he did not trust much to Kinchela, who had now gone beyond his knowledge, and had never before been to that part of the continent—he was rather uneasy, while following the main stream, to find that he was making much way to the north; however, he knew that he should still be in the track of settlers, and having no apprehensions for food or water, he freely gave himself up to the enjoyment of the beautiful country through which he passed—so much less monotonous than that of the west, and so much more fertile than that of the south. The climate, however, was much the same, and to him always delicious; for there was a buoyancy and elasticity in the atmosphere, both of east and west, which he had never experienced in any other quarter of the globe; and gave him both the power to travel, and the unfailing hope of ultimate success. There were many familiar forms of soil, vegetation, and animal life. Where the first was poorer than usual, the Casuarinæ were so numerous as to form a scrub, and the soft breezes sometimes swept their stringy and leafless branches, the sounds of which an imaginative person could easily have compared to the tones of an Eolian harp; a few beautiful parasites hung gracefully over them, and adorned this dark, gloomy tree with red blossoms tipped with green. A pale Mantis, with green and pink wings, often seemed to fly before him, as if a guide, and when he took it in his hand, it would turn its head round and look at him; the spur-winged Plovers again uttered their pretty, but plaintive cries; and beautiful varieties of Pigeons, especially the broze-winged, abounded; there was a large white Ibis, that was very picturesque, and the Parrots and Cockatoos were more beautiful and varied than ever; the Crinum often whitened the whole plain; there was also a shrub which looked like a white Lilac, the Calostemma raised its bunches of purple bells, and the Amaryllidæ were of a beautiful straw-colour. Heath-like shrubs now and then entangled Tiger's feet, and marked the presence of a loose sandy soil; while the Acacia pendula always prevailed in the fissures, on which snails were often found.

Having pulled up under the shade of a lofty tree, some birds on the lower branches appeared to be as much astonished at the presence of our travellers as other two-legged creatures had been. These birds had a peculiar chirp, which Captain Spencer imitated, upon which they flew round him with great familiarity, and some even perched on Tiger's back; he then whistled, and they replied, varying their answer with a number of the sweetest notes, very different to their chirp, which had been harsh and grating; the males and females seemed to differ much in plumage, especially about the head; they had not been seen before, and were not again; and on this solitary occasion they were disturbed by Charlie, who, when he saw them clustering round Tiger, dashed in among them, screaming, "Rogues! scoundrels! ho! ho!" the unbrotherly terms with which he always saluted other birds; and they dispersed. The Gum-trees, at times, formed the most charming, open forests, in which beautiful shrubs perfumed the air; Kangaroos were numerous; the most delicious yellow Sorrel sprang up under their feet, which afforded an excellent salad; and the river, when it occasionally swelled into a lake, was covered with Wood Ducks, whose long legs, formed for perching on trees, made them an easy prey to Kinchela, who dived under the water, and caught hold of them. There were, also, other kinds, frequenting the profuse quantities of Cyperus, which pushed forth their globular heads of flowers; and on these a spider, covered with spines, spun its geometrical webs.

Gipsy one day came upon a ball of spines, which she rolled about with her paw, nevertheless she was a little afraid of it; and when her master took it up, he found it was a living creature, and putting it gently down, and quietly watching it, it unrolled itself, and then he knew that it must be the Spiny Ant-eater, with spines, not only all over its body, but in the roof of its mouth, and also where the teeth of any other animal would have been. The Santalum often varied the landscape, with some of its branches drooping, while others stood erect, and with its elliptical leaves a **foot** and a half long. A small sort of Melon,* with not much flavour, but very cool and refreshing, was often found in the plains; and they saw some old women gathering them, who carried mummied bodies on their backs, under their opossum-cloaks: one of whom was more hideous than anything which Captain Spencer had ever seen in human form; her under-lip projected frightfully; her hair was short and gray, which is never becoming to dark complexions; she was like a living skeleton; and she chattered and screamed at the travellers as they passed, with a hurried fiery glance, and threatening gestures. There were traces of natives in every direction, such as broken mussel-shells, heaps of grass, ashes, &c.; and Kinchela found a rude implement, formed of a piece of iron stuck on to a stick with cement of gum. There was a purple Eremophila, a curious Jasmine, growing like a shrub, and an exquisite Abutilon; while Honeysuckles, large Bindweeds, and a magnificent Coral-tree, the seeds of which had a sweet, kernel-like flavour, were all spread before them to gladden their senses. Tiger revelled in new grasses; and new birds as well as new plants seemed to present themselves at almost every step. A Solanum, with tempting-looking berries, would have been avoided by the Englishman, from the fear of its being poisonous, but Kinchela unhesitatingly

* Cucumis pubescens.

stepped forward, and ate some of the fruit. They supped upon that of a trailing plant, which was shaped like an egg, and, when roasted, was excellent. The rains had commenced earlier in this part of the country, and this accounted for the greater development of fruit.

A tramping of many hoofs startled Captain Spencer from his watch, and Tiger also, who had been quietly sleeping on the sod. He rose suddenly, and stood with dilated nostrils, fore-legs stretched out, and his tail half raised, when a troop of horses came up, as if to claim him for their companion; their eyes flashed, they neighed, retreated, returned, and played all sorts of antics, being only kept off with the handle of a spear. For a moment poor Tiger was tempted to follow his brethren, and made a rush towards them; but the voice of his master recalled him, and he trotted back, and rubbed his nose against him, as if to say that he was sorry for having yielded, even for a moment. Kinchela was excessively alarmed at the appearance of so many big dogs, and gladly, but tremblingly, assisted his master in making several large fires around themselves, to keep away what he looked upon as monsters. They hovered about the party for several days, and caused considerable annoyance, for they came near enough to kick, and one even tried to bite Tiger. "Are these indigenous to Australia?" thought Captain

Spencer. "No; they must have escaped from the herds of settlers, and become irrecoverable." The marks of cloven hoofs were often visible on the soft banks of the river; but there were no signs of a spur to any of them, and the conclusion was that these were caused by unrecovered cattle.

Glimpses of very distant blue mountains now began to appear from time to time, when the travellers happened to mount a hill, and which Captain Spencer thought promised vicinity to civilized habitations, for he knew that a chain existed in Eastern Australia. On descending from one of these hills, they came upon a wide reach of the river, and determined to pass the night on its fertile banks. Beyond it, on the other side, was a thick wood; and before they could take up their position, from its covert issued merry and loud sounds, some of which Captain Spencer fancied were composed of English words, and his heart beat quickly at the hope of meeting his countrymen. Shortly after, thousands of cattle emerged from the trees, and rushed down the sloping bank which bordered the river. From another part came eighty or a hundred horses; and in advance of them was a man on horseback, wearing a round hat covered with oil-skin, mackintosh leggings, short jacket, and a short-handled whip, with an immensely long lash. Behind the cattle were three others, also mounted, and several natives with spears. The first had evidently come to reconnoitre, and to find the best spot for crossing the river; and there was something about him which seemed to say that he was the master of the lively and numerous procession.

It so happened that Captain Spencer, in following a native track, had stopped opposite the ford; but now fearing that he and his companions would be overwhelmed by the multitude as they came across, he removed to some distance. He tucked Gipsy on to his knapsack, and she peered over his shoulder; Tiger stood quietly by his side, with Charlie on his back; Kinchela, spears in hand, eagerly contemplated the unusual scene; and Captain Spencer himself stood still, resting on his gun. The grouping was beautiful, and the master of the herds was evidently struck by it, for he paused, and seem to scan it with a curious gaze. At last he called out, "Are you an Englishman? and do you know anything about the ford?" "I am an Englishman," replied Captain Spencer; "but as it is the first time I and my servant have been here, we are both ignorant of its depth; its situation is most probably where you now stand." The owner of the cattle plunged into the water, and ascertained the nature of the locality; he then returned, gave the signal for crossing, and himself assisted in driving and urging the beasts into the proper direction. It was a most animated scene: at first, horses and cattle refused to enter the water; then came the shouts and exclamations of the Europeans, the slashing of their long whips, the screams and cries of the natives, mingled with the snortings and bellowings of the beasts, and the barkings of large dogs. The refractory, instead of crossing, rushed along the side of the river, and, by their bad example, dispersed the others; then their masters galloped after them, the blows rained thickly on their hides, and they strove to regain the bush, or forest. The mounted horses, turning sharply on their haunches, got a-head of them, and their riders drove them back, forming a display of horsemanship which would have done credit to an Arab; and Captain Spencer longed to unload Tiger, and go to their assistance. At last, a few beasts, more docile or more frightened than the rest, were slashed and pushed into the water, and in a few minutes a large extent of the river was covered with heads and horns, the dogs swimming round and round to keep them from being too widely scattered.

At length all were safe over, and were driven to the plain beyond the hill, where there was excellent grass; and when collected into two parties, a watch was formed, and fires made at close intervals all around, both to prevent the herds from straying, and the incursions of natives. With

Gipsy still on his back, and his two other companions following him, Captain Spencer then advanced, his heart thrilling with pleasure as he heard the principal stranger say to his chief man, " We have done it well this time, and the horses and cattle are well broken in; we never passed a ford with so little trouble; but who can this be coming to us?" " He has been doing the same as ourselves," replied the driver, " and is now returning." " No, no," said the first speaker; " he has never driven a herd of cattle, I am sure; a pack upon his horse—which, by the by, is one of great value— an unknown bird on the top of the pack, a dog upon his knapsack, his clothes patched, and a native servant—who can he be?" Captain Spencer was much amused at the audible observations of the cattle-owner, who seemed to be quite careless, or unconscious that he was heard. The traveller was himself scanning the new arrival, who was a remarkably fine young man, about five-and-twenty years of age; and whose appearance, even in his travelling garb, was strikingly that of the gentleman, while the bronzed cheek told that he had been long exposed to the sun. The thick, clustering curls on his neck, the short, full, and glossy beard which encircled the lower part of his face, the clear sparkling eye, the broad chest and shoulders, the firm yet good-natured mouth, and the frank and animated expression of the whole countenance, would have made him a remarkable person anywhere; but to a wanderer, who had been so long from his own countrymen, and who had just been living entirely with savages, he looked like a being sent from another world. He dismounted, and stood to receive the soldier's salute, who, even in raising his misshapen grass hat from his head, created a favourable impression; and the courtesy was returned with a grace and polish of which even cattle-driving in the wilderness could not deprive a man of birth and education. "Have you come from Adelaide?" asked he. "No," replied the military man, "and I can scarcely tell you in a few words where I do come from. It is now some months since I have seen the face of an European, and very many since I heard my native tongue; I am Edward Spencer, Captain in the —— regiment of Bombay Native Infantry. Wounds and fatigue sent me in search of health; my vessel was wrecked on the northern coast, and I have found my way from thence to where I now am; part of the time with only my dumb companions, but since then, the native whom you see has been added to my followers, and to which addition I probably, under God's blessing, owe my existence. I could not have traversed the desert without his assistance. It is now my turn to inquire who—"—"Philip St. John, an Overlander," said the young man hastily, holding out his hand with frank cordiality; "all travellers are, or ought to be friends; you must share my damper to-day." "I do not doubt that damper may be very good, better food perhaps than I can give to you; but I am the oldest inhabitant of this part of the country, and therefore I must be allowed to provide your supper. Kinchela and I have a tolerable stock just now, but our mode of eating is very rough; therefore if you have a canteen with you, you had better furnish yourself with fork and spoon." Mr. St. John smiled, and said, "I accept your offer with as much friendliness as you make it; and while you prepare this noble repast, I will settle my men and my beasts for the night, and when we have eaten, you will tell me some of your adventures, will you not? I never had such an insatiable curiosity to know all about a person, as I have had ever since I caught sight of that plume of cockatoo feathers in your hat." "Agreed." said Captain Spencer; "people like to talk of themselves."

When Mr. St. John returned, the supper was set out in pieces of bark, in a profusion which surprised him. There were stewed Kangaroo meat, baked Duck, boiled Trefoil, which resembled Spinach; Sorrel salad, Cray-fish, and cakes of Grass-seed by way of bread, some powdered dust which resembled mustard,* and salt was supplied by small pieces of the salsolaceous plants. The native Melons, and the fruit of a Solanum, which tasted like an Apricot, formed the dessert; and the Overlander's surprise was frequently expressed in warm terms. "You will excuse the absence of wine," said his entertainer; "my friend Kinchela, with all his cleverness, has not been able to find that." "I have brandy," said Mr. St. John, drawing the flask from his pocket. "No, keep it all for yourself. Such things and I have long been in separate quarters; the only substance with which I have been able to flavour water here has been honey." "I must say, if this is your usual fare in the desert, I cannot pity you." "It is not always so abundant; this is a fertile spot, and we know how to take advantage of it, but there have been times when our hunger-belts have been drawn very tightly round us. Even here our bill of fare might be more meagre, if there had not been rain lately." "Yes," said Mr. St. John, "the great bane of Australia is the occasional droughts, which I am told are of rarer occurrence on the western coast. To the east we have been lately without rain for three years; and it is the observation of every one, that the climate is much less humid than it was when first inhabited by white men. But what

* From the wood of a Gyrostemon, which is a tree with bluish leaves.

have you made your bread of? it is ten times better than my damper, which is only flour, water, and salt." Captain Spencer told the Overlander, and then produced meal from roots, which he said he should taste on the morrow. "Have you found a substitute for tea? for there are some trees here which are said to taste like that plant." "I believe I know what you mean; I tried some once, but did not like the flavour, and I have done very well without." "But a cigar will perhaps be a treat?" "I smoked a great deal in India, but being now totally weaned from the habit, I will not resume it. I have had a great many lessons to learn; but I am thankful for them, and hope to be wiser in future." A fine dog, who had found out his master, now bound towards them, and received a portion of food, after which he made advances towards Gip, who received the civilities by showing her teeth and growling. Mr. St. John ordered the dog to be taken away; and while Kinchela put everything in order, and his master gave him instructions for the morrow, the Overlander made his final inspection of his stock and men, and then returned to Captain Spencer to enjoy his narrative. Kinchela wrapped himself in his kangaroo-skins, Tiger lay down by his master's side, and Gipsy seated herself on his knees; Charlie, however, was not to be seen. "My cautious bird," said his master, "is, I believe, frightened at numbers. I must whistle him back." The accustomed signal was given, and answered, and the bird flew to the spot, exclaiming, "Charlie's coming, all's right! Boccolo, Sahib, Ned Spencer!" "What an extraordinary creature!" said the Overlander; "how can he know what to say?" "He has been a great amusement to me," replied the traveller, "and I have taught him certain sentences for certain occasions, so that when these occasions recur, he always repeats them; I cannot tell you what a comfort this bird was to me, when I had no other thing to speak to; and he really is a droll, sensible creature, full of sly gravity and impudence." "I hope you are not sleepy," said Mr. St. John, "for I must have your history directly." The talking continued far into the night, Mr. St. John occasionally interrupting the narrator by his observations and questions, and then both slept from exhaustion. In the morning, when they had bathed, and resumed their dress, Mr. St. John, tucking his arm within that of his new friend, said, "Come with me and inspect the men and the stock; my drovers are good, honest fellows, and come from Scotland; and the natives make very good servants in this way, for here they are not tempted to drink. Do you know that I cannot go away to-day? I mean to be still your guest, as you have already taken upon yourself the office of host. I must talk a great dea' more with you, and hear about the capabilities of Western Australia for cattle-farms."

The friends breakfasted, and then the Overlander said, "Spencer, you must turn back, and come with me to Adelaide; I expect to make a good round sum of my cattle there, and you shall share it, and start with me on another expedition. You know the country, you know many of the natives, and I suspect we must shortly find a new field, into which we must conduct our enterprises; already the Murray, the twin river of the Darling, and much the finer of the two, has its banks lined with cattle stations, and the whole country will soon be covered with them; we are the pioneers, and perhaps we might, for our lifetime, find spots enough between this and Adelaide. But the mining property there increases, and the agricultural must, in a measure, suffer. Where we now stand, there will probably, in a few years, be the homestead of some settler; the plain will be divided into pastures, and the hills into sheep-folds; but you will come with me, Spencer?" "You forget," replied his friend, "that I am a soldier on leave of absence, and that I am not my own master. I confess, that were it not a point of honour and duty, I should be somewhat tempted; for if my wanderings have brought suffering, they have not been without their charms; and with such a companion as you are, I would willingly go all over the ground again, except the stony desert." "But what is your black fellow about in the river?" interrupted the Overlander. "Diving for fish, for our dinner." "Really, you know all the resources of the country; you are exactly the man: I should blunder through with that heavy damper, brandy and mutton, which we cook in a great pot; while you, with your more acute perceptions, turn every thing to account with absolute refinement. "And yet," said the soldier, "it has only been for the gratification of my appetite." "Depend on it, it would be the same in everything." "You are complimentary; I must teach you some of our secrets; come and see our oven, now going to work upon the stock for our future journey. I have had the supply doubled for you, which may last a few days."

Mr. St. John was so pleased with the oven, that he called his men to inspect it, and watched the process of Kinchela's and Captain Spencer's arrangements: the steaming with wet grass was first performed; then the oven was cleaned again, heated, and made fit for baking, and just as it was closed for that purpose, Charlie flew back, saying, "Boccolo, Ned Spencer; such a row!" and stationed himself near Tiger. "There are natives near, and in numbers, too," said his master; "I have taught him to give me this warning, and I would advise you to be on the look-out for them.

They are always more or less afraid of cattle and horses; but some of the tribes about here are very mischievous, and where you least expect them, the plains will teem with their numbers."

The guns were loaded, and watch set, when Kinchela, mounting a tree, told his master that there were "plenty black fellows" to the west of them, and Captain Spencer advised that a volley, of powder only, should be fired in that direction, which would probably disperse them. The orders were given and obeyed, and the hostile party decamped; but the travellers now joined the Overlanders, and took their turns in watching.

Kinchela was most successful in his captures and cooking, and so pleased at the praises which he received, that, of his own accord, he again repaired to the river, and when the Overlanders departed, had a quantity of fish ready for them. "That native lad," said Mr. St. John, "is already half-civilized." "I have done my best," observed Captain Spencer, "and I am surprised at my own success; I believe he now prays with a tolerable notion why he does so; the trial will be at Sydney, where I may not be able to attend to him as closely as I could wish. But why do you not try to educate your natives?" "Because I never thought of it, in the first place; and in the second, I should have much to undo; they have all either been born among white men, or lived with them from their earliest age, seen the worst of our people, and their slight degree of taming has taken from their energy, without planting anything in return. It has often come across me, how unjustly we, generally speaking, behave to these aborigines." "Among them," observed Captain Spencer, "are some of superior intellect, such as Warrup and Ugat; but I do not know if they are capable of receiving instruction; has it been tried?" "Yes," answered Mr. St. John; "I do not know much about Sydney, but there are schools there, and at Adelaide they have learned to read, write, and cipher with facility. I do hope that the amount of their degradation will be diminished at every new settlement, and that we shall never again hear of their being fired upon like so many wild beasts, or being executed according to our laws, which they do not understand, and in utter ignorance that they had committed any crime. Their greatest vice about Sydney is their intoxication, which, you know, prevents all progress. What you told me last night, about their inherited hunting-grounds, prevented me from sleeping soundly, and long before you were awake, my mind was labouring under a feeling of usurpation, which made me very uncomfortable; and yet, how are they to be civilized, and receive the blessings of Christianity, unless we come among them? That aboriginal question is a difficult one to settle, and only of two things can we be certain—that we have no right to treat them ill, and that we cannot blame them, when, after we have usurped their lands, and driven Kangaroo away, as they say, which, in other words, is to deprive them of their sustenance, they strive to turn us out by the only means in their power, physical force, administered in the only style of warfare with which they are acquainted."

"Did you not see the Murray at all?" continued Mr. St. John, after a pause. "I cannot answer any geographical questions," replied Captain Spencer; "without a chart, and with an erring compass, I can but guess at what I saw, further than that I was in the Bight of Australia, to the east of King George's Sound, and that I believe I skirted Lake Torrens. You tell me we are now on the Darling." "It is well for me," returned his friend, "that you are here, because I have met you; but you would have been delighted with the Murray, which is never, like this river, reduced to a chain of ponds. but flows continuously, and overflows its low lands every year, at the rate of an inch per day, and has a course of from thirteen to fifteen hundred miles. In many places it is bordered by yellow, perpendicular cliffs, in which are to be found not only shells, but various bones and sharks' teeth. The land to the south of it is grassy, and full of beautiful flowers, chiefly Orchidæ of every colour; and beyond this are low sand-hills, leading to flats like dry sea-marshes, covered with salsolaceous plants, which are very wholesome for the occasional feeding of cattle. There is a sort of liquorice, too, which grows on these plains, and the beautiful Nitraria Australis is abundant on the southern bank, which the natives eat raw, stem and all. I presume that what are called the Darling Downs will be converted into cattle stations, and I do not see why they should not be as fine a pasture district as that of Port Philip and its neighbourhood, called Australia Felix; though the distance from a sea-port would make the transport of wool, hides, and tallow, rather difficult."

"You were speaking of the mines of Adelaide,' said Captain Spencer; "what do they find in them? The natives with whom I lived told me they knew Adelaide well, and said there were many men there who went to the mountains, dug very deep holes, and got heavy stones out of them. I am sure I have almost everywhere seen plenty of iron in large pure masses, as well as mixed with sand and other things; also copper, after I left Lake Torrens, and I suspect gold." "Just the very things," replied Mr. St. John; "both Mount Barker and Mount Lofty, which, by the by, are fossiliferous, are crossed by igneous rocks, containing rich metallic veins, and Adelaide stands upon the same sort of soil. In Mount Lofty, on which grow large stringy bark trees, is what is called the Burra Burra stone, which yields an enormous supply of copper, and in Mount Barker lead is found; but it is difficult to say where metals do not exist in that district; the small quantity of gold which has been met with is of the purest kind, and there are indications of quicksilver. The copper was discovered in 1848, by a Mr. Dutten; and considerable difficulty arose in making the mines profitable, from being obliged to send the ore to England to be smelted, which was very expensive; now, however, some one has come from England who has established smelting works, and the mines go on like wild fire. The Burra Burra galleries are cut through solid blocks of ore, and every precious stone has been found there except the Diamond, especially Opal of the most precious kinds. The mines are worked by associations, or companies, and more than a thousand men are employed in them. The Burra Burra last year yielded a profit of 52,000*l*., which was distributed among individuals." "How far are these mines from the town of Adelaide?" asked Captain Spencer. "Ninety miles," was the reply: "the district in which they are situated is very barren, and separated from the rest of the colony by a range of high hills, which is rather an obstacle to the conveyance of the ore to the port. At present it is all carried by bullock-drays; and much difficulty would, I think, be found in making a tram-road across. The expenses of working will, I suppose, be diminished by the discovery of coal near Sydney; but a mine of that mineral near Adelaide would be invaluable." "Could I not see these metallic mountains from Lake Torrens?" inquired Captain Spencer. "I should think not," said Mr. St. John, "for they are not of great elevation; they run from north to south, and are about fifteen or twenty miles broad. No one knows what may happen there; for two shocks of earthquakes have been felt in Adelaide, and these cannot occur often without causing alterations. Among other odd things, I was once at Adelaide, when some remarkable visitations of birds* occurred in the town and neighbourhood; you could almost have walked upon them, and they reminded me of locusts, only that they were not destructive. They were never before seen there, and have never returned."

"With these mining riches I should suppose, then, that Adelaide will never be conspicuous as an agricultural colony." It has many capabilities for such; and there is a sort of cotton-tree there, very like the real Gossypium, called Sturtia, after that brave Captain Sturt, who has been further into the interior than any one else; unless, indeed, you exceeded him." "I dare say I did not; for

* Tribonyx.

he probably carried water and food with him.' "Well! you have done wonders. I cannot think how you contrived to find out what was good to eat when left by yourself." "I certainly was puzzled, because the general knowledge which I possessed turned out to be of little or no use. I knew that it was dangerous to meddle with Umbelliferæ; but I only met with two specimens in the West, one of which was the Wild Carrot; but when a man depends entirely on himself, his wits are sharpened, and thoughts are put into his head. I made one or two mistakes, as that of the Zamia nuts; and of course, without Kinchela, I should never have thought of eating the roots of the Gumtrees, and some other things. Tiger's sagacity often directed me, and Gip brought me many a meal. But a word or two more concerning the natives; if I have spoken favourably enough of them to interest you in their behalf, it is not because I am insensible to their defects; for while I make allowance on the score of their being savages, I must not conceal from you that, in some points, their morality is even more lax than any I ever heard of; and I should think the females the most degraded and ill-treated of the human race; yet they are capable of gratitude and attachment. All these people know they must be conquered eventually by the white race; but this does not subdue their energetic spirit. While I try to enlist you in their behalf, I must caution you against the extreme cunning, which they consider to be a virtue. Recollect they are never without their weapons; and while they appear to be unarmed, their spears and clubs are concealed close by. Even while they have advanced with boughs in their hands, as tokens of peace, they have been dragging their spears through the grass between their toes, not for any premeditated attack on me, but fear that I should be treacherous. Nomadic as they are, you may meet with my friends; and I am sure my name, Boccolo Tence, as they call me, will awaken kind recollection; but on this they may build extortionate demands. I owe them some reparation for the life which self-preservation obliged me to sacrifice; and I should like to extort a promise from you, that you would never fire upon to hurt them, till you have given time for their first impulse to subside; nevertheless, trust them not, entirely, at any time." "But you trust Kinchela?" "I do, because I consider him as peculiarly situated, and utterly separated from the influence of tribe and relations; and moreover my destruction would probably involve his own. But you start to-morrow, you say?"

"Yes; and I feel that some account of myself is due to you. Brought up at Eton, and a younger son, I was intended for the army; but in peaceful times your Indian service is the only one of activity, and I felt myself full of enterprise and strength. I therefore asked my father to give me my younger son's portion, and let me make my own way. My lady mother—kind, good soul—was shocked at the idea of my coming to a convict land, which was all she knew of it; but I talked her over, and here I am. This is my third overland journey, and I have been successful. It was my intention to return as soon as I had acquired a certain sum; but at present there is a charm in this wild life which attaches me to the place, and I feel as if I could not as yet go back to the old-world forms. Moreover, from your conversation, new thoughts have come over me, and I appear to have a higher purpose. If I do ever acquire influence, I promise to do all the good I can. But how shall I hear from you; for you must nurture the good feelings which have sprung from you? I must make you a chart for your guidance, and while I do so, give me your instructions." Thus speaking, Mr. St. John took some paper from his pocket-book, and sketched the route which his friend ought to follow. He then wrote an introduction for him to a Mr. Onslow, the proprietor of an estate on the Hunter river.

Putting the papers into Captain Spencer's hand, the Overlander continued to speak, saying, "I have noted down a few landmarks. You must make northing, and then come south again, and you will have to cross yon blue mountains. My friends, the Onslows, will receive you with affection for my sake, and will put you in the way of getting to Sydney. Hospitality is everywhere shown in this country; but do not be tempted to stay anywhere except with the Onslows. I think you will be at first taken for a bush-ranger; in fact, that was my first opinion of you, and I believe it was your elegant hat that put it into my head." "Not a word against my hat," interrupted Captain Spencer, with mock gravity; "it is a sample of my genius, and the most comfortable head-covering I ever had." "Well," resumed his friend, "ask your commander-in-chief to adopt it in the regiment; but I must put you on your guard against these escaped felons, for you are coming into their neighbourhood. Their impudence and daring are sometimes even laughable, and their cool courage worthy of a better cause; but they are, nevertheless, troublesome companions, and murder is not unfrequent among them. Now for your address." "I had better give you that of my agent in Bombay; always put your name outside your letters, as I shall have especial orders about them. I can scarcely believe that we met as strangers the day before yesterday, and now that it is such pain to part." "My dear fellow," said the Overlander, "believe that this feeling is mutual. I am sure we shall meet again." "If not here," said Captain Spencer, lifting the despised grass hat from his head, "we shall when both are called up for our final judgment; and may we be admitted together into that Heaven which is, or ought to be, the object of our existence! My lonely travels, my marvellous preservation, the majesty of the wilderness, have made me a deeper thinker than I have yet been; and I have no doubt the best lessons for both of us have been learned in Australia."

A pause ensued for a few moments, which was broken by the quick, ardent Overlander. "Do not suppose," said he, "that I am unobservant of the highest of all duties; your books were all drowned, therefore you shall have my pocket Bible." So saying, he put the sacred volume into the hands of the traveller. A flush of pleasure crimsoned the sun-burnt cheek of the soldier. "It is, indeed, a treasure," he said; "but what can I bestow in return? unless, indeed, you will have my hat?" "Not your hat, but bestow the plume upon me, which I will keep for your sake for ever; but we can exchange pistols, though not shots," added he, smiling, "and that will be another remembrance between us: the superior value of yours shall be your present; you will soon manage mine. Teach Charlie to say Philip."

Fish and roots were supplied as plentifully as time would allow by Kinchela, who had been active in procuring and preparing them; the cattle were in motion, the friends shook hands in silence, but a liquid lustre glistened in the eyes of each. Captain Spencer watched the Overlanders till they were about to enter a wood; handkerchiefs were waved for the last time, and then he thoughtfully and sadly turned towards the river. "Come, Kinchela," said he, "let us cross directly; and since we have a sheep for our dinner, we need not stop to get more provisions." "Boccolo too much sorry," said the native; "but we soon see plenty more white fellows. Kinchela get roots." The little party forded the river in safety, and taking the direction pointed out by Mr. St. John, they bent their way to the long-desired settlement.

CHAPTER XIII.

Captain Spencer romantic — Birds — Native — Captain Spence. catches him, and relieves his hunger—Fairy-like plains—Bul comes down the hills, and gentlemen on horseback after him—Insects, and their webs and nests—Harry Blunt attacks Captain Spencer—Harry caught and overcome—His companion stunned—Captain Spencer kind to the bush-ranger—Captain Spencer goes on—Forest flowers—Wooden pear—Lemons—Flying foxes—Native cherry—Beautiful plants—Green frogs—Lizards—Out-station—Shepherds—Laughing Jackass—Robin—Knife-grinder—Fish and its nest—Storm—Sorcerers make storms—Pine forest—Plants—Metamorphosis of beetle—Head keeper's station—Captain Spencer hospitably received—Tall black man's history—Harry Blunt's visits—Head keeper and wife very kind and hospitable—Untidy and deserted stations—Deserted townships—Ascend mountains—Meet drays—Ants—Come to the river—Arrival at Mr. Onslow's farms.

THE spirit of romance came strongly upon Captain Spencer, and a lingering regret that he had not turned back with Mr. St. John seemed to fetter his endeavours to move fast onwards. Early in the evening, he seated himself where, from the rising ground, through the open forest, he could at some distance behold the spot where he had parted with his friend, and calling Charlie to him, he endeavoured to teach him that friend's name. The bird, however, stammered so much at the surname, and pronounced it so badly, even after repeated efforts, that his master was obliged to confine himself to the word of Philip; and Charlie most triumphantly for a few days screamed out "Friend Philip," as he always did every new acquirement, and then laid it by in his memory to come out with it again when least expected. As his master sat with his eyes still gazing in the direction taken by his late most congenial companion, his reverie was suddenly interrupted by the Laughing Jackass, and its merry peals seemed to mock his sadness. "Vile bird!" he exclaimed; again came the cheerful sound, repeated in various directions, till at last Charlie himself caught the note, burst into a loud "Ha, ha!" and seemed to go into fits of laughter: it was irresistible; Kinchela caught the infection, both Tiger and Gip pricked up their ears, and Captain Spencer himself joined in the chorus.

There were still many weary miles to go, and the travellers started early on the following day. The scenery became more than ever beautiful, and birds, insects, and flowers multiplied upon them, the former to a much greater degree than Charlie liked, for Cockatoos, Parrots, Parrakeets, common as Sparrows in England, drove him to Tiger's back, where he sat muttering to himself, "Rogues! scoundrels!" Then there were Pigeons, Quails, the native Turkey,* with its small portion of

* Talegalla.

brains, having a nest constructed like that of the Leipoa; the noble Crane,* the Wood-Swallows,† which huddle together like a swarm of bees; immense Nightjars, which lie under the trees and bushes all day; and many old acquaintances from the south and west, all affording food, or subjects for admiration. On watching by the fire in the night, however, Captain Spencer heard the notes of several new birds, and the little flying Opossum dropped from bough to bough. Both men never slept at the same time; for the country was thickly inhabited, and as they passed during the day, they frequently saw natives peeping at them from behind the trees. On one occasion, Gip, whose recent education had taught her not to bark suddenly, raised her head, and gave a low whine. "It is a native," thought the Englishman; "I wonder if he be going to spear me." He made the peculiar cry which he had learnt of the tribes on the other part of the Darling, but no answer was returned; he uttered another, and another, but there was no response. "We are mistaken, Gip," said he, and he rested his head upon his knees. In about half an hour Gip was again uneasy, and sat upright; the noise was repeated, and it was scarcely louder than if a fly had touched a leaf, but it was a little nearer. Captain Spencer's gun was close to him on the ground, the

* Antigone Grus Australasianus.   † Artamus sordidus.

rustling was repeated, and Gip had an inward convulsion, as if to stifle her bark, and then there was a slight movement of the gun. "Aha!" thought the traveller, "you do not know that it is fastened round my wrist with a leathern thong." A hand was laid upon the gun, and Captain Spencer grasped it. "To him, Gip!" said he, and in a moment the dog had a leg between her teeth. Kinchela was roused. "Kinchela, get up," said Charlie, half asleep: and although he made violent efforts to escape, the intruder was caught. "You speak Inglis?" said Kinchela; the man was silent. "Boccolo very good man," continued Kinchela, "only black fellow say if plenty more wid him." No notice was taken of this speech, and then Captain Spencer tried to make him speak, by addressing him in a gentle tone of voice. The man fell on his knees before him, and in broken English entreated that he might be allowed to go away. "Where do you come from?" asked Captain Spencer: "why did you try to take my gun?" "Oh, massa," said the man, "they hunt poor black fellow, they kill him; he want gun to save him, he no touch massa; let him go, poor fellow, let him go." "Are you hungry?" asked Captain Spencer. "Berry hungry," was the answer. "Kinchela, blow up the fire, so as to let me see the man, and then give him something to eat." Provision was now put into his hand, and Captain

32*

Spencer said, "Here is something to eat; never take anything from a white man which he does not give you. Let go, Gip," and then relaxing his own hold, the man was free; he paused for a moment, as if wishing to say something, but the words died within his lips, and he darted away with almost incredible speed. "That black fellow," said Kinchela, "do something very bad." "Why do you think so?" "Because he not got spear, not got waddie, not gin. He run away when Boccolo good to him."

The next morning the travellers were up early, and a short time after, they found a bag on the ground, such as the women carry. "That black fellow had his gin," said Kinchela; "here is her bag." "Look into it, and see what is inside," said Captain Spencer. Three snakes, some small mucilaginous fishes, and a woman's skull, were all the contents. "What is this for?" asked the Englishman. "For black fellow to drink out of," answered Kinchela; "perhaps it was the gin's mother." Captain Spencer shrugged his shoulders, and said, "put some cakes of meal into the bag, and leave it where you found it. I dare say the woman will return, and is not very far off even now."

Leaving the river, the party crossed some exquisite and fairy-looking plains, bounded by sandhills; and as they came near to the latter, they saw a large bull leaping and gliding down the very steep sides as if it were mad. As soon as it gained the level ground, it started off as rapidly as possible, with its tail erect; and made for the forest which Captain Spencer had just left. Immediately after him came two horsemen and their dogs, down the same apparently impracticable descent. One of the large dogs lost his footing, and rolled down; but, after stopping a minute to recover his breath, he got up, shook himself, and bounded after the others, in pursuit of the noble bull. The horses slid down upon their haunches, the riders (evidently Englishmen) keeping a sharp pull upon their mouths; and when arrived at the bottom, away they went as hard as they could, without seeing Kinchela or his master. "That is the boldest riding I ever saw," said Captain Spencer; "they must be hunting stray cattle; but this makes it evident that we are now approaching the precincts of white men; and strange to say, my caution and vigilance must be redoubled." He looked well to his rifle and pistols, and told Kinchela to keep his spears ready, but to be sure not to throw them without orders.

On went the quartett, through forest and glade, traversing the most luxuriant country. An infinite variety of insects were to be seen; curious-looking, spotted Caterpillars with turned-up tails; brown Butterflies; a variety of large brown or yellow Locusts with black marks; Moths with fringed antennæ, of peculiar shape; Pangolin Flies, which stung Tiger; Phasm Beetles of singular form; Spiders with thick hairy legs; Epeiræ, which spun yellow webs as they do in Borneo; and numbers of curious insect-nests, hanging so plentifully upon the trees as to look like fruit. They were formed of a very thick web, and strengthened outside with pieces of small twigs, neatly rounded at the ends, and made to adhere to the web. Captain Spencer destroyed one, and found it lined with a soft, white, silken web, within which was a large white caterpillar; a discovery which he did not impart to Kinchela, fearing he would stop and destroy all the nests for the sake of eating the inhabitants. There were many ants of different kinds, one of which amused Captain Spencer, as he sat at breakfast one morning, by making a perpendicular hole in the ground, round the entrance of which it built a wall, sloping outwards in the shape of a funnel. While watching this clever little workman, he heard a noise like the growling of a dog, and thinking it might be a Dingo come to attack Gip, hastily turned to drive it away; but he saw nothing save a black Beetle, as big as a bird, and carrying another insect, something like a Grasshopper, and he was convinced that the sound proceeded from this creature.

On the borders of a lovely little lake, surrounded

on three sides by verdant hills, which were speckled with half-wild cattle, the travellers on the fourth side met with a wood, through which they had to pass, and where, as he rested in the shade, Captain Spencer was surprised at the salutation of "Halloo there! pull up, I say! Harry Blunt wants to see what's in your pack, and perhaps he wants to swop horses with you." "And who is Harry Blunt?" said Captain Spencer, drawing one of his pistols from his belt, and putting it on full cock. A man on horseback rode immediately in front of the traveller, clad in boots, leathern leggings, fustian jacket, and a white hat stuck on one side of his head, ornamented with different coloured ribbons, altogether presenting a reckless appearance. For a moment he seemed to quail before the steady, unshrinking gaze of the stranger; but he dismounted from a horse which had evidently been ridden long and hard, and with an impudent swagger went up to Tiger. "Touch him at your peril," said Captain Spencer, pointing his pistol at him; "you are a dead man, if you lay but a finger on him." Harry had both pistol and rifle, but he did not offer to use them; he, however, drew a long knife, and was about to rush on the stranger; who, with great presence of mind, dashed his arm to the ground, and fired through the top of Harry's hat. The man staggered, but recovering himself, he was about to make another sudden attack, when

Kinchela came up from behind, and thrust a spear into his arm, and Gip plunged her teeth into his leg-coverings. At this moment appeared a still more lawless ruffian, leading a horse in still worse condition than Harry's, and walked up to Tiger. The well-known order to dance was given. Tiger's paws came into action, and the man lay senseless on the ground. "Hold," said Captain Spencer to his antagonist; "I have traversed this wild country north, west, and south, and have escaped injury from its savage inhabitants; shall one of my own countrymen behave worse to me than they have done? I guess what you are, Harry; your companion is disabled, you are pinned through the arm by my servant, and you may consider yourself in my power. I do not belong to any of the settlements in this country, and have therefore no authority to make you my prisoner, consequently you shall pass on without further molestation; Kinchela, withdraw your spear." The native obeyed, and the blood gushed from the wound; the man looked at his arm, then at the party before him, and remained motionless. "Come," said Captain Spencer, "I am an old soldier, and will bind up your wound; it is not made with a war-spear, and will soon heal." Harry stood almost passive as his jacket was removed, the shirt-sleeve tucked up, the edges of the wound drawn close together, and then bound up tightly with one of Captain

Spencer's handkerchiefs. "Are you hungry?" asked the latter. "Yes," said the man: "we have ridden far to-day, and I have no powder, or you would not have conquered me." "Well," said the traveller, "you shall have something to eat. Kinchela put some meat and cake out. Now eat," he continued, " and we will do something for your jaded horses—leave go, Gip—your companion is stunned, not killed; but he will scarcely be able to ride to-day. My horse and I are inseparable; if you take him, you take me, and I am an awkward person to deal with." Harry hung his head; half sulky and half ashamed, he devoured the food which was put before him, while he appeared to be much astonished at the treatment which he experienced, and he looked around as if he suspected there was some stratagem. He seemed to be also surprised when Kinchela and Captain Spencer washed the horses of himself and companion, and rubbed their legs. The poor animals were of great beauty and value, evidently accustomed to care, and turned their large eyes gratefully upon those who were now doing their utmost to administer to their comfort; they looked as if they had not been long from the stables of one of the settlers.

Harry's fierce hunger appeased, and his heart softened by the unusual manner of his new acquaintance, his face now assumed quite a different expression. " Harry," said Captain Spencer, as he ate with him, " there is something in your look which tells me you would be a better man if you had the opportunity of becoming so." Harry coloured, and said, " I have gone too far." " It is never too late," said his entertainer. " I would give anything to be what I was once," continued Harry, with much emotion; " I was tempted, fell into bad hands and bad courses, and was transported. I was set to work, and beaten by the overseer for a fault of which I was not guilty. This maddened me, and I struck him a heavy blow, under which he fell. I did not intend it should be fatal, but it was supposed to be so. I was, of course, closely imprisoned, and I found myself along with that man; he told me that I was sure to be hung; he had prepared everything for his escape, and I consented to accompany him; he contrived to file away our irons; we were strong and active, and could swim well; we threw ourselves out of a window, crossed the water to escape the blood-hounds, and have led a bush-life ever since; he, poor fellow, breathes, but I think it will be long before he recovers himself; and I dare not stay with him, for I know the officers are upon our track. He has made me worse than I was before, and put me foremost on all occasions because I was the best-looking.* I am glad, however, to say that I did not kill the overseer, for I have seen him since, alive and well. Whoever you may be, sir, you have spoken kindly to me, when it was in your power to kill me, and when you would have been justified in doing so in self-defence. This is the first act of kindness which I have received since my sister took leave of me in an English prison. If you would add to your goodness, sir, by not betraying me, I should be grateful."

But as no murder can be brought against you, Harry, why not surrender, submit to your punishment, and try by good conduct to regain some degree of respectability?" "You know not what it is to be an escaped convict, sir, or what a man has to undergo if retaken." "You are sure to be that, sooner or later, unless you are killed in some encounter with the police. However, I shall not give any information concerning you; my way lies in that direction, and I expect you to take an opposite course; and as I do not wish to expose you to destruction, I caution you against those hills to the north-west, for gentlemen are among them, hunting stray cattle. Here is your knife—I shall not give you any powder, for I dare not trust you with it, but here are some fishing-hooks; the river will afford you plenty of food; besides which, make yourself a spear, and use it for other sorts of provision, as we have done. I shall place meat by your companion, in case he should recover, and I think he will." "God will reward you, sir, if such a one as I may say that." "Ask him to forgive and help you, Harry: here is some meal for present wants; do not press your poor horses too much." Harry coloured, hesitated, was about to speak, then stopped himself; and Captain Spencer asked him if he wished to say anything more. "I should like to know your name, sir," was the reply. Captain Spencer told him; and Harry then took off his hat, and stood gazing at the travellers as they departed, with his eyes full of tears; and when they last looked back at him, he was still standing, as if to catch a final glimpse of them. The horses would have gladly associated themselves with Tiger, but Captain Spencer knew not where to take them; he, therefore, was forced to resign one to Harry; and he tethered the other so as to be able to procure grass, until his rider should recover.

The forest through which Captain Spencer now passed was of Gum-trees; but they did not grow close to each other, and occasional openings made the path exceedingly beautiful. Wherever the sun could penetrate, the most exquisite shrubs and flowers adorned the glade. "Surely," thought he again, "the eastern side must be the most beautiful; and yet several of these gorgeous forms are familiar to my eyes. I must have passed several without particular notice, in my earnest wish to press forward, and my anxiety about sustenance;

but although I saw several Casuarinæ, I never saw these two plants hanging over them as they do now." One had nothing to recommend it, apparently, but its exquisite scarlet blossoms, with their fragrant odour, like that of a Honeysuckle;* but as he stopped to examine the other,† Kinchela gathered one of its parasitical roots, and asked his master to follow his example, and eat it; he did so, and found it to be full of starch, and to smell like ottar of roses. "Certainly," continued Captain Spencer, "I did *not* see those weeping-willow Acacias, nor that white flowering shrub, whose flowers are red in the centre,‡ nor that peppery plant, with its strong scent, and long, narrow, drooping leaves.§ Then, again, that plant with dark shining leaves, which are white underneath, and hang round the stem like a staff-officer's plume, is new; and this charming Ranunculus, like the Buttercup of my childhood, never gladdened my eyes before. But what have we here? this must be the Wooden Pear, which cannot be eaten."‖ Captain Spencer tried to put his teeth in it, but in vain; it was like a feather in weight, and the leaves of the tree were very small. "Tiresome thing," said he, throwing it away; "I suppose you would not be here, if you were not good for

---

* Loranthus linearifolius. † Cymbidium.
‡ Damasonium ovalifolium. § Geijira parviflora.
‖ Xylomelum pyriforme.

something; but you are very tantalising. These, however, are delicious little lemons; and that is the rose-coloured Eugenia. Kinchela, we must have some of that fruit." Kinchela dropped his spears, climbed the tall tree, and brought down some of its refreshing, but astringent apples. "Boccolo know better than black fellow," said the native; "Kinchela not see it before." "But you know this, Kinchela?" said his master, holding up a fruit, turning black from green and amber-colour. "Yes, Boccolo, very good!" returned he, devouring a handful.

The Flying Foxes in these parts appeared to live upon a small, but oval, acid fruit, with a stone in it, having a bitter kernel; and more than once, what the Englishman knew must be the native Cherry* was to be seen. It looked like an Arbor Vitæ, and now thought he, " I shall see the outside stone. Why, the berry is like that of the yew, and just as insipid in taste. Certainly, if it be the land of flowers, Australia is not the land for fine fruits. Yonder, however, is a magnificent specimen of beauty."† It was a plant six feet high, as straight as a walking-cane, having large green leaves, like those of an English Oak in shape and colour, all the way up, and the whole crowned with a wide-spreading tuft of scarlet and crimson petals, surrounding a cone or pyramid of trumpet-

* Exocarpus cupressiformis.   † Telopia speciosissima.

shaped florets in the middle, five inches high; and it sometimes put forth branches like a candelabrum. "There is a blue starry flower, like a very open Harebell, and a deep rose-coloured Convolvulus, among the grass; but can this be a Fuchsia? the berries are like currants. I have seen this before; it is a sort of Cranberry, I think; and there is a splendid Bignonia,* with glossy green leaves, and flowers like cream-coloured Foxgloves."

"Are you going to eat those pretty, brilliant, green frogs, Kinchela?" said his master; "we have plenty of food without taking them." "They very good," said Kinchela, putting them into the fire which he had lighted for cooking their supper. "Look there, Boccolo," continued he. Captain Spencer turned his head, and saw a round piece of the soil lifted up like a trap-door, which fell back as if it had a hinge. "Gip, come here, and don't disturb that creature," said Captain Spencer, much interested, and the dog's curiosity had been equally excited. A hairy, gray spider came out, peeped all round, and then went back and sat just inside, so that it could not be seen above. No prey arrived, and the spider walked out, which gave the human watcher an opportunity of examining its dwelling. It was some inches deep, had a curve at the end, and in order to prevent the earth from falling in, it was lined with a fine web; the

* Bignonia Australis.

lid, covered in the same way, being formed within of earth, and the hinge also of web. Two lizards were not far off; one a bloated, broad thing, lying with its mouth open, and showing a blue tongue. It did not get out of Gip's way; and when she turned round and worried it, it started up fiercely, and had she not been very nimble, would have inflicted a serious bite. The other was much larger, and more active, and was climbing a tree; its tail was twenty inches long, it had a sharp knowing head, was speckled black and white, was covered with close, hard scales, and its teeth were movable, like those of a snake. The party encountered numbers of the latter reptiles, some of which were handsomely marked; especially one, which was like Mosaic work. Those which were brown and black, Kinchela said, were all fatal. There were also scorpions, and two sorts of centipedes.

Some days after the adventure with the bushranger, the travellers came upon a beautiful valley surrounded by at least a hundred small hills of limestone, which occasionally peeped out from the grass with which they were otherwise covered; some slender streams wound between them, and were shaded by trees and shrubs. "What a charming place for a station!" thought Captain Spencer; and others were of the same opinion, for sheep were grazing upon the hills, and a solitary wooden hut stood at one end of the valley.

Captain Spencer went to it, and found that it was occupied by two men, one only of whom was at home, and who was much surprised at the traveller's appearance. He seemed to eye him suspiciously, said he was glad to see any gentleman, but that he had little or nothing to offer, except damper. Captain Spencer assured him that "he did not require any assistance; that he should take his food outside the hut, and stay all night; for his friend, Mr. St. John, had told him he would find honest men there." "Oh, indeed, sir!" said the man, "you are a friend of his, are you?" his countenance lighting up as he spoke; "he is a very good gentleman; he did not take sheep with him last journey; but he did the time before, and picked out all the finest of our flocks; he is as good a judge of sheep as if he had been brought up to it, though his father is a lord. Perhaps, sir, you are come to choose some? you can see them to-morrow before they leave the folds." "No, friend," replied Captain Spencer, "I am only a traveller in this country, and am now on my way to the Hunter River, from whence I mean to go to Sydney." At these words the man's countenance lengthened again, and he said, "If, sir, you would like to go a few miles further, the moon will be up, and you will there come to the head station, and plenty of room and company too for that matter; and he involuntarily glanced at the sword, gun, and pistols. "No, I thank you," answered the soldier; "but I see you are not quite satisfied about me. I give you my word I am neither a bush-ranger nor one of the police, but am here against my will." He then related as much of his adventures as would explain his appearance there, and after that the man became communicative, and cast off all suspicion. "Do you always live here?" asked Captain Spencer, after he had supped, and turned Tiger loose; but before the man could reply, Charlie flew up, and seeing a white man, said, "Friend Philip!" His master thought friend Philip would not have deemed himself complimented, and replied, "No, Charlie, friend Philip's not here." "Not here, not here," repeated the bird; "all's right!" and perched himself on the top of the hut. The hut-keeper stared, and said, "You did not get that bird here, sir; we have plenty of magpies, and all sorts of talking birds, but we never teach them to speak. There is a Shrike which comes to us in winter, with a fine, clear note; but he is dreadfully mischievous. Our most amusing bird is the Laughing Jackass, which makes us merry sometimes; the whole place often rings with the laughs of these birds; one beginning, then two, three, and four following, till at last the whole flight sets off." "I must have heard them, then," said Captain Spencer. "I have no doubt of it, sir," resumed the man; "they are very numerous just here, and we like them, not entirely because they are so cheerful in these solitary places, but because they eat so many snakes and lizards. Then we have a bird which we call the Knife-grinder; for his note is just the same as the grating of the blade upon the stone, as it turns. We like to know something about all the animals near us, living as we do in such a lonely spot. There is one bird which we take pleasure in calling a Robin, because it has a red breast;* but its back and wings are black, with white bars across, and a white spot is on the crown of its head. It is so gay, with its bright black eyes, so frolicsome and sociable, that it is a great favourite. But here comes my chum." "Do you two keep this station?" "Yes, sir; I am the hut-keeper, and always stay within, do the washing, the cooking, and keep watch all night; for we are always obliged to be on our guard against the Dingoes and the natives." "Does no one come to see you?" "Master comes sometimes, or the head man, or one of the young gentlemen." "How far off is the head farm?" "About thirty miles, or thereabouts; but the keeper's is only ten miles, and he often has company." "And do you like this sort of life?" "Why, it is very easy and quiet, sir." "How much do you get?" "Twenty-five pounds a-year, and allowances of sheep, flour,

---

* Petroica ebenacea.

and tea; and we can't spend anything, except for clothes." "How do you pass your time?" "My comrade has enough to do with his sheep, and I have a bit of a garden. Sometimes the natives, who are friends with us, come and make a Corobbery, and master gives us flour, tomahawks, and other things as presents, to keep them in good humour, and we never lose anything. They are, however, but poor savages, and some of the hut-keepers have been attacked and murdered by them. One of master's men had a grand fight with some of them, and five of the natives were killed. This made the others retreat a little, and their dead companions were buried before the door, when it was known that their friends were looking on. They never have come near the place again, and never will, for they will not cross the spot."

The sheep had by this time arrived, and, with the assistance of the dogs, which were of the sort called Kangaroo, were folded for the night; and the shepherd touching his hat to Captain Spencer, seemed to hesitate about speaking. "This gentleman is a friend of Mr. St. John's, Bill," said the hut-keeper; at which the newly arrived man seemed to be quite relieved, and then joined in the conversation. He said this station was one of the best in the whole country for sheep; because when it was wet in the valley, they could go on to the hills; and that young Mr. Gordon had had a hard push to get it, for a place of that sort was always the right of those who reached it first. After it was discovered, and when he and several others started to come to it, he pretended he would not go any further, and the rest thought he had turned back; but he dashed over everything, having marked the highest hill with his eye, and he never stopped or turned till he gained the point; so, when the others came in, they found him seated, quietly lighting his cigar, and they could not say anything, because they would all have done just the same. "Do you ever see the bush-rangers?" asked Captain Spencer. Both the men coloured, and one replied, "Yes, sir, we do; and to tell you the truth, at a distance you looked like one, only you came in leisurely and peaceably, and they are always in a hurry, because they are hunted down. There is nothing here for them to take, except a little damper, or pork; besides which, master trusts us; and we should have a hard fight with anybody who touched what belonged to him; but we never betray them, because many of us have been in trouble ourselves." "I dare say not," observed Captain Spencer, "especially if they do no harm to you; it is much easier to get into trouble than to get out." Seeing that Captain Spencer and Kinchela were spreading their skins, in order to lie down, they asked the former to sleep inside; but he told them it was so long since he had slept under cover, that he would rather remain where he was, but he should like to see the inside of the hut. He accordingly entered, and found that the cook had prepared slices of bacon and kangaroo, to be fried for supper; that the men took it in turns to sleep, on what they called a stretcher, which was a piece of canvass supported upon a frame, nailed to four upright posts; that they had plenty of blankets, for they said they often had frosts in August; and though there was not much cold weather, they sometimes felt chilly. The hut itself was built of what would be called plank in England, but they call these pieces slabs; they were raised on four posts, and thatched with bark.

Very early next morning, before sunrise, Kinchela was out to renew his stock of bulrush roots, and the new friends took a lesson from him in preparing them. He brought a curious fish to his master, which the shepherds said was what they called the Jew-fish.* He also said that it had been constantly swimming round a ring of sand, the inside of which was filled with stones. The hut-keeper informed the travellers that it was only at certain times of the year that they watched it, and they believed that it was the nest of the fish; though how the stones came there, they could not tell, for such were not to be found in the neighbourhood. Captain Spencer was not incredulous.

* Ptotosus tandanus.

because he knew that there were fishes in the Chinese seas which made nests and guarded them in the same manner. Just after the return of Kinchela, the air was like a furnace, and the most tremendous lightning opened the thick clouds; it became almost dark, so that a light was required within the hut; a rushing noise was heard, the men sought their blankets, and throwing them over their shoulders put out their light, which was only a piece of rag lying in mutton fat, and said, "Stand clear of the hut." All moved out of its reach, and during the few still moments which ensued, the sheep-keeper said, "We don't often have these things, but they do sometimes come from the south-west; and I am glad it happened when I and the sheep were in the hollow; for we should have been blown about like straws on the top of the hill." "What do you expect?" asked Captain Spencer. "A hurricane, sir," was the reply; "and after that, heavy rain." Captain Spencer then said to all his followers, "Come close; smother the fire-stick, Kinchela." This was immediately wrapped in a piece of thick skin, and, going to a still deeper hollow, and taking off all his clothes, he put them under his coverings, and sat down with the rest, in as compact a body as possible. Charlie, with his usual sagacity, creeping under the skins. "I am sorry we have not a better shelter to offer you, sir," said the shepherd; "but our hut is sometimes blown down; for these hurricanes make playthings of all that come in their way, and they lay down even the biggest trees; when there is hail, if the trees are not knocked down, every leaf is stripped from them." The storm came, and was as tremendous as any Captain Spencer had experienced, and he thought sadly of his poor Malays; it was, however, no sooner over than he was dry and comfortable, and the shepherds were lost in admiration of his plan. "I am used to such storms, here and elsewhere," said the traveller; "now, you see, I have dry things to put on after my shower-bath." "Very bad sorcerer made that storm," said Kinchela; "more bad than we see anywhere, Boccolo." "I am sure we could learn many things of you, sir," said the man to Captain Spencer. When he inquired if the hail ever killed the sheep, the outwatcher said, that on one occasion they had lost forty, and that the valley became one broad sheet of water; for as the rain always ran rapidly off the soil, the hollow places were filled in an instant.

Captain Spencer, taking a friendly leave of the shepherds, and receiving particular instructions from them, at once proceeded towards the head stock-keeper's house, where he thought he should find a guide to the Hunter River, for he fancied he often wandered very much from the proper track. The storm had cleared the atmosphere;

Tiger, who had appeared drooping the day before, was now as bright as ever, and Charlie hurra'd, and said, "Good-bye, all's right!" to the great entertainment of his new acquaintances, and soared up into the air; but the man who went out with the sheep, accompanied the travellers for a mile or two. The birds, which had taken refuge in the trees from the storm, had not left their coverts as they passed, and numerous were the Choughs, Crows, and Pigeons; among the latter was the Harlequin Bronze-wing,* which the shepherd told him laid its eggs in low bushes, in the middle of plains; the Common Bronze-wing wheeled round and round in immense numbers as they approached, and took their flight to the grassy flats, where the seed was ripe. On parting with the shepherd, the wayfarers went through a portion of an extensive pine forest, interspersed with a few other trees; the former was seventy feet high, full of cones, and Kinchela knocking one which lay upon the ground, it fell to pieces, and both men ate the aromatic seeds which lay between the scales. On the other side of the forest was a small open space, covered with Cassias, Sensitive and Ice Plants, and in which grew a large tree, about thirty feet high, standing by itself. It attracted Captain Spencer's attention, and, on going up to it to ascertain what it was, he found it to be a fearful Nettle,

* Phaps histronica.

and pointing it out to Kinchela, he warned him never to touch it; to which the man replied, " Yes, but Boccolo always tell Kinchela ;" a proof how completely he had made up his mind to remain with his master, and how entirely he trusted him. On the outskirts of the pine forest were webs of dark yellow silk, yards in length, and reaching from tree to tree, which were made by some bright green spiders. They rested under a clump of trees, when they chased away some scorpions; but a most interesting process was taking place at the foot of the tree under which they sat; some insects, looking like heavy, lumpy, brown beetles, an inch and a half long, with scaly coats, and their claws like those of lobsters, crept from under the turf, and were about to emerge into another state; their backs burst, and out of the slit came a head, body, and legs, looking as if they had boots on; then a pale creature issued and stood upright. Two odd-looking tufts of membrane, crumpled into a thousand folds, spread into opaline wings; and Kinchela said he had often seen them, and if they came out when the sun was hot upon them, these wings became so stiff that the insect could not fly. In walking along that same afternoon, they saw a number of small, yellow circles, formed of the bits of a Cistus blossom, which some ants had divided, and were carrying to their deposit, while others dragged them into the holes of their nests. They tried to ascertain what these little creatures were like: but they all rushed into the earth when they approached, and hid themselves.

A low thatched house, surrounded by a neat and pretty garden, in which the owner was at work, proved to be the residence of the person to whom Captain Spencer had been recommended by the Overlander, and opening the gate, and walking up to him with only Gip by his side, the traveller at once accosted him by saying, "I am come, by the advice of my friend Mr. St. John, to request you will let me take a few hours rest at your house, and then that you will put me in the way of finding Mr. Onslow's farm on the Hunter River." The person thus addressed was a tall, respectable-looking man, whose broad shoulders, and well-shaped limbs, curling brown hair, and clear blue eye, showed that he was of that Anglo-Saxon race now spreading itself over the whole world, and showing itself superior to all others in energy and perseverance. "I am very glad to see you, sir," was his reply, "not only for Mr. St. John's sake, but for your own, for you look as if you had been travelling some time. Wife," he said, going into his house, "see what you can do for this gentleman, while I get something for his supper, and have his horse and servant put up." A rather shy, but pretty young woman made her appearance, while two children stood peeping from the inner room. It was so long since Captain Spencer had seen a bright English complexion, that he could scarcely persuade himself she was not the most beautiful female he had ever beheld. As to Kinchela, when he first cast his eyes upon her, his astonishment was so great as to bewilder him; and he afterwards told his master he thought she was a good spirit, such as he had told him of as living in Heaven. Tiger was unloaded, and about to be led to a stable, but Captain Spencer requested that he might be allowed to graze in a pasture close outside the garden. Kinchela went there with him, Charlie also adhered faithfully to Tiger, and Gip remained with her master.

Mr. Richardson, for this was the name of the stock-keeper, brought in some lamb for the supper of the strangers, which his wife immediately prepared, and with some potatoes put it into the oven. "Pray, sir," said he, "did you see a tall black fellow on your way, anywhere about here? I suppose you are come from an overland, which is a great wear and tear for the clothes, and the body too." "I am not an Overlander, my friend," said Captain Spencer; "nevertheless, I come from a great distance. I did see a tall, black man, who tried to take my gun from me; but I caught him, and when he resisted, my dog just pinned him by the leg; and as he was very hungry, I gave him something to eat. He said he was hunted, and wanted my gun in order to defend himself; and if he be the same, I should like to know what he has done?" "Why, sir, he has committed murder; and the police are riding him down in every direction." "Where did he commit it?" asked Captain Spencer. "Thank God, it did not happen here, sir, but at one of Mr. Wilde's stock-keeper's; if it had been here, I think my little wife would have gone out of her mind. A black fellow hung about the stock-keeper's house for some days, and seemed as if he wanted to be taken as a help; but the men there could not quite understand what he said. They fed him, and at last began to trust him; so one wet night they asked him to sleep inside the house on the floor of the keeping room. They do sometimes make very good servants, and this one seemed, poor fellow, to be quite handy. That same night that he came into the house, another black fellow—the very rascal whom you saw, I suppose—knocked at the door, and begged so hard to be let in, that, considering it was such a rough night, they gave consent, and he laid himself down in one corner. Every body went to sleep, and in the night it is supposed that he stabbed the other to the heart with a large knife, which was found sticking in him. The rascal lay down again, and slept till morning. When the stock-keeper got up, he was of course dreadfully frightened, but he secured the man, and sent for the nearest police. When they came, the rascal denied that he had touched his countryman; but they handcuffed him, and marched him off to be tried. On the way, he leaped, handcuffed as he was, from a precipice into the river, and disappeared. Great search was made for him, and although they did not find the body, the police thought he was drowned. All pursuit would have been given up, had they not afterwards heard that he had dived and swum under water, till he had completely baffled them. Now they are again after him; but so determined a fellow as that is not easily overtaken." "I suppose he thought me to be one of the police, then," said Captain Spencer; "and that was why he did not answer when I made the native call. There was little doubt that he had tracked his enemy to the house of the stock-keeper, and taken revenge for something he had done, which, however dreadful to us, was only according to his notions of justice."

The supper was ready, Gip was fed, Kinchela had a portion carried to him, and all things were in repose, when the stock-keeper, who was evidently (although he tried to conceal it) very curious to know who his guest might be, said, as he smoked his pipe, "Perhaps, sir, you have also seen Harry Blunt, the famous bush-ranger? you **may,** in fact, be come after him." "No, indeed," answered Captain Spencer; "I seem to have met with the most famous characters of Eastern Australia, but I have not sought them. I have seen Harry Blunt, and in fact only parted with him a few days ago. Was it from here that he and his companion took those two valuable horses?" "Sure enough it was," said the stock-keeper. "We had long heard that rangers were about, but as the story came from the natives only, who take great delight in raising all sorts of false reports, we did not alarm ourselves, or make preparations to receive them by sending for the police. At last, however, some of our own people saw them, and then we tried to be ready whenever they might come. We constantly kept watch, night and day, sat with our guns loaded, piled lots of things against the windows for a month, till at last we were tired out, and thought they must have taken another direction. But about a week after we had relaxed a little, two horsemen rode in at the gate while we were at dinner, and one of them wore a white hat with red ribbons hanging from it. Before we could rise he was in the house, saying he must have something hot for dinner; while the other put the muzzle of his rifle in at the window, so that he could have shot any one of us had we stirred to get our own arms, which were hanging up, so we dared not refuse; and as to Sally," continued the narrator, " I never saw her so over civil in all my life ; she got up and waited upon him a great deal quicker than she ever waits upon me ;" and he looked archly at his wife, who exclaimed, " Oh, James !" and blushed deeply. " Well, sir, you see we were fairly caught ourselves ; so we set all that we had to eat before Harry, and he ordered us about as if we had been his subjects, taking care to let us see that he had a large knife, and a brace of pistols in his belt. When he had eaten enough, he took one of the pistols, cocked it, and kept guard with it in his hand, while his companion, a much worse rascal than he, sat down in his turn and made a good dinner ; they then called for tobacco and brandy, and Harry said he would leave his card for the police, and thereupon carved his name upon the table, as you may now see. He spoke well enough, but he took what small articles he fancied, such as a powder-horn ; changed his old hat for my new one, and secured a few trifles, as he called them ; he then winked at his companion, who slipped out, and soon returned with two of our best horses, saddled and bridled, leaving in their place two jaded creatures. Harry filled my gun and pistols with water, to prevent me from firing after him ; and thanking us for our civility, they both mounted our horses and rode off, saying we should hear from them again. There was no one at home but Sally, myself, and a boy, who was so frightened that he hid himself. We fed and got the horses round which they had left, and soon found their owners. Ours, I dare say, will come back in just the same condition.

"They treated one gentleman in these parts in a very different manner. He was not at all prepared for their coming, and his men were all at work; the first notice which he had of their arrival was a rustling noise as he sat at a table reading; he turned his head, and saw his fire-arms in their possession, but he tried to spring upon Harry, and get his pistols back again; however, as he was no match for the fellow, he was bound and obliged to remain quiet, while they took whatever they liked, and ransacked his drawers. Then Harry told him he knew him to be a tyrant over his men, so he must punish him; they tied him to a tree, and began to flog him; but after his companion had whispered something in Harry's ear, they rode off as hard as they could, leaving the poor gentleman fastened to the tree. A party in search of the rangers came up in a few minutes; and as they stopped to release the victim, the scamps got out of reach."

"Your dogs are of the same sort as those of Mr. St. John," said Captain Spencer; "what do you call them?" "They are half-bred Greyhounds, sir; and we call them Kangaroo-dogs, because they are so useful in hunting those animals, which required two of them, and a fast horse, to be a match for them. They are also capital for catching the Dingoes." Captain Spencer smiled when he recollected how Gip and he had caught many of the former, but he asked if the native dogs in the neighbourhood were numerous. "Yes," replied his host, "they are the greatest plagues we have; their step is so light and stealthy, that we never know when they are coming, and they lie in wait for their prey in the long grass, or rocky places; they sometimes come alone, and at others five or six together, and sometimes run well for a little while, but soon get frightened when they are pursued. They, however, die hard, and often pretend to be dead, so that they may be left; they then suffer themselves to be beaten, kicked, and dragged about without flinching; hanging their heads, and making you believe they are done for; then they get up, and run between your legs, or spring over your shoulders, in order to escape. Our dogs will kill them, but nauseate them afterwards, and always plunge into water after hunting them; there is, however, a good breed between them and tame dogs. They are the greatest sheep and calf worriers in the world, and do not kill their prey first, but eat it bit by bit while it is alive. They have been known to eat off the tails of the cattle as they lay asleep." It was now time for the stock-keeper to perform his duties for the night;

nis men, flocks, and herds were come in, and it was necessary to go to them. While he was absent, Captain Spencer visited Tiger, and talked to the children, who at first had been frightened at him, but now hung about him as if he had been an old friend; he went outside the door, and whistling for Charlie, treated them to some of his conversation; he asked their names; "Jim and Tom Richardson," was the reply; and Charlie, who happened to be in a good humour, repeated the words, to their great surprise and enjoyment. Then came the time for rest; and taking his cloaks from the nail on which they had been hung, the traveller prepared to join Tiger and Kinchela, who had already laid themselves down. This caused much astonishment to Mr. and Mrs. Richardson; but he said he had been so long accustomed to the open air, that he preferred it, and would join them at breakfast the next morning. The good couple for awhile remonstrated; but finding their visitor inflexible, with true hospitality suffered him to do that which he liked best.

Breakfast was ready at an early hour; the sheep and cattle were already gone to their pastures, and the exquisite climate and scenery seemed to make his spot the beau ideal of a pastoral life. The whole of the neighbouring country was apparently in the possession of settlers, and its wild products were consequently less abundant; still, so accustomed had the traveller been to find ample sustenance in the desert, that he was about to start on the second morning without taking thought for future provision. Mr. Richardson, however, said, "I shall make up a parcel of eatables, for you and your servant, sir; your horse and bird will find plenty to eat, but human food will be scarce." Captain Spencer started, for the idea of difficulty had not occurred; but recollecting himself, he expressed his thanks, and asked if he should not find any inns on the way. "Yes," replied the stock-keeper, "more than one, sir; but I would not advise you to trust to them, for they are often so full of riot, drunkenness, and quarrelling, that a gentleman like you will scarcely be willing to put up at such places." Captain Spencer smiled, and looked at his dress; his host understood him, and added, "I know a gentleman, sir, whatever clothes he may wear. You are not an Overlander, so I suppose you are a traveller, and travelling quite spoils the dress." "True, friend," said the soldier, "I am a traveller against my will, and have come a great way; and now I recollect myself, I have none but Indian money, and a letter of credit, which will not be of much use at a wayside inn." "I have but little to lend you, sir," said the honest stock-keeper; "but I can let you have a few shillings; you can send them back to me some how or other, when you get your own money." "My good friend," said the soldier, offering his hand, "this is true hospitality; stranger as I am, you trust me, and I shall never forget your kindness. After having found my way, partly without human assistance, across a large portion of this extraordinary country, I can do with very little; Gip will, I suppose, find Rats and Opossums, Charlie insects, Tiger grass, and if all these things set aside on the dresser are for me, Kinchela and I shall have enough for many days; but if not, Gum-trees would supply our wants." "Gum-trees!" exclaimed Mrs. Richardson, with an astonished look. "Yes, I have more than once lived on the bark and roots for many days." "Oh! sir," continued she, with an uncontrollable impulse, "if you would but stay with us a day longer, and tell us all that has happened to you, it would not take my husband from his work, because this is slack time with us. When I have made the place tidy, if you would be so kind, it would give us such pleasure, and we should talk all our lives about your adventures. We have read our books so often, that we are tired of them; but we should never weary in talking of you." Captain Spencer smiled at the earnestness of Mrs. Richardson, and willingly consented to reward his host and hostess for their kindness by an ample account of all he had seen, suffered, and enjoyed; nor did he ever feel more pleasure in narrating his history than in imparting to those simple persons, who seldom interrupted him, and when they did, it was with some artless expression of wonder and sympathy, or by some apt question which only gave him fresh zest to continue. When he actually did depart the next day, he gave each of the children a gold coin to keep in remembrance of him; and Richardson and his wife took leave of him with tears in their eyes. "You have taught us a lesson of trust, sir," said the stock-keeper, "which I hope we shall never forget. Few leave their own country for ever of their own accord, without having suffered much, and I have had my share; but it now seems to me as if I had not trusted enough to God. Besides which, you have put his goodness in a new light, by teaching us the uses of many things, which have till now been wasted on us; and what is more, you and Kinchela have given me new feelings about the blacks, which I should never have had without you, for I have judged of them only by those which I have seen about the colony. Ah, sir! you will be grieved when you see the poor drunken creatures lying about like beasts; but I must not talk any more, and so prevent you from starting. We shall pray for, and never forget you, and I hope you will always remember farmer Richardson, the superintendent of Oakley Farm." Assurances to this effect were warmly given; and Edward Spencer and his companion again set out upon their travels, the heart of the soldier refreshed by this short intercourse with such specimens from his own country.

Deeply did the English traveller, as he passed along, regret the beautiful wilderness which he had left behind him, for the country which now met his eye was only half what is called "redeemed from the waste." Some of the ground was enclosed for the purposes of agriculture, in other places the white trunks of trees lay scattered on the soil in disorder. The labour of man had not replaced Nature's prolific treasures; untidy hovels, few and far between, composed of slabs stuck up like palings, and thatched with bark, sheltered the cultivators of the soil; but even these were frequently in a state which showed that the emigrants there were not of Britain's orderly children, or were of that unruly portion which every race of human beings presents. The thatch was frequently hanging in shreds, the broken windows were stopped up with rags, the doors were off their hinges, and fragments of bottles, cinders, and rubbish were lying around the immediate vicinity. Captain Spencer smiled when he met with a finger-post, informing him in what township he was, without seeing even a trace of a dwelling; reminding him of what he had read of allotments of land in America; and he now saw the force of what the stock-keeper had said respecting the difficulty of

35 *

finding food for himself and Kinchela. He had received ample instructions as to the way in which he was to proceed, and found himself, in obedience to those indications, going south, and mountains rising up before him. "Kinchela," said he, "we must pass over these mountains." "These bigger than other mountains far, far away," replied Kinchela. The party bent their steps towards them, and hourly received fresh proofs of the capriciousness of the rains in Australia. They were now in a district which had evidently been without them for a long time; the dry rivulets, the rusty leaves, the dusty roads, deserted cattle and sheep stations, seemed to show that no moisture had gladdened the earth; a tale that was familiar, having drought for its burden. The only food for Tiger was maize, the plantations of which having been deserted, his master not only suffered him to browse on it, but the bags were filled with it in case of future scarcity. The approach of the travellers scattered from it immense flights of green, blue, yellow, and crimson Parrots, Cockatoos of various kinds, Pigeons, Finches, Swallows; in short, all the birds of eastern Australia, and most of those from the other portions of the country seemed to congregate in these fields of grain, affording a rich harvest for the sustenance of the strangers, who rested there to secure a stock of food; and Captain Spencer was amused to see how carefully Kinchela avoided the destruction of Pigeons, as if he had a superstitious reverence for them.

The path by which Captain Spencer ascended the limestone mountains was narrow and steep, but slabs of wood occasionally made them a little more passable. They met five heavily-laden drays, just like those of English brewers; two men attached to each, which had conveyed the produce of their owners' farms, such as hides, tallow, and wines, either for home consumption in Sydney, or for exportation, and were returning with the goods which they had received in exchange. Captain Spencer drew up on a crag above the path, and watched them as they passed; each covered with a tarpauling, and drawn by eight or ten oxen, having no other harness than bows, ropes, and yokes, and all going on so quietly and patiently, that they needed no other. The drivers seemed to be very much astonished at the party above, and one asked if they had met with any water lately. Captain Spencer informed the man of a muddy pool, and he in return gave him a knowing wink; and turning round to his companion, said, " A queer chap that. I can't think what he is; he's too near to be a ranger, and not a bit like a police." " He's a travelling merchant, Dick," said the other man, " with that pack on the horse's back; and yet," continued the man, looking once again, " the horse is a beauty."

On getting higher up the mountains, the climate became raw and cold; and as poor Kinchela wrapped his Kangaroo-cloak round him, his master began to think that he was placed in an awkward dilemma. He was going to a civilized dwelling, and had no clothes for his servant; the whole of his own wardrobe was on his back, and that in such a wretched condition that he every day dreaded it would yawn too widely ever to come together again. He saw, with some degree of comfort, that Kinchela's cloak was unusually long, and he hoped that the ladies of the family would not be too fastidious. When he looked back upon all the difficulties which had beset him, he could not help smiling to find that dress should be so perplexing, and even cause him annoyance. They began to descend, and a sharp turn in the path opened to them a lovely landscape, whose sudden fertility and verdure, owing to the permanent nature of some of the streams, formed a striking and cheerful contrast to the dreary, parched region which they had just passed, where frequent and tall columns of dust, at least one hundred feet high, had passed them, gliding rapidly and mysteriously along, at an immense rate. On the mountains themselves, they had been much tormented by swarms of Ants, some with black bodies, red heads and legs, and yellow forceps, which jumped at them as they passed, emitted a nauseous odour, and bit Kinchela severely.

The route still continued along the side of the mountain, now and then cheered by a patch of shrubs, or a trailing plant, such as one of the Kennedias, and again did the travellers meet with Grass-trees, and resting for the night close by one of them, Kinchela set fire to it, and created an immense sensation, as Captain Spencer afterwards heard, among the inhabitants of the plain below, whose curiosity and surprise induced them to rush out of their houses to behold the men and the fire on the mountain. At length they saw the river, which had been described to them, and descending as soon as possible into the valley, they wound along its banks, delighting their eyes by looking at old friends in the shape of tall trees, reeds, and frogs; and new ones in the form of flowers, one of which was like a fringed Violet. There were, however, new torments; for stinging flies worried Tiger, who, after trying to get rid of them by sundry antics, rushed up to his master, as much as to say, Rid me of my persecutors.

The river became gradually wider; small and beautiful islands studded its clear waters, which were adorned with exquisite shrubs, the habitations of splendid birds and insects. Trees descended to the water's edge, or retreating to a distance left a green, grassy slope, on one of which they rested for the night. The next morning they retreated from the river, and following what appeared to be a road, they met a party of farm-servants with a horse, and themselves nearly covered with a quantity of boughs, belonging to a very beautiful shrub. Its leaves were like those of the Horse-chestnut in shape, but the upper side was dark-green, and the under quite pale. The starry flowers were placed like sprays at the end of the twigs; all the flower-buds were of a greenish-white; but as they advanced towards maturity, they passed from pure white into rose-colour, and at last became quite crimson. They smelt like new hay; and the men were laughing under their burdens, by which they were so blinded, that they had not seen Captain Spencer. He asked them in which direction he should find Mr. Onslow's farm; and then they all moved the leaves from before their eyes, to stare at the strangers. "Up the hill yonder," said one of the men, peeping from his leafy covering; "we are his servants, and as this is Christmas eve, we have been to fetch flowers for dressing up the house." Dressing the house for Christmas-day! What a happy sound did that convey to a poor wanderer, who had been so long deprived of Christian worship, except in his own heart. Reminiscences and a host of feelings crowded so thickly upon him, that he could not speak. "If you will follow us, sir," continued the man, "we will show you the shortest way to the house." The laughing had ceased; and the whole party, looking at Captain Spencer, whispered conjectures to each other, as to who and what he might be. "Do you know Mr. St. John?" said the traveller. "Oh, yes, sir!" was the reply; "he was here a few months ago, bought stock of my master, and was going with it, by the Darling, to Adelaide." "It was by the side of that river I met him, and he gave me a letter for Mr. Onslow, which I will thank you to take to him." "Certainly, sir. Do you know how stock has been selling at Adelaide?" asked the man, eyeing Captain Spencer from head to foot, and evidently taking him for an Overlander. "I have not been there," he replied, "nor did I meet with any one coming from thence."

CHAPTER XIV.

Description of Mr. Onslow's farm—Cordial reception of Captain Spencer—Clothes supplied—Conversations about Aborigines—Mr. Onslow wishes for Kinchela to enter his service—Kinchela refuses—Dingoes, sheep, cattle—Mrs. Onslow's garden—Hunt stray cattle—Wayside inn—Captain Spencer's courage and nerve—Tiger's good behaviour—Letter from stock-keeper Richardson, describing an interview with Harry Blunt—Endeavours to persuade Captain Spencer to settle in Australia—Conversation with Mr. Onslow—Description of woods—Mare eats a foal—English plants spring up in the neighbourhood of cattle—Tarantula—Native cat—Adventure of the pumpkins—Parting—Mr. Onslow goes to Sydney with Captain Spencer—Kinchela rides with them—Mrs. Onslow's courage when attacked by natives—Arrival at Sydney—Charlie—Attempt of Gipsy, Tiger, and Charlie to accompany their master—Harry Blunt taken—Captain Spencer obtains a mitigation of his sentence—Harry afterwards becomes a faithful servant to Mr. Onslow—Captain Spencer sends presents to all his friends—Arrival of all the travellers in Bombay—Letter from Mr. George Onslow about the Gold-mines.

The whole party had reached the top of the bank, which they had ascended by way of making a short cut, and Captain Spencer paused at the charming scene before him. On a rising ground stood a long, low, white house, plastered in imitation of stone, thatched with bark, so skilfully put on that it looked like a smooth, symmetrical covering; a green verandah shaded the front and sides of the house, and it was raised a few steps from the ground; a small lake on one side communicated with the river, an extensive kitchen and flower-garden encircled the house, beyond which was a paddock for saddle-horses, another for milch cows and working bullocks, and close by was a vineyard. A line of low buildings, stables, sheds, cattle-yards, &c., occupied the other side; and the trees in the garden, and the hills at the back, rendered it a perfect picture of a settler's home. An air of neatness, and even of elegance, reigned over the whole, and showed that the establishment was conducted with the most consummate care and skill. "This is reckoned one of the finest farms in the country," said Captain Spencer's conductor; "my master and the young gentlemen do and see so much to everything themselves, and my mistress is so fond of her garden, that it is full of the plants and fruits of all countries." It was not compact enough to be English; but the repose, the cleanliness, the comfort, and convenience, showed that English habits were there practised; and so occupied was the soldier by it, that only when they reached the inner gate of the domain, did he recollect the leaf on which Mr. St. John had written his introduction; he stopped and pulled it from his pocket, the man deposited his load on the shoulders of another, and took the message to his employers. While he was gone, Kinchela came up to his master, and said, "Spose, Boccolo, very big man live in that house." "Why?" said his master. "Because it very big house," was the reply. "We shall soon see," returned his master, "for here come two of the gentlemen." Mr. Onslow had read the paper, and his sons had looked at it over his shoulder: scarcely giving themselves time to get to the end, they both bounded to the gate, and Mr. Onslow went into the house to tell his wife and daughter. Each of the young men seized a hand of the stranger, the eldest saying, "Any and every friend of St. John's is most welcome here. Walk in, Captain Spencer; my father himself is coming to meet you." Captain Spencer hesitated, and looked at Tiger, Gip, and Kinchela. "There is room for all of you," said Mr. Onslow, who now came up and read the traveller's thoughts; "we are right glad to see one coming from St. John. Your servant can put your horse into a comfortable stable, while you and your dog come with us." Captain Spencer raised his hat from his head, and bowed his thanks; and he then said, "I have yet another companion;" and he gave the signal for Charlie. In half a minute the bird flew on to his master's shoulder, exclaiming, "All's right, Charlie's coming!" and looking round him at the group, added, "What a row!" The astonished owners of Onslow's farm burst into a laugh. "Now go to Tiger, good bird," said his master, and Charlie perched himself on the horse's back

The love of these two for Kinchela was now only secondary to that which they felt for their possessor, so that they went contentedly with him; and Gip, who had already been welcomed by various members of the canine race, leaped into her master's arms, where she was buttoned up inside his jacket, so as not to incommode him in returning the kind salutations which met him on all sides, and not the least from the ladies. They said tea was about to be served; and he was therefore at once shown into the room he was to occupy, where the luxury of soap and towels made him revel in the resumption of long-lost comforts. A servant entered to ask if he should fetch his things from the stable; at which Captain Spencer smiled, and replied, "that he must appear as he was, for he had no other clothes, and that he would himself go to the stable before bed-time." His chief annoyance at that moment was, that it should be discovered he had no linen; and he buttoned up his jacket, and combed his handsome beard carefully over his bronzed throat, flattering himself it was not deteriorated by the sand-scrubbing which it had so constantly received. He gave his whole suit a good beating; and when he had made his last effort he recollected that there was a looking-glass in which he might contemplate the effect he had produced. He not only started, when he looked at himself, but he remained so astonished at the alteration, from the yellow, sickly face, which he had last beheld, that he was still standing before the mirror when Mr. George Onslow came to tell him tea was ready.

The impression made by Captain Spencer's voice and manner had been too favourable to suffer his shabby habiliments to lessen the respect felt for him; and when he found himself so suddenly transported from the wild woods into the society of ladies and gentlemen, he felt as if in a dream. He looked round him instead of eating, and saw the refinements of polished life, books, work, musical instruments, and heard the low, sweet voices about him, as if they were not real, till they noticed his abstraction. "Forgive me," he said; "I do not feel as if I were myself. My first astonishment and doubt was occasioned, however, by seeing myself in a looking-glass, and now—I think you must turn me out again, that I may be sure of my own identity." The night was far advanced when the parties separated; the traveller's adventures were related and heard with so breathless an interest, that there was no commentary, except an exclamation, and no inquiry, for fear of interruption. "You must stay with us as long as you can," said Mr. Onslow, "and when you must go I will accompany you to Sydney." "I should only be too happy to remain for a time." answered the guest,

but I am too poorly clad to delay reaching a

place where I can get freshly accoutred." "We can help you," said both the young men, "and to-morrow morning we will have a consultation; my father's things will be much too wide for you." The stable was visited, and the three travellers there were found fast asleep. Kinchela was awoke, with a strict injunction not to appear without his kangaroo-cloak: and Gip returned with her master, to sleep by his side on the bed-room floor.

All masters of farms keep stores of clothing, of which they dispose to their workmen, and from these Kinchela was equipped with new shirts, for his own had been entirely worn out since he left the *Marie;* and Captain Spencer was supplied by the young men, who, at an early hour, entered with all they could find which they thought might be useful. "My father is always saying we are extravagant," said George Onslow; "but I am sure he will now be very glad that we have enough for a friend." Between the two tall youths, the handsome soldier was well equipped; the beard was reduced to a short fringe, and Edward Spencer was himself again. The house was decorated for the festival: and after breakfast, Mr. Onslow assembled all his men, and read prayers, among which he offered up a thanksgiving for the safety and preservation of his newly-arrived guest, whose heart swelled with gratitude, and who hailed the **return** of this glorious anniversary with a **depth** of devotion which few can conceive who have not been the object of such signal mercies as he had experienced.

Time passed swiftly; and Captain Spencer became so interested in the settler's occupations, that his friends, who quickly attached themselves to him, entreated of him to abandon the soldier's life, and come among them to live, saying, that with his influence, his knowledge of native customs, his acquaintance with their languages, he might not only benefit himself, but save the aborigines from some of the degrading consequences which the vicinity of white men seemed to entail upon them. "At Sydney," said Mr. Onslow, "and indeed we need not go so far for such sad examples, you will see the state to which they are reduced, as it were, upon their own soil; but I hope the time will come when it will be thought criminal to fire upon them, as if they were a flight of crows invading our fields of grain, whereas it is we who are the invading crows. The settlement of Moorundi, near Adelaide, has already produced a humanising effect; and your Kinchela is a proof how much may be done, at least with some dispositions. We employ several about the farm, and find them useful, docile, and intelligent; how far they would be faithful in any attack from their own tribe, we have no opportunity of judging, nor do we wish to have; but we take great care to keep what they call fire-water from them, for that destroys both body and soul." "But has no effort been made to christianise them?" asked Captain Spencer. "Yes, many," was the reply; "we have missionaries and schools in the townships, as well as the head colony, and success has altogether equalled expectation." "It surprises me," resumed Captain Spencer, "that these people should always have been reported lower in the scale of intellect than any other savages; they argue shrewdly, comprehend much, have rules of government, extraordinary ceremonies, although not of a religious nature—a quiet submission to what they think justice, and well-defined notions of landed property—all of which betoken a much more advanced condition than that with which they are credited. Perhaps it is the treatment of their women which has given rise to the stigma." "Oh, in that respect I have nothing to say in their favour," replied Mr. Onslow.

"What are you going to do with Kinchela?" said Mr. Onslow one day to his new friend. "I have promised to take him with me," replied Captain Spencer, "wherever I go, though I confess I shall find some difficulties with him in India, among the jealous Hindoos; but there I think I can keep the gin-bottle from him." "I was going to ask you to leave him with us, as house-servant." "It would be much to his advantage to do so, especially as you would not spoil him. At present I must confess your men have made so much of him, that he is in a complete state of puppyism; however, we will ask him." Kinchela was summoned, and Mr. Onslow's proposal stated, at which the poor fellow at first looked astonished, then angry, and at last putting up his hands, and tears rolling down his cheeks, he implored his master not to forget his promise of taking him wherever he went: "Boccolo stay," said he, "Kinchela stay; Boccolo keep here, Kinchela glad; Boccolo go away, Kinchela go away, and glad too." He was assured that he should do as he pleased; and he then repeated that it was "best for Kinchela to be with Boccolo, Gip, Tiger, and Charlie." "It would be wrong to press him any further," said Mr. Onslow; "but if you ever wish to part with him, while he is as he is, send him to us; unless, indeed, you yourself bring him." "I have thought much about settling here," was the reply; "but I do not deem it would be honourable to quit the service in which I am engaged, while I can be useful in it; but perhaps I may pay you a visit. Now I linger in this charming circle as a sort of repayment for all my sufferings; but I feel that the duty of a soldier, in spite of an extended furlough, is with his regiment." "You must not talk of going yet," said Frederick Onslow, who now came up, "we have a hundred things for you to see and do: we are going into the bush, to try and bring back some stray cattle, and, of course, you will go with us. Fortunately we have just shorn our sheep, and to-morrow we begin folding and packing, so that our time will be more our own."

The next morning the traveller found his way through the cattle and sheep folds, to a long, low shed, devoted to the wool, where Mr. Onslow had already stationed himself, to superintend the process which was going forward on a large table. "Which is the best breed?" asked Captain Spencer. "The Merino," answered Mr. Onslow; "and we form our flocks into five, of 800 heads, which are watched as you have seen; but occasionally, if they lie far out, the shepherds sleep in a mere box, and this is necessary on account of the Warragles, or Dingoes. We are obliged to be very strict with our shepherds, or they would grow indolent and careless, and we deduct the value of the missing sheep from their wages. They never are fit for anything else, after leading so monotonous a life. Next to the Dingoes, our greatest nuisance with the sheep is a burr, the seeds of which are set with hooks, which turn backwards,* mix with the wool, as you see here, and it is next to impossible to get them out. I have farms entirely for sheep, and others for cattle; for unless under your own eye, it is best to have them separate." "How many have you at these farms?" "At one I have

* Calotes uncifolia.

20,000; less than 5000 will not answer. As to my cattle, it would be difficult to count them to a nicety, for they are always straying to a distance; but all are branded. The branding is a most exciting affair; for the men stand with their hot irons ready, while others drive the animals to them, and you will suppose the difficulty there is in getting them to the proper spot." "What is that long line of sheds for?" asked Captain Spencer. "For my working men, who are very comfortable in them, I assure you." "And now, as I am in an inquisitive vein, do tell me why you have that gallows in your yard; do you take the law into your own hands?" "You shall soon see," said Mr. Onslow, "for there is a movement near the cattle-yard, and the slaughter took place last night." As he spoke, some men brought a bullock to the gallows, and by a pulley hoisted it to the top, where it was to be cut up. "That is the extent of my penal avocations," said Mr. Onslow.

"Captain Spencer," said a cheerful voice, "for a man who professes to admire flowers, I do not think you have paid sufficient respect to my garden." "Indeed, Mrs. Onslow, I have; my walks in it take place every morning before you are up, although you are a very early person; but I now challenge you to a *tête-à-tête* walk in it this evening." "You had better not," interfered Miss Onslow. "for if you do you will stand a chance of not going to bed: mamma never knows when to finish if she gets on horticultural topics; and I warn you that she means to coax you out of some seeds from India." "I will promise them beforehand, and I shall trust to you to come to my rescue, when you think I have received as much instruction in gardening as will be good for my shallow intellects."

As soon as tea was over, Mrs. Onslow rose, saying, "You are not to mind that impertinent child, Captain Spencer, but come now and see all I have done. The fact is," continued she, as they walked along, "Mary has had only the sweets, and I the labour; for to form a garden in this country, which shall be all you wish, requires much patience and trouble. Sometimes the insects come and eat up everything; then an overwhelming flight of birds one year destroyed all my grapes,* for I include the vineyards in my occupations. I was the first in this part of the country to make wine, and now it forms an important article of exportation. Then come those terrible droughts, which, if they do not kill, make everything languish. I try, by watering as much as possible, to counteract them, but this takes my hands, and they cannot always be spared, nor can I ask for it when I see our poor cattle dying for want of this life-giving moisture, and when we are obliged to have it brought from

* Zosterops dorsalis.

great distances for household purposes. My little lake, which Mr. Onslow had made for me, in consequence of being so successful with the vines, is a great resource for them. I fill my garden-engine from it; but even that became dry in a drought which lasted three years. That is why you see such large plantations of maize for the horses, pigs, and poultry, as wheat will not grow in dry seasons. Now stop and look at my two Norfolk Island Pines; did you ever see more beautiful specimens of the cone tribe? what strength, majesty, and symmetry combined, as they lessen by degrees towards the top, where that tiny cross adorns the summit! I assure you I am very proud of them." "I have often stopped to admire them," said Captain Spencer, "and wondered where they came from, for I had not seen any in the country through which I have passed." "No, they are all brought from Norfolk Island; but, as you see, this place suits them very well. I have endeavoured here to get round me whatever is good in all countries, and even those which grow in the bush; for who knows but that cultivation may make many plants valuable acquisitions? For instance, here is a fruit called the Loquat; you see it is a handsome tree, with large, long leaves, and bears clusters of white fragrant blossoms, which turn into golden gooseberries. Mr. Onslow will not let me have any of the beautiful Acacias of Australia, because he says there are too many in the bush, and they are the torments of the settlers' lives; but I have the Botany Bay Lily, and the splendid Iris, just the colour of ultramarine. Then, you see, I have Figs, Bananas, Guavas, and Oranges; but my Lemons are rather a failure, for they look like misshapen Seville Oranges. The Pomegranates I have cultivated for the sake of their bright blossoms; but of all things I cherish the English fruits and trees, which give me a feeling of home whenever I look at them. I tried to environ myself with the forest-trees of the dear old land, for everything here grows at such an enormous rate, that even my life might be long enough to enjoy their shade; but they only succeed on the hills, and Gooseberries and Currants are only to be reared on the heights. If I could, I would have a garden at one of our out-stations, and ride over to it once a week; but Mr. Onslow only laughs at me. Apples and Pears will not grow in these lower districts; but in the south, and in Van Diemen's Land, they are excellent: they may well call the former Australia Felix, for everything flourishes there. At supper you shall taste my Quandang jam, which is made from the Fusanus* fruit, which you have seen in the bush. I cultivated this Coral-tree,† because its leaf is just like a human hand, and its two bright scarlet peas

---

* Fusanus acuminatus.   † Erythrina vespertilio.

are so beautiful in their pods. I smuggled in some of the Jasmines for the sake of their fragrance, as well as those bushes which remind me of Mint,* and Thyme,† and the broom-like plant,‡ from the bush. Look at my large white Datura; I am obliged to have it far from the house, its odour is so strong. I have a fine Orchis, with a bright-blue flower, and gold and black inside, which I have had great difficulty in rearing; but it is not in blossom now. You can see my beautiful Nelumbium, with its large leaf, and its stalk eight feet out of the water. Its tuber looks as if it were good to eat." "That and its seed are both edible," said Captain Spencer: "I tried it in the west, and you may make use of almost all tubers by boiling them in two waters, which washes out all the acrid properties."

"To tell you the truth," continued Mrs. Onslow, "I have a little secret in that corner. I am trying what can be made of that which they here call the Cotton-tree;§ and, if it should answer, I have a project for spinning the cotton on our own estate." "You must get St. John to bring you the seeds of the Sturtia from the neighbourhood of Adelaide," said Captain Spencer; "they say it affords very good raw material." "Thank you for telling me," resumed Mrs. Onslow: "I will cer-

---

* Stenochilus.   † Prostanthera odoratissima.
‡ Jacksonia.   § Cochlospermum gossypium.

tainly try it. I have vast plans in my head," she continued, her bright eyes kindling with enthusiasm, "and we have surmounted so many obstacles, and done so much already, and in this country the spirits are so elastic, the energies so strengthened, and nature so vigorously responds to our endeavours, that I seem to live two lives in one. I have visions of a native school, in which not only book-instruction shall be given, but other things taught, such as carding and spinning; and who knows but weaving and bleaching may be accomplished? But, first of all, we must have a church." Captain Spencer smiled, and said, "From what I have seen of the natives, I think no sedentary employment will suit them; and it will take two or three generations of taming to fit them for such purposes. To me their wildness seems to be unconquerable, and I even look forward to Kinchela's straying occasionally; my best security in India will be the wild beasts, of which he will be horribly afraid."

"Look, Captain Spencer," again continued Mrs. Onslow, "I have your Bamboo from India; Mr. Onslow has condescended to approve of this importation, and has even made a plantation of it for himself, because it is so good for fences. Here is a native plant* which will please you; it has pods just like Chili peppers." "And much more aromatic," said Captain Spencer, tasting them. "Here

* Hœmodorum.

comes Mary to call us in," cried the mamma. "I hope I have not teased you too much." "On the contrary," answered Captain Spencer, "I have been much interested, and I shall use my best endeavours, when I return to India, to procure as many plants and seeds as I can for you." "Oh, thank you, Captain Spencer; that is the only thing which can reconcile me to your going, and for which promise I now give you an English rose, one of the dear roses which I brought from Wimbledon; I look at them every day, and think of my dear friends there, and the most beautiful garden in the world; and only my especial favourites are allowed to have any of the blossoms."

"I am come to the rescue," exclaimed Miss Onslow, as she approached; "my mamma will teach you horticulture, papa agriculture, and George and Frederic will complete your education by talking to you forever about wild cattle." "And you, Miss Onslow," whispered the officer, "will perhaps favour me with the last polish, by remarks on Overlanders." Miss Mary's deep blush, and hasty exclamation of "Here come the boys!" succeeded by a hasty flight, showed not only the keenness, but the truth of the soldier's penetration.

"Well, Spencer," said George Onslow, "we start in the middle of the night, and I have ordered a good feed of corn to be given to Tiger. Kinchela wants to go; but as he cannot ride, neither he nor

Gip can go with us." "Certainly not; I leave them both in charge of Mrs. Onslow." "You must not take one of your awkward tin cans," continued the young man; "we shall equip you like one of ourselves, with a tin pot, some damper and corned beef, flint and steel in your pocket, your rifle at your back, and your pistols in your belt. We will allow you to wear your grass hat; for that cap and gold band are really too dashing; but take your opossum-cloak. We sup early, that we may go to bed and have a good sleep before starting. We shall breakfast at the inn close by the creek through which we go."

Tiger was in high spirits, full of corn and animation after his long rest; poor Gip had been carried to Mrs. Onslow's bed-room, and Charlie was left perched upon a rack in the stable. Kinchela looked very disconsolate; but Captain Spencer raised his importance by telling him he must take care of all his things while he was away, and this was some consolation. After riding a few hours, the party came to the inn, which even at that early hour was a scene of intoxication; and the drunken swearing of the master, on being awoke, promised badly for the ensuing breakfast. The inn itself was a pretty little building, with a garden, flowers, and good accommodations; but within all was disorder; black and white men were lying on the floor, sleeping off the effects of the night's excess;

the pretty young mistress herself coming to the gentlemen guests with a stupid look, and evident signs of not having been undressed all night. "What a dreadful picture!" said Captain Spencer; "surely no colonies can prosper where this frequently occurs." "It is the curse of many new colonies," observed George Onslow; "the income of a wayside inn is chiefly derived from cattle-keepers, half-reclaimed convicts, idle emigrants, and people of a loose description, who lead the master of the establishment into temptation; he leads his wife; and you know how soon such habits are formed. My men, however, know how to manage, and I see they are lighting a fire to cook bacon and eggs for us, the staple commodities of such places. There is a milk cow in the yard, can you draw it?" "No," answered the soldier; "I never tried." "I can," said Frederic, "if we could but get a clean jug or basin into which we could put the milk." "I will take charge of the horses, for both your stock-keepers are busy." So saying, Captain Spencer led them to a shed, where he gave them hay and water. Frederic met him on his return with a wash-hand basin full of milk. "This is the only thing which I could find," said he, "which did not smell of beer or gin; and in getting it I awoke a servant-girl, more drunk than her mistress, and quite insensible to some of those pests which are falsely distinguished as belonging peculiarly to London."

The breakfast being finished, and a provision of hard eggs and bacon secured for the next meal, one of the stock-keepers thrust the money for their entertainment into the pocket of the querulous host, and proceeded up the creek. "Do you call this a creek?" said the stranger. "To be sure," was the reply; "have you been so long in this country, and not know that a creek means either a dry water-course, such as has not held water during the memory of man, or an open space in the forest, with or without water? We have many incongruous terms; such as going down the country, for going to the capital." "Then the interior of this country is full of creeks of the former description," said Captain Spencer; "but I suspect some mighty torrents of water have at some period or other rushed through them." "And perhaps may again," observed George Onslow; "the rains of Australia run off at once, as if they never sank into the soil; and I have seen creeks suddenly flooded in the most terrific manner."

Early in the evening the party arrived at the dwelling of Mr. Onslow's principal stock-keeper, from whom they had received the request to come and help in the regaining of the stray cattle. "Do they often go away, Mr. Graham?" said Captain Spencer to the intelligent-looking man before him. "Yes, sir, often," was the reply: "these have been tempted by beasts which are half wild, of which there are vast herds in the interior; if not, they would have returned, for they are always inclined to come back to their pastures, as we know when we want to move them; and even when they have been driven by a circuitous route, they will reach the old places by a straight direction. For some reason which we do not know they often separate into distinct herds, and always remain divided after that." "But do not the natives attack them?" "No, sir, they are too frightened at them; and I have seen a whole tribe clamber into the trees at their approach."

Supper was eaten, and soon after midnight the cattle-seekers started, with the addition of Mr. Graham and one of his men; the former observed that Captain Spencer ought to be warned of the danger incurred in hunting bulls. "They are very dangerous, sir," he said; "and you must be able to turn your horse round as sharp as if he were on a cabbage-leaf." They proceeded through an open forest, at the termination of which the brightness of the moon enabled them to see the tracks of the cattle. "The black fellows told me I should find them by this path," said Graham; "but let us see which way the wind is, because we must go against that, or they will smell us out, they are so acute in this particular. They are

HUNTING THE STRAY CATTLE.   [Page 441.]

somewhere up in these ridges, I am pretty sure. I will go and reconnoitre." Dismounting, and giving his horse to his man to hold, the stockkeeper crept stealthily up the hills, and when he arrived near the summit, he went upon hands and knees and peeped over. Then returning, said: "There they are, on the other side, as friendly as possible with the wild ones; and there are two big bulls among them which seem to be the leaders, the one black, and the other red." "I, Captain Spencer, and you, will take the red bull," said George Onslow, "and Fred and the men shall have the other; we will divide into two parties, single out these two, and sacrifice them." "That is right, sir; but you had better take a mouthful before you begin, and let the horses also take a slight bait and rest, for we shall want all their strength and courage." This being done, the two divisions took their way without speaking; the fiery steeds of the young men were with difficulty restrained, for they knew what was coming, and panted to be off; even Tiger began to fret; but his master's hand and voice, saying, "We must go very gently, good horse," quieted him immediately; and his pretty slender legs seemed almost to skim the turf, and make neither sound nor impression "I could let that horse walk right over me," said Graham, looking at the Arab with great admiration.

They reached the top of the ridge, and had crept partly down the other side, when one of the bullocks snuffed the air, gave a mighty bellow, and rushed across the level ground at full speed; the other bull answered him, and the two herds galloped on, the sportsmen after them at their utmost speed; and, dashing in among the cattle, they fired at the leaders. Captain Spencer, who knew the sensitiveness of sportsmen, especially when young, had not fired, but kept his eyes steadily fixed on the object he had to pursue. The black bull turned upon his pursuers, but they were so scattered that he was uncertain which to choose; and being inexperienced, he became bewildered, and knew not at which to take his aim; he therefore attacked them all in their turns, and caused them to perform marvellous feats of horsemanship; they fired repeatedly, but not being mortally wounded, he kept them long in suspense; and at last fell upon the ground, faint from loss of blood, where he was soon despatched. Not so the red bull: Mr. George Onslow and Graham both fired, but missed the mortal part, which is just behind the shoulder; Graham and his horse were overthrown, and would have been gored to death, had not Mr. Onslow presented himself as a new object for the bull's fury: but the well-tried horse turned away as he rushed at him, and his horns went through empty air; then he caught sight of Captain Spencer, who remained perfectly still to receive the attack; "Stand, good horse," he said, "and trust your master." The noble steed remained motionless; but his flashing eyes, erect ears, and raised tail showed a consciousness of his danger. The bull came on, but when two yards distant a pistol-ball went into his forehead just between his eyes; he staggered, and fell dead.

"That's the finest thing I ever saw," said George Onslow in the enthusiasm of the moment, shaking his friend warmly by the hand. "You forget," said that friend, laughing, "that I am a soldier, and a hunter of wild beasts. Now let us go to poor Graham." But Graham and his horse had risen, the latter a little strained, and he somewhat bruised; but they all assisted in collecting the herd, and drove them back in triumph to the stockkeeper's yard, where they were secured; the wild, no longer having a leader, going with the rest." "You must find the owners for these," said Mr. George Onslow to the keeper. "As soon as possible, sir, for they will be very troublesome among my poor beasts." "I think, sir," continued Graham, turning to Captain Spencer, "now I hear your name, I have a message for you from Richardson, the overseer, which has come through several stations, and reached me the day before yesterday. We shall find it at my house."

On arriving at the station, Captain Spencer received the following:—

"Honoured Sir,—My wife and I hope you have got safe to Mr. Onslow's, and pray for a continuance of the same. This is to let you know that we have had another visit from Harry Blunt, who was very civil, but having, as usual, surprised us, was going to lay his hands on whatever he could carry away, and opening the drawer of my wife's table, he was about to pocket the gold coins you were so good as to give to the children. My wife then burst out a crying, and pleaded so hard he would leave them, that he asked her why she was so fond of them; she told him it was because a very good gentleman, a captain, who had been all over Australia, had given them as keepsakes to the boys. On hearing this he turned very red, and left the house without taking anything: saying, as he went away, 'For the sake of the only man who has shown me kindness for many a long year, I will never touch anything which belongs to his friends.' In a few days our two horses came back, each with a piece of leather tied round its neck, on which was written, 'Returned for Captain Spencer's sake,' and really they are not in bad condition. Since then I hear that Harry has been caught; and if you should see anything of him, perhaps you might do him some service, for I do think there is some good in him at bottom Sally and the boys send their duty to you, sir, and desire me to say they never forget you.

"I am your dutiful and obliged servant to command, JAMES RICHARDSON."

"Poor Harry!" said Captain Spencer, "I should be very glad if I could be of any service to you."
The party returned joyfully to Onslow Farm; the young men loud in the praises of their new friend and his horse. I do not know which to admire most," said George Onslow, "the firm courage of the rider, or the entire obedience of his steed." "Make allowances for military education and Arab origin," said Captain Spencer. "And now, my friends, I must reluctantly think of my departure; I ought not to stay longer." The necessity was unwillingly admitted, and Mr. Onslow said he should be ready in a few days; that the drays should be packed and started, and then he would set off on horseback; Kinchela might go with the drays. "Agreed," said Captain Spencer; "my tin cans shall be made over to your garden, Mrs. Onslow; I can roll my grass hat in my opossum-cloaks, and fasten them upon my saddle." "Ay, preserve that as a trophy," was the general cry. "I will take your tin cans under my especial care," said Mrs. Onslow. "Charlie can fly with us, and Gip will ride inside my coat," continued

the soldier; "so all is well arranged." Kinchela, however, when he heard that he was to be separated from his master, was in such an agony of distress, that Captain Spencer was extremely puzzled what to do with him. One of the men about the farm, hearing of this, respectfully accosted the officer as he stood thoughtfully near the stable, and said, "I beg your pardon, sir, but Kinchela has been learning to ride while you have been away, and if master would lend him a horse, he might go along with you; he was so sorry when you went to hunt the cattle alone, that he begged to be taught, and we all like him so much, that we took pains with him, and he can sit his horse very well." "Then all difficulties are smoothed," said Mr. Onslow, "for he can have one of my horses. Come, Spencer, and take a quiet walk with me round the new plantation for the last time."

"There are some great drawbacks to living in this country," said Mr. Onslow; "the young are apt to think that everything must prosper, and get too confident; and as yet we have so few places of worship; the latter will, I hope, be remedied now we have bishops; the former I dare not hope will be checked by adversity. We have just passed through a season of suffering, which has nearly overwhelmed us, and I hope we shall profit by the lesson, and go steadily on; but even that steadiness is at such an enormous rate of progress, that it would seem almost frightful in the Old World. I suppose the western part will be peopled from Swan River."

"Have you any convicts employed about you?" asked Captain Spencer. "Certainly, more than half my men were transported from England; some are perfectly reformed, and not only make excellent servants, but excellent characters; while others require to be watched. I do not know what we should have done without convicts, as so many of the emigrants come out with the notion that they are to be their own masters, or that they are to be well paid for doing less than in Great Britain; whereas every one in a new colony must work hard." "Which are the best emigrants?" asked Captain Spencer. "The Germans are admirable; but I think Scotch and English are the best; the Irish are idle. It is a curious fact, that the Scotch are the worst of all convicts; I suppose, arising from the circumstance that they are never transported except for some very serious crime."

"I presume," continued Mr. Onslow, "that you possess a knowledge of all the natural resources of the country." "Not its mineral riches," replied Captain Spencer; "except the prominent features." "We have almost all," returned Mr. Onslow; "our coal is excellent, and one of the most valuable of our possessions. St. John told you of all that has lately been found in the neighbourhood of Adelaide ; and the enlightened Count Strzelecki has given a learned account of what is to be met with in New South Wales." "I am very much puzzled," interrupted Captain Spencer, "by the names given to the trees, which appear to me to be rather fanciful." "We delight in giving English names from real or fancied resemblances ; that for the Casuarina is the She Oak ; the Stringy Bark, which grows chiefly on the tops of hilly ranges ; the Blue Gum, which is of immense size, has large, white, gnarled branches, and whose bark breaks off in angular pieces ; the Iron Bark, the Balm-tree, which abounds most in sandy creeks, the Thyme, the Red Gum, the Dwarf Gum, the Box-tree, the Mahogany tree, which springs up to a height of forty or fifty feet, or even more, without a bend or a branch, are all Eucalypti ; and then the Rose-wood, the Raspberry-jam, which smells like that preserve, the Violet-wood, which yields just such a perfume as that flower does, the Myall, of which the cattle are so fond, the Malga, with its hard wood, are all Acacias, of which there are at least two hundred sorts, all useful for their wood, their gum, and their bark, which is excellent for tanning ; and the two latter substances form articles of export. Besides these, we have, as you know, the Callitris Pine, with its yellow, compact wood ; the Bidwelliana Pine, with its invaluable straight trunk ; and the

Cypress, which smells like a Cedar, with a red and white wood." "It strikes me," observed Captain Spencer, "that some of the grasses would be highly useful." "I am quite of your opinion, and I think their excellence often makes our cattle stray; but we all of us try to imitate the mother country, and have a sort of prejudice towards new productions.'
"If I mistake not," further observed Captain Spencer, "there is also a very good native Tobacco, with white blossoms and smooth leaves; and it appears to me that your vegetable resources are either not sufficiently known, or that you do not sufficiently turn them to your advantage." "I perfectly agree with you," said Mr. Onslow; "but newly-established farmers cannot try experiments; and when they know that, if a fair quantity of rain comes, they procure twenty-five bushels of wheat from an acre, and sometimes more than forty, and even heavier crops of barley, in a light, sandy soil, you cannot wonder, at the preference in their favour. It is a curious circumstance that certain English plants spring up spontaneously wherever we turn our English cattle to graze; for instance, the Horehound and the Couch, or Dog's-tooth grass. But what is the cause of that commotion in the Horse-yard? let us go and see. "What is the matter, Brown?" asked Mr. Onslow of the nearest man. "One of the mares has killed her foal, sir; she always was vicious."

"These unaccountable things happen every now and then; sometimes to such an extent," said Mr. Onslow, "that all the foals of a herd will be destroyed. You say you met with herds of wild horses, and they are those we have lost; they treated Tiger civilly; but very often they will not let a strange horse come near them; our saddle-horses are trained so as to graze within two or three miles of the farm; but in several instances the wild herds have forced them away."

As Mr. Onslow and Captain Spencer entered the inner gate, Frederick Onslow ran to meet them with a pair of tongs, between which a small, dark object had been nipped, and was partly hanging out. "We have found a whole nest of Triantelopes, father," said he, laughing, "behind my grandfather's picture; and I came to present the venerable patriarch of the family to Captain Spencer; he will probably find it an interesting acquaintance." "What a mercy you have found them!" said Mr. Onslow. "I saw something dark," continued Frederick, "suddenly emerge from behind the frame, and on inspection found the colony: George and I demolished them all; my mother and Mary ran away." "Perhaps you have seen them already," said Mr. Onslow, turning to Captain Spencer, "for they constantly live between the bark and wood of old trees." "No," was the reply, "I never have; but your colonial name is very extraordinary." "Yes, but if you were to talk to the farm-servants of a Tarantula they would not understand you." "Are their bites fatal?" "No, though very severe; and their web is so strong that you can scarcely break it." "Your dogs," continued Captain Spencer, "brought in a little animal this morning, gray in colour, with white spots, and having a thin, wiry tail, which I have seen, but Gip has never caught it." "Oh, you mean the native Cat,* which comes and eats our fowls and even turkeys; it is a pretty creature, but very vicious; and it often masters the dogs." "One more question on natural history and I have done. What is the reason I have never met with the Lyre-tail Birds?" "Because they belong more properly to the south-eastern portion of this continent, where the Spiny Anteater† also most abounds, though occasionally found near the Darling. We have had both, but the latter disappeared, and is perhaps in the lake at this moment; and the former died."

The night after the above conversation was to be the last which the traveller was to spend among his kind friends; and, as he lay awake, thinking with regret of the approaching separation, he heard a most tremendous noise; he started up and listened, and it occurred again, sounding as if it were an attempt to break open a door; he hastily

---

* Dasyurus. † Echidna.

threw on his clothes, and George Onslow burst into the room, saying, "I see you have heard them, Spencer; it is either a company of bush-rangers or a body of natives trying to break in; they must have come over the hills at the back. I cannot understand why the dogs have not given tongue." "Gipsy has," said her master. "Take your pistols, and come with me," continued George; "it is in the new part of the house." The friends issued from the door, and at the head of the stairs met Mr. Onslow, half dressed, with a sword and a light. "Put out the light," said Captain Spencer, "and let me come first." "Certainly not," cried Mr. Onslow, and pushed past him; in doing which Captain Spenrer blew out the candle, thereby obscuring some white forms, which had anxiously but partly issued from their doors. Frederick Onslow now joined them; and as he did so they heard a parley. "Go back, Mary! Mother, you have no business here." "Can't we help you load the pistols?" "No, we are quite sufficient to keep them at bay, till we can, by our firing, alarm the men about the premises." Another thump, louder than ever, threatened to burst the door open, which was near the foot of the stairs. "Let us stand here," said George Onslow, "and we shall catch them as they enter." At last the door was burst open, and a flood of moonlight streamed in. Mr. Onslow made a furious lunge, and fell; for an instant only there was silence, but then a wild scream of laughter burst from the young men. Captain Spencer looked around him for the explanation, when something rolled against his legs, and made Gip hop away. "Oh, my mother's pumpkins!" at last said the young men; the laughter was renewed. But Mary, who had followed, cried, "Pick up my father; perhaps he is hurt." "Hurt!" said Mr. Onslow, "I can't move for laughter. O Ellen! Ellen! your horticultural propensities will be the death of me." A rustling noise, and the shutting of a door, told that the innocent cause of the alarm had made her escape from the taunts which she knew were coming. She had made a stack of pumpkins in one of the new and unoccupied rooms; something had disturbed their equilibrium, and they had given way. Such was the explanation of the mystery; but there was no more sleep that night; the young men sat up to talk; but a loud laugh burst forth whenever the adventure was thought of, especially the appearance of Mr. Onslow, his fierce plunge, and his roll among the enemy. He went back to his bed; but his wife had taken refuge in that of Mary, where she buried her head in the pillow, to avoid hearing the reiterated bursts of her sons. It was with difficulty that Captain Spencer assumed a serious countenance when she came to the early breakfast the next morning. "I could not let you go," said the lady, "without taking farewell, or else I would not have appeared this morning. I am more sorry than I can express to lose you; but I never before saw Mr. Onslow go away and felt so much pleasure at his departure; I do not mind Mary and the boys, but he really is too unbearable." "I do assure you," said Captain Spencer, " that if I were not so sad at parting with you I should be as vociferous in my merriment as they are ; so it is well that I am going."

The travellers departed with sadness and sorrow at their hearts, for affection had been cemented between all parties by circumstances, which had played the part of time, and they were old friends in heart, though not in days. The soldier's duty never seemed so hard as at that moment, and he was almost tempted to make a promise to return; but he found sufficient firmness to forbear. It was some time, however, before he could be amused, as Mr. Onslow was, with the pride of Kinchela, who, equipped in trousers and shoes, given him by his friends at the farm, had issued from the gate in the midst of a loud "Hurrah!" which Charlie echoed, laughing with all his might, bawling out the names of all the family, "George, Mary," &c. The servants loudly applauded him; nor could those who were sad refrain, when he flew round and round in token of farewell, and as his last salute screaming "Pumpkins, pumpkins!" which

Frederick Onslow had been at some pains to teach him that very morning.

"I should have thought," said Captain Spencer, "after the first pangs were over, that, with your establishment, and the extent of settlement and cultivation around you, you were not in danger from an attack of natives." "Nor do I think we are," said Mr. Onslow; "but this I do think, that, on the very outskirts, our colonists are not sufficiently careful; it is difficult, however, to divest ourselves of old habits and feelings. I did not doubt last night that the noise was occasioned by natives; it was my boys who imagined bush-rangers, because they are often hearing of their exploits. I must now tell you an instance of Mrs. Onslow's courage, as a reward to her for so much teasing about her garden. I was at Sidney at the time, and it was during our first establishment on our land, so that we had no neighbours to help us, no resources but in ourselves, and scarcely any defence. It seemed that some of the natives had been ill-treated, or fancied they had been ill-treated, by some soldiers and constables the day before; and their tribe, to the number of 400, assembled, and came to revenge themselves upon us. They were all fully armed after their own fashion, and we had only four guns and a pistol, which, however, were prepared for action. As soon as they came to the house, my brave little wife went to them, by herself, inquired into their grievances, soothed them with kind words, and gave them tobacco and corn ; she, however, told them that there were people inside the house, who would shoot them if they committed any violence. Surprising to say, this kind but dauntless conduct on her part produced the most favourable results, for they went away, only taking with them what she had given, and some articles of clothing, which they had found in the men's huts when they ransacked them. Our overseer went among them, after her first address and reception, as in fact, did the whole family, and as our people gradually assembled round Mrs. Onslow, they all endeavored to make friends with the enemy, and behaved very well, so that we did not suffer much ; but I attribute our preservation (of course under Providence) entirely to Mrs. Onslow's conduct, for frightful murder and outrages were committed by them within thirty miles of us lower down the river."

The magnificent entrance to Port Jackson, and the beautiful appearance of Sydney, one of the fairest cities of the earth, struck Captain Spencer as the finest scene which he had beheld in Australia; and the more so, considering that, only fifty years ago, the native inhabitants performed their savage dances under the trees on its site. The two dark, lofty rocks, which seem to form the gates of the harbour, were passed; a noble estuary presented itself, decked with the loveliest bays, inlets, islands, villas, cottages, and gardens, and the silvery sand of the beach formed a glittering border. Captain Spencer at once proceeded to the principal hotel, where, sending for a tailor, the adornment of the outer man was speedily accomplished; then came presentation to the Governor, introductions, calls, and fêtes; and all the ceremonies and usages of polite life, with the hospitality of the colonies, were put in practice for one who was naturally the hero of the day. But this hero soon became tired of the gaiety which he was obliged to share; and although grateful for kindness and attention, he was weary of long, dusty George street, of luxurious dinners which he could not eat, and of hot rooms where he thought he could not breathe, and every hour increased his impatience to depart. Tiger was well housed, and Kinchela was constantly with him, for his countrymen claimed him, and he did not covet their society; the white servants laughed at and jeered him, and Tiger was his best companion in the absence of his master. Gip was of course often left behind, and her consolation was to lie upon her master's cloak. As to Charlie, he, every morning, very cleverly flew off, and returned at night to Tiger: and, one day, when Captain Spencer was riding through the Hyde Park of Sydney with some gentlemen, one of the latter exclaimed, "Is that you, Captain

Spencer, whose name is so vociferously called by a strange voice? it is probably one of your friends from the bush." The traveller listened, and looked round, and presently, "Ned Spencer, Ned Spencer! here's Charlie, Ned Spencer!" met his ear. He whistled in the usual manner, and Charlie flew on to his shoulder with every mark of delight. "I could not think where the poor fellow went to every day." said he; "but I was easy about him, as he came back every evening." "All's right, hurrah!" said the bird, and flew away. "I would give 100 guineas for that bird," said one of the gentlemen. "I would not take 500 for him," observed his master; "his voice, day after day, was the only sound which cheered me in the wilderness, and I can never part with him." In consequence of this, Charlie was a marked bird among all the inhabitants of Sydney, and was consequently safe from harm as he flew backwards and forwards to and from the hotel.

On one occasion, when some ladies called in their carriage to take Captain Spencer to the racecourse between Sydney and Botany Bay, as he was about to get in, something touched his shoulder, and there stood Tiger, preparing to go with him, with Charlie on his back, and Gip was unceremoniously running up the steps of the carriage. They had all made their escape, and of course, thought they could not do wrong by accompanying their master.

The ladies were so pleased, that they entreated the horse and bird might be suffered to accompany them, and Gip was received into the carriage. Kinchela was mounted in the rumble, to his infinite enjoyment; and from that moment the whole party was included in all the invitations where they could be admitted, no pic-nic taking place without Charlie.

Captain Spencer passed several gangs of convicts at work, and he scarcely dared to look at them, for fear he should see Harry Blunt among their number; but it was not there he found him. On returning to his hotel one day, he saw a crowd at a distance, and, on going through it, heard that the famous bush-ranger, Harry Blunt, who had so long eluded pursuit, was at last taken, and brought in by the police. Harry was committed to prison, where his friend visited him, and heard that an engagement had taken place between him, his companion, and the parties sent out after them, in which he, seeing no chance of escape, had surrendered without further resistance. The more Captain Spencer saw of this erring man, the more did he hope for his reformation; he expressed himself as if he were sincerely penitent, and Captain Spencer made use of all the influence which he possessed for the mitigation of his sentence. He related to the proper authorities all that he knew of him, employed counsel for him, and Richardson's letter being read in court produced a favourable impression.

The working in chains was thus commuted for imprisonment, which his friend thought would be almost as irksome to bear, and he obtained a mitigation of its length. To his surprise, however, Harry expressed a firm determination to bear his punishment patiently, saying "it was the least he could do after such kind exertions had been made for him."

Captain Spencer entreated that the strenuous efforts of the chaplain of the jail might be used on his behalf, and this gentleman was so pleased with the conduct and improvement of the convict, that when, on going out of prison, Mr. Onslow offered to take him into his service, he gave him his best commendations, so that it was an inexpressible source of happiness to the Australian traveller, to think, when his friend wrote him, that Harry Blunt was a faithful and attached servant, that he had been allowed to act as an instrument in saving a fellow-creature from perdition.

Presents were sent to Mr. St. John, Richardson, the Scotts, the Onslows, and even the stock-keepers at the out-stations, so that none could imagine themselves to be forgotten; and Captain Spencer embarked on board the *Asia* with mingled feelings of regret and pleasure, each of which were surmounted by gratitude. Kinchela, Gip, and Tiger, were very happy on board ship, and Charlie had the sagacity not to attempt to roam during the voyage.

"Have you heard the news? Spencer is come back, better than ever he was, with his horse, dog, and *such* a bird;" were the exclamations of all who had known him in Bombay, directly after he had reported his arrival. Hearty greetings saluted him on all sides, and he seemed to live in a whirl of pleasure and excitement. Great was the astonishment felt at his adventures and sufferings, and honourable were the distinctions with which he was received in society. He, however, joined his regiment as speedily as possible, where, among old and dear friends, he could calmly consider and talk over the past, and as often as he did so, he became more and more impressed with gratitude and submission towards his Heavenly Protector.

As frequent a correspondence as opportunities would allow, was carried on between Captain Spencer and his highly valued friends the Onslows; and during a period of two years, no event of import ance occurred, except the marriage of Mr. St. John with Miss Onslow, and their subsequent settlement on a farm within a day's ride of her parents. Then came a letter from Mr. George Onslow, couched in the following terms:—

My dear Spencer,

All our endeavours to tempt you to come and settle among us have signally failed, and I grant you that your reasons are cogent; therefore do not suppose that the present epistle is intended as a renewal of our efforts. I merely lay the circumstances before you; and when you have weighed them all, your own right feeling and good sense will enable you to determine the course you ought to pursue.

It is some time since I last wrote, owing to the great difficulty I have found in procuring a conveyance for my despatches; and perhaps it is well it should have been so, for by the delay I can now put you in full possession of an important discovery, which, although taking place in the farthest retreat of civilization, bids fair to influence the whole world. It is neither more nor less than that of finding prodigious quantities of gold in our soil, which far exceed the amount yielded by California, tidings of which have of course reached you through the newspapers.

To begin at the beginning. It seems that the great geologist, Sir Roderick Murchison, when he examined the specimens of rocks, and heard the accounts of the eminent traveller, Count Strzelecki, was struck with the resemblance of the former to those of the Ural mountains, which you know supply Russia with gold; and he then foretold that we should, sooner or later, meet with the precious metal in our territory. Still no search was made. Now it is known that an old shepherd actually brought several pieces of gold for sale at Sydney, and on being questioned as to where he had procured them refused to give any information. Strange to say, that although it was known he came from the district of Bathurst, no one followed to see from what spot he dug the treasure; in fact, no pains were taken to profit by his discovery.

At last, a Mr. Hargreaves returned from California, with nothing but experience in gold-finding as the result of his visit to those regions. He applied his knowledge to Bathurst and Wellington, and after riding over some hundreds of miles, he gave tidings of a rich harvest of gold in the Crown lands. He made arrangements with the Government, went to Bathurst, assembled the principal inhabitants of that place at an inn, showed them four ounces of gold which he had procured after three days' labour, and succeeded in awakening them to a search for more. From that time the golden mania has been raging, and weekly increasing in strength; the emigration from the British empire, which had languished, is now beginning to flow again, and hundreds have arrived, and still come; our new towns have been in a measure deserted, and two thousand persons were in one week known to go to Bathurst, consisting of all classes, and various ages. I can scarcely describe to you the condition to which some of the settlements have been reduced; respectable clerks have thrown up valuable situations, even men of substance have not disdained the enterprise, apprentices have broken their indentures, tillage has been neglected, not even seed sown for future crops, buildings suspended, sheep have wandered about without shepherds, and in Adelaide the famous copper-mines have stopped working for want of miners.

You will readily suppose that such a sudden change in everything, such a sudden rupture of the bonds which link society together, have produced strange results, and laid the foundation for much after inconvenience, if not suffering. The regular supplies derived from our crops must fail, the prices of most things will be raised, our exports stopped, our flocks and herds will have irrecoverably strayed, it will be difficult to reduce the enormous wages given to those who have remained faithful to their duties, and the fair, the refined, and the delicate have been, and may be again, forced to perform those offices for which they are unfitted by health or education. These seem to me quite enough to think of, without troubling myself with the financial changes which such an influx of gold may occasion in other parts of the world. Various are the surmises and speculations on this head; but who can tell?

As these mountain ridges which contain gold generally assume a meridional direction, fresh explorations took place to the south, and now still more prolific deposits are found in the province of Victoria. A native shepherd in the service of Dr. Kerr, at Louisa Creek, fifty miles from Bathurst, stumbled upon a spot which yielded 4240*l.* sterling to his master. A party of diggers, six in number, procured 900*l.* worth in one day. One man, seeing his neighbour about to wash a tin dishful of slate-coloured clay, at a venture offered 50*l.* for it, the possessor asked 75*l.*, this was refused; and the owner had reason to rejoice, for it yielded 100*l.* The value of 350*l.* was dug up in a few hours, from earth which had lodged round the root of a tree. A blacksmith, in one hole, found the worth of 440*l.*; and a poor man met with 8lbs. of gold in one spot, after the labour of only a few minutes, which he compared to digging potatoes. All these occurred in the Sydney deposits. At Mount Alexander, in Victoria province, a party of four men from Adelaide, after working for a few days, returned home with 11,600*l.*

I will not weary you with further statements of success, nor will I trouble you with the losses, which appear but trifling in comparison; such losses are, however, not rare. Government has assumed the conduct of these diggings, and each person must take out a license, which costs 1*l*. 10*s*. per month, and which entitles the holder to appropriate the produce of a certain portion of land, called a 'claim.' These claims not unfrequently turn out to be wholly destitute of gold, and the parties do not even repay their expenses. These uncertainties are easily explained by the supposition that quartz is the matrix of the gold; this has been broken or disturbed by some great convulsion, and the shattered fragments are rolled from their original bed; sometimes arrested by an insignificant obstacle, and accumulating, and at others passing over, and leaving the course bare. This theory also accounts for the presence of the metal in other formations, such as blue clay and clay slate; and the fissures of slaty rocks have presented most lumps or nuggets (as they are called), they having, as it were, caught the quartz as it has rolled along. It is asserted that in Argyle, granite is the matrix, and thus stones containing gold have been applied to the building of bridges, and used for pavements. Does not this remind you of the stories told in former times of the streets of Timbuctoo being paved with silver? Stories which we can now beat, without exaggeration, by the assertion, that Bathurst is paved with gold.

After long exemption, at length Fred and I were seized with the universal fever; but when we owned its influence to my father, he shook his head, and as our men stole off to the diggings, we felt it would be very hard upon him to deprive him of our help. At length St. John came, fully determined on tempting us to join him in an excursion to the diggings. Mary came with him, to remain with our father and mother during our absence; it was not a busy time just then, and at length the project received approbation. We persuaded our neighbour, young Montague, to complete the number of four, which is said to form the most convenient party; and promising high wages to two of the men who had remained with us, we first started for Sydney. At one time we wished to have Harry Blunt with us, but he wisely preferred staying to take care of the farm; saying, that a love of gain had once led him into evil, and he would never put himself in the way of temptation any more.

At Sydney, we bought the rough dresses which were to stand the water and hard labour, which we knew we had to encounter; we provided ourselves with a tilted cart, which held us all, and to which we harnessed two horses from the farm. We had pick-axes, spades, buckets, tubs, files, wedges, scales and weights, tin dishes and cradles. We did not forget our mattresses, plenty of thick blankets, a tent, cooking apparatus, and a stock of provisions carefully selected by my mother and Mary. We arrived in safety, left the care of our property and the cooking to the men, and helped each other to dig, to wash, to rock the cradles, &c. It was even rougher work than any we had hitherto encountered, for there must be no relaxation, and no shrinking from wet garments.

I must not forget to tell you, that we took Lion, the mastiff, with us; and the dear old dog was one of our most useful auxiliaries. When a suspicious character approached the tent, he gave the alarm, and as we were well armed and slept lightly, it was scarcely possible to take us by surprise.

It was a curious sight to see so many hundred tents together, looking more like a vast fair than a military encampment; and from the number of those who had preceded us, it was difficult to choose our claims, or establish our temporary dwelling. We exerted all our thought and skill, and being a party of brothers, as it were, our experiment turned out well; for in six weeks we, between us, realized 15,000*l*., beside some extra gains, (which we gave to our men for their faithful conduct to us,) and the selling of our claims when we left the ground. We every week sent our gold by the armed escort provided by the government, to Sydney; so that we never had any great accumulation by us, and thus we did not know how much we had realized till we returned to the capital.

It was not a life that tempted us to remain long, and we were glad to return to our homes. St. John and Montague, being lately settled, find their portions advantageous to their farms and stock. Fred's has enabled him to become independent, and mine is thrown into the common purse between me and my father.

You will probably think that I have given you too favourable an idea of the scenes which we witnessed, and of the hardships which we encountered. With regard to the latter, it must be recollected, that they came lighter to us as settlers, than to those who pass their lives at the desk, or in professional employments. The health of many gave way under the toil and exposure, and probably many will, all the rest of their days, feel the effects of their exertions and exposure. With respect to the former, the day was quite enough, for most of those present were devoted to their all-absorbing occupation; but at night, the return of so many lawless characters to the camp, of necessity produced some frightful scenes. Such a din of firing guns, shoutings, frightful oaths, drunken quarrels, and barkings of dogs! Robberies are frequent, and murders are sometimes committed; and it requires incessant watching to retain your horses and other property. Still all these are

40

nothing to the horrors which we hear of in California; and as police and military force are being established, still greater order will prevail. One thing struck us very forcibly, which was the observance of the Sabbath; and perhaps this, as well as some forbearance from evil, may be ascribed to the sprinkling of gentlemen who come to share the chances of the rest. It is true that such enterprises are great levellers of caste; nevertheless, superiority of mind, morals, and acquirement, must exercise an influence wherever it may abide.

There is an abundant attendance of those who seek to gain a more certain profit by the exercise of different callings necessary to the wants of such a multitude; and they do not fail to take advantage of the necessity which arises for their labours. The charges for washing are enormous; a trifling derangement of your tools, or damage to your cart, cannot be remedied without incurring heavy expense, and you are forced to submit to the most extortionate demands. Provisions are decidedly cheap. I have not yet described the cradle, which is so named on account of its resemblance to that accompaniment of childhood, in its outward form. A square box is fitted into its head, at the bottom of which is a sheet of iron, pierced with holes the diameter of my little finger, like a sieve. Across the bottom of the cradle are three thick iron bars, one of which is placed at the lower end, and the other two divide the cradle into three equal parts. An upright bar of wood fixed on one side forms the handle, and by means of this one person violently rocks the machine with his left hand, while his right, with a stick, stirs or beats the soil put into the iron sieve. A second person dashes water upon it. The cradle is put in a slanting position in which the sieve is the highest; the particles of gold fall to the bottom, where they are arrested by the bars, and the muddy water runs off at the foot. This gold is afterwards put into the tin dish which I have already mentioned, and carefully separated from the pieces of iron stone, and other heavy substances, by further washing.

If you will join us, dear Spencer, we will make a second expedition, and turn our steps towards the Victoria diggings. It is true that the disorganization of Melbourne is beyond my powers to describe, if all be true that we hear. Robberies are committed in the streets by daylight, and nothing but superior force is an efficient protection. You, however, are not one to shrink from hardship or danger; come then and make your fortune.

My father and Fred write you all family news, and therefore I have now only to subscribe myself your faithful friend,   GEORGE ONSLOW.

Captain Spencer wisely thought it very possible that he might mar, instead of make his fortune by going to the diggings, and declined the above invitation, remaining perfectly satisfied with the majority which he had just attained. The great extension of steamboat navigation soon, however, enabled him to have more frequent intercourse with his friends, and to be a personal witness of their prosperity.

THE END.